THE BOOK OF
HYMNS

Edited by
IAN BRADLEY

Testament Books
New York

This 2000 edition is published by Testament Books™,
an imprint of Random House Value Publishing, Inc.,
280 Park Avenue, New York, NY 10017,
by arrangement with The Overlook Press.

Testament Books™ and design are trademarks of Random House Value Publishing, Inc.

Random House
New York • Toronto • London • Sydney • Auckland
http://www.randomhouse.com/

Printed and bound in the United States of America

Library of Congress Cataloging-in-Publication Data

The book of hymns / edited by Ian Bradley.
p. cm.
Originally published: Woodstock, N.Y. : Overlook Press, 1989.
Includes index.
ISBN 0-517-16241-5
1. Hymns, English—History and criticism. I. Bradley, Ian C.

BV315 .B54 2000
264'.23—dc21
00-059372

8 7 6 5 4 3 2

CONTENTS

Introduction	1
The Hymns	5
Further Reading	469
Index of First Lines	470
Index of Authors, Translators and Composers	474

This book is dedicated to the memory of my brother

DAVID WILLIAM BRADLEY

Born 12 June 1952   Died 27 May 1987

'We may not know, we cannot tell, what pains he had to bear'

INTRODUCTION

We are often told that ours is a post-Christian society. If that is, indeed, the case, and I myself am not at all sure that it is, then the songs of the defunct cult which we are supposed to have passed through have a remarkable staying power. Every Sunday morning millions of Christians around the world gather in churches to sing hymns of praise to God. Others tune into religious broadcasts, both on television and the radio, to hear the hymns Christians have known for centuries.

Hymns are sung and enjoyed not just in churches, but in schools, community get-togethers, at football matches and in pub sing-songs. They are perhaps the strongest expression of the folk religion which is still deeply embedded in our so-called secular society. For many people they provide a more familiar and accessible source of teaching about the Christian faith than the Bible. There can be few who do not know the opening verses of 'There is a green hill far away' or 'Abide with me'. Half-remembered verses from childhood hymns and choruses remain a great source of inspiration and comfort to many who would not count themselves as regular churchgoers or committed believers.

For me, one of the greatest glories of Christian hymnody is that it is a truly ecumenical enterprise. Hymn-singing really does cross denominational barriers and unite Christians of every persuasion. Roman Catholics happily sing the lyrics of Charles Wesley, while Baptists and Presbyterians equally happily sing the words of John Henry Newman.

This book prints the words of 150 of the best-known hymns in the English language with an accompanying commentary on each. It is a personal selection, but I hope a representative one, which covers every branch of hymnody in the English language, from translations of the office hymns of the Early Church, through metrical psalmody, seventeenth-century devotional verse and the classics of Wesley and Watts to American gospel songs and contemporary choruses. The only category which I have excluded is Christmas carols, and that is simply for reasons of space. They really deserve a book to themselves.

Inevitably the selection which I have chosen will not please everyone. For many, a favourite hymn will have been left out, while for others, no doubt, one that they do not much care for will have been included. Let me just say in my defence that although what follows is inevitably a personal choice, reflecting my own tastes, I have also taken extremely careful note of lists of the most popular hymns on both sides of the Atlantic, such as the 'Songs of Praise' Top Hundred most requested numbers and the US Ecumenical Hymnody index.

Those who like statistics may be interested in the following information about the 150 hymns which make up this collection, ninty-three are English in origin, 17 American, 6 Irish, 5 Scottish and 2 Welsh. Of those that have been translated from foreign languages, 11 were originally in Latin, 9 in German, 2 each in Italian and Greek, and one each in Swiss, Swedish and Danish.

Sixty-nine of the hymns in this collection were originally written in the nineteenth century (this is not counting translations of earlier hymns), 35 in the eighteenth century, 14 in the seventeenth century and 12 in the twentieth century. Three date from the sixteenth century and the remaining 17 are translations of hymns from the Early Church and the Middle Ages. Not counting the Psalms, which form the basis for many of the greatest hymns in the English language, the oldest hymn in this collection is from the second century.

A denominational league table of the original authors would be headed by Anglicans with 63 entries, followed by Roman Catholics with 21 (including all the pre-Reformation hymns just mentioned), Methodists with 16, Independents or Congregationalists with 11, Lutherans and independent Evangelicals with 8 each, Presbyterians with 5, Unitarianis with 4, Quakers, Greek Orthodox and freethinkers with 2 each, Baptists, Mormons and Swiss Reformed with 1 each. Fifteen of the hymns were written by women.

Although I would myself admit to a particular fondness for

nineteenth-century Anglican hymnody, I do not think the preponderance of hymns that fall into this category in the pages that follow reflects simply a personal bias. Surely few people would dispute the fact that hymns have been one of the Church of England's greatest gifts to the English-speaking world and that the nineteenth century was the golden age of hymnody.

By no means all the verses that appear in this collection could be counted as great poetry. A good hymn is different from a good piece of devotional verse – it gains its effect from being sung rather than from being read. I am very conscious that in presenting the words of hymns without the tunes that are their essential accompaniments, this book does not do full justice to its subject. But I trust that those who read through the verses in this collection will do so with the familiar tunes to which they are used to singing them in their minds – indeed, I imagine that there are many like me who find it impossible to read the words of a well-known hymn without mentally singing it through.

Wherever possible, I have printed the full original texts of the hymns included in this book. Often these diverge quite considerably from the versions with which we are now familiar. I hope readers will find it interesting to see what the authors originally wrote and why their words have been changed. I have also printed the original titles given to the hymns by their authors.

Can I end this short introduction with a plea to the clergy, whose ranks I hope shortly to be joining. Would it be possible to introduce into services some brief words of explanation about the hymns which are going to be sung, such as are increasingly given before readings from the Bible? Hymns form one of the most important elements of public worship, and yet they are often announced as though they had little to say and were to be got through as quickly as possible. I think congregations would appreciate learning a little about the authors of hymns and the circumstances in which they were written. I modestly offer this book to all who find themselves conducting services of worship in the hope that they may find it helpful in preparing a few words to introduce the hymns. I hope it may also prove interesting to all those who enjoy lifting up their hearts and letting their mouths show forth the praise of God, whether in cathedral, church, mission hall, open-air rally, or in the privacy of their own homes.

The words of the following hymns are in copyright: Nos. 47, 50, 56, 59, 82, 84, 86, 97, 122 and 141. A note giving details of the owners of copyright will be found at the end of each of these hymns. I am extremely grateful to them for giving me permission to reproduce the words.

I.B.

1 A SAFE STRONGHOLD OUR GOD IS STILL

This great work by Luther is an appropriate first entry in an anthology of well-loved and much-sung hymns, for it is from the Reformation that the tradition of congregational hymn-singing comes. Although, as we shall see, there are several verses dating from medieval times which are regularly sung today, they were not written for congregational use.

Martin Luther (1483–1546), the German monk who is generally regarded as the instigator of the Reformation, deplored the largely passive and silent role played by the congregation in traditional Roman Catholic worship. He wrote a total of thirty-seven hymns for congregational use, mostly to be sung at important points during the Mass. Instead of being in Latin for chanting by choirs, they were in the language of the people.

'*Ein' feste Burg is unser Gott*', to give this one its original German first line, is not, in fact, a liturgical hymn. Rather it is a defiant song of battle against the forces of evil in the world and perhaps also against the power of the Roman Catholic Church. Certainly many commentators have interpreted the 'ancient prince of hell' in the fifth line of the first verse as referring to the Pope as well as to the Devil. The opening of the hymn is based on Psalm 46: 'God is our refuge and strength, a very present help in trouble.' But Luther soon departs from the language of the Psalmist to create his own powerful imagery.

For a long time it was thought that the hymn was written shortly before Luther's celebrated appearance in front of the Emperor Charles V at the Diet of Worms in 1521 to account for his published attacks on the Catholic Church, and that he sang it as he entered the town. But in fact he almost certainly wrote it eight years later for the Diet of Speyer. It was at that Diet that a number of German princes protested to the Emperor at the suppression of religious liberty and so gained the name 'Protestants'.

'*Ein' feste Burg*' was first published in 1529 in Wittenberg, the town where, twelve years earlier, Luther had nailed up his famous ninety-five theses attacking such practices as the sale of indulgences. It rapidly became not only, in Heinrich Heine's words, 'the Marseillaise of the Reformation', but also the anthem of German nationalism. During the Thirty Years War it was sung to the accompaniment of trumpets by the massed forces of Gustavus Adolphus as they prepared to do battle with the Catholic forces at the Battle of Leipzig. Frederick the Great called it 'God Almighty's Grenadier March' and it was taken up by the German forces during the Franco-Prussian War of 1870.

Although the hymn was first translated into English by Miles Coverdale in 1538 (as 'Oure God is a defence and towre'), it was not widely taken up in the English-speaking world until the nineteenth century. The translation printed opposite, which was made by Thomas Carlyle (1795–1881), the Scottish historian and essayist, and first published in *Fraser's Magazine* in 1831, is probably the best-known in Britain. It has been described by the distinguished hymnologist Erik Routley as 'the greatest translation in the whole field of hymnody'. Carlyle himself said of the hymn, 'There is something in it like the sound of Alpine avalanches or the first murmur of earthquakes: in the very vastness of which dissonance a higher unison is revealed to us.'

In his massive *Dictionary of Hymnology*, John Julian lists no less than forty-seven different English translations of Luther's hymn. Others still regularly used include 'God is a stronghold and a tower' (Elizabeth Wordsworth, 1891), 'A Fortress sure is God our King' (Godfrey Thring, 1882) and 'A mighty fortress is our God' (F. H. Hedge, 1852, a version particularly popular in the United States). Altogether, '*Ein' feste Burg*' has been translated into more than fifty languages.

The tune, known as *Ein' feste Burg*, or sometimes as Worms, was also written by Martin Luther. Mendelssohn included it in the last movement of his 'Reformation' symphony and Wagner incorporated its theme in his '*Kaisermarsch*' written to celebrate the triumphal entry of German soldiers into Berlin after the Franco-Prussian War.

Der XXXXVI Psalm. Deus noster refugium et virtus

A safe stronghold our God is still,
　A trusty shield and weapon;
He'll help us clear from all the ill
　That hath us now o'ertaken.
　　The ancient prince of hell
　　Hath risen with purpose fell;
　　Strong mail of craft and power
　　He weareth in this hour;
　On earth is not his fellow.

2　With force of arms we nothing can,
　　Full soon were we down-ridden;
But for us fights the proper Man
　　Whom God Himself hath bidden.
　　　Ask ye who is this same?
　　　Christ Jesus is His Name,
　　　The Lord Sabaoth's Son;
　　　He, and no other one,
　　Shall conquer in the battle.

3　And were this world all devils o'er,
　　And watching to devour us,
We lay it not to heart so sore;
　　Not they can overpower us.
　　　And let the prince of ill
　　　Look grim as e'er he will,
　　　He harms us not a whit;
　　　For why his doom is writ;
　　A word shall quickly slay him.

4   God's word, for all their craft and force,
        One moment will not linger,
    But, spite of hell, shall have its course;
        'Tis written by His finger.
            And, though they take our life,
            Goods, honour, children, wife,
            Yet is their profit small;
            These things shall vanish all:
        The city of God remaineth.

2 ABIDE WITH ME: FAST FALLS THE EVENTIDE

Voted seventh in the poll conducted among viewers of 'Songs of Praise' in 1985, this Victorian hymn is particularly associated with funeral services and has given hope and comfort to many facing death or bereavement.

The author, Henry Francis Lyte (1793–1847), was born at Ednam, near Kelso in the Scottish borders, and educated at Trinity College, Dublin, where he won the prize for English poetry three times. He was ordained in 1815 and served as a curate in churches in Ireland and the West of England. In 1823 he became perpetual curate of the parish of Lower Brixham, a seaside and fishing village in Devon. There he remained for the rest of his life, increasingly dogged by illness.

Lyte wrote a large number of sacred poems and hymns, most of which were published in two books, *Poems chiefly Religious* (1833) and *The Spirit of the Psalms* (1834). 'Abide with me' was not, however, published until after his death. For a long time it was thought that he had written it in his study on his last evening in Lower Brixham, 4 September 1847, after he had preached a farewell sermon to his congregation. The following day he sailed for the South of France where he died of consumption just over two months later.

It now seems more likely that the verses were composed in 1820 when Lyte was just twenty-seven and still in good health. The inspiration for the hymn seems to have come from a visit that he paid to an old friend, Augustus le Hunte, who was in his last illness. The dying man kept repeating the phrase 'Abide with me' and these words so impressed the young curate that he constructed a set of verses around them. When Lyte came to the end of his time at Lower Brixham and knew himself to be close to death, his mind went back to the hymn he had written more than a quarter of a century earlier and he gave the manuscript to a relative who subsequently secured its publication.

The scriptural inspiration for the hymn comes from St Luke 24:29, where the disciples journeying on the road to Emmaus beseech Christ: 'Abide with us: for it is toward evening, and the day is far spent.' It is printed opposite in its full original form. In most modern hymn-books the third, fourth and fifth verses are omitted.

Lyte composed his own tune for 'Abide with me' and it was also sung in its early days to the Old 124th, St Saviour, and a tune called Troyte's Chant. However, when *Hymns Ancient and Modern* was being compiled, the editors felt that none of these was satisfactory and the musical editor, William Henry Monk (1823-89), organist of St Matthias, Stoke Newington, was asked to write a new melody. His tune, Eventide, accompanied the hymn in the first edition of the new hymn-book which was published in 1861, and has been its inseparable companion ever since.

The story goes that Monk wrote the tune for 'Abide with me' in ten minutes following a committee meeting of the compilers of *Hymns Ancient and Modern* and while a piano lesson was going on in the same room. But his widow recalled that '"Abide with me" was written at a time of great sorrow. Hand in hand we were silently watching the glory of the setting sun (our daily habit) until the golden hue had faded . . . then he took paper and pencilled the tune which has gone all over the world.' In fact, these two versions of the circumstances in which the tune was written are not totally incompatible. Several of the compilers' meetings took place at Monk's house and it is quite possible that he wrote Eventide after such a meeting and after a walk with his wife.

'Abide with me' was much parodied by soldiers in the First World War. The most common version, heard more in training camps in England than in the trenches of Flanders, was: 'We've had no beer, we've had no beer today.' In its original version the hymn gave much comfort to Edith Cavell, the British nurse imprisoned and condemned to death by the Germans in 1915 for helping wounded soldiers to escape. On the night before she was shot, she sat in her cell singing it with a British chaplain.

Abide with us, for it is toward evening

Abide with me: fast falls the eventide;
The darkness deepens; Lord, with me abide:
When other helpers fail, and comforts flee,
Help of the helpless, O abide with me.

2 Swift to its close ebbs out life's little day;
Earth's joys grow dim, its glories pass away;
Change and decay in all around I see;
O thou who changest not, abide with me.

3 Not a brief glance I beg, a passing word;
But as thou dwellst with thy disciples, Lord,
Familiar, condescending, patient, free,
Come not to sojourn, but abide with me.

4 Come not in terrors as the King of Kings,
But kind and good, with healing in thy wings,
Tears for all woes, a heart for every plea –
Come, Friend of sinners, and thus bide with me.

5 Thou on my head in early youth didst smile;
And, though rebellious and perverse meanwhile,
Thou hast not left me, oft as I left thee,
On to the close, O Lord, abide with me!

6 I need thy presence every passing hour;
What but thy grace can foil the tempter's power?
Who like thyself my guide and stay can be?
Through cloud and sunshine, O abide with me.

7 I fear no foe, with thee at hand to bless;
Ills have no weight, and tears no bitterness.
Where is death's sting? where, grave, thy victory?
I triumph still, if thou abide with me.

8 Hold thou thy Cross before my closing eyes;
Shine through the gloom, and point me to the skies:
Heaven's morning breaks, and earth's vain shadows flee;
In life, in death, O Lord, abide with me.

3 ALL CREATURES OF OUR GOD AND KING

This fine hymn of praise for God's creation is based on the *Cantico di fratre sole* (Canticle of the Sun) composed by St Francis of Assisi (1182–1226) towards the end of his life. It derives much of its imagery from Psalm 148 ('Praise ye the Lord, Praise ye the Lord from the heavens').

St Francis, known to his contemporaries and followers as 'the gay troubadour of God' and remembered for his love for all animals, was the son of a wealthy merchant. At the age of twenty-five he renounced all earthly possessions and, in his phrase, wedded Lady Poverty. He founded the order of poor brothers known by his name which became one of the largest religious orders in Christendom.

There are conflicting stories about the precise circumstances in which his poem, which is also known as the 'Canticle of the Creatures' was written. It seems probable, however, that it was composed over a period of time. The first four verses seem to have come to St Francis during an hour of ecstasy after he had kept vigil for forty nights in his rat-infested hut at San Damiano. The fifth verse, with its strong call for the spirit of forgiveness, is said to have been added after a quarrel between the Bishop of Assisi and the local magistrates had caused division in the community. The sixth verse, welcoming death, was composed when, racked with pain and almost completely blind, the saint had a vision indicating that his own sufferings on earth would soon be over.

St Francis's canticle was regarded by the nineteenth-century French philosopher Joseph Renan as 'the most perfect utterance of modern religious sentiment'. The most faithful translation into English, which preserves the metre of the original, was made by Matthew Arnold in 1865. It begins:

O most high, almighty, good Lord God,
   To thee belong praise, glory, honour and all blessing.
Praised be my Lord God, with all his creatures;
   And specially our brother the sun, who brings us the day and
      who brings us the light.
Fair is he and shines with a very great splendour:
   O Lord, he signifies to us Thee!

The version printed overleaf is a rather freer and more singable translation by W. H. Draper (1855–1933). He wrote the hymn while he was rector of Adel in Yorkshire for a Whitsuntide festival of schoolchildren in Leeds.

Educated at Keble College, Oxford, and the translator of many hymns from the Greek and Latin, Draper was a product of the Oxford Movement, the High Church or Catholic revival that swept through the Church of England in the mid nineteenth century. It is because of that movement that translations of many of the great canticles and hymns of the early Church are now found in English-language hymnals. The Tractarians, as those involved in the Oxford Movement were called, sought to restore all that was best in patristic and medieval liturgy.

The tune *Lasst Uns Erfreuen,* to which 'All creatures of our God and King' is almost invariably sung, first appeared in a German tune-book called *Geistliche Kirchengesang,* published in Cologne in 1623. Its first appearance in Britain was in 1906 in the first edition of the *English Hymnal* where Draper's hymn was set to it. The man responsible for this perfect matching of tune and words was the composer Ralph Vaughan Williams, who was musical editor of the new hymnal.

Laudato sia Dio mio Signore

All creatures of our God and King,
Lift up your voice and with us sing
    Alleluia, Alleluia!
Thou burning sun with golden beam,
Thou silver moon with softer gleam,

    O praise him, O praise him,
    Alleluia, Alleluia, Alleluia!

2   Thou rushing wind that art so strong,
    Ye clouds that sail in heaven along,
       O praise him, Alleluia!
    Thou rising moon, in praise rejoice,
    Ye lights of evening, find a voice:

3   Thou flowing water, pure and clear,
    Make music for thy Lord to hear,
       Alleluia, Alleluia!
    Thou fire so masterful and bright,
    That givest man both warmth and light:

4   Dear mother earth, who day by day
    Unfoldest blessings on our way,
       O praise him, Alleluia!
    The flowers and fruits that in thee grow,
    Let them his glory also show:

5   And all ye men of tender heart,
    Forgiving others, take your part,
       O sing ye, Alleluia!
    Ye who long pain and sorrow bear,
    Praise God and on him cast your care:

6   And thou most kind and gentle Death,
    Waiting to hush our latest breath,
       O praise him, Alleluia!
    Thou leadest home the child of God,
    And Christ our Lord the way hath trod:

7 Let all things their Creator bless,
  And worship him in humbleness,
   O praise him, Alleluia!
  Praise, praise the Father, praise the Son,
  And praise the Spirit, Three in One.

4 ALL GLORY, LAUD, AND HONOUR TO THEE, REDEEMER, KING

This popular Palm Sunday hymn is another translation of verses dating from the early Middle Ages. The Latin original on which it is based, 'Gloria, laus et honor tibi sit, rex Christe redemptor', was the work of St Theodulph of Orleans (c. 750–821).

Born in Italy, St Theodulph became abbot of a monastery in Florence, and was then brought to France by Charlemagne and consecrated Bishop of Orleans around 785. He retained this position for more than thirty years until he was suspected by the Emperor Louis I of plotting against him and imprisoned in Angers in 818.

It was almost certainly during his imprisonment that St Theodulph wrote his hymn, which celebrates Christ's entry into Jerusalem on a donkey as described in St Matthew 21:1–17. It ran to thirty-nine verses and was designed to be sung in the long processions which many churches had on Palm Sunday. Legend has it that Theodulph himself sang it from the window of his cell as Louis went past in procession on Palm Sunday, 821. The king is said to have been so moved by the hymn that he ordered the release of its author. St Theodulph was only to have a brief taste of liberty, however, since he died later that year.

From early in its history the hymn was incorporated into Palm Sunday processions throughout Western Europe. The opening verses were often assigned to seven boys who were posted at a high spot on the processional route, perhaps to commemorate the imprisoned bishop.

The English version printed overleaf was the work of John Mason Neale (1818–66), a prominent member of the Oxford Movement who translated many early Latin and Greek hymns into English in an effort to restore the medieval and Catholic heritage of the Church of England. His biography can be found in the notes accompanying hymn No. 23.

Neale first translated 'Gloria, laus et honor' for his book Medieval Hymns in 1851 and it is that version which is printed here, except for the first line which was originally 'Glory, and laud and honour'. The compilers of Hymns Ancient and Modern altered the fifth verse of the hymn, with Neale's permission, to the form which appears in all modern hymnals:

> To thee before thy passion
>   They sang their hymns of praise;
> To thee now high exalted
>   Our melody we raise.

'All glory, laud, and honour' uses only a small part of St Theodulph's original hymn. Neale noted that 'another verse was usually sung until the seventeenth century, at the quaintness of which we can scarcely avoid a smile'. It went:

> Be thou, O Lord, the rider,
>   And we the little ass,
> That to God's holy city
>   Together we may pass.

The usual tune for the hymn, known as St Theodulph, Melchior, or Kronstadt, was written by Melchior Teschner, cantor and pastor at Fraustadt in Germany, and first published in Leipzig in 1615. Bach incorporated the melody in the St John Passion.

Gloria, laus et honor

All glory, laud, and honour
To thee, Redeemer, King,
To whom the lips of children
Made sweet hosannas ring.

2   Thou art the King of Israel,
    Thou David's royal Son,
    Who in the Lord's name comest,
    The King and Blessed One.

3   The company of angels
    Are praising thee on high,
    And mortal men and all things
    Created make reply.

4   The people of the Hebrews
    With palms before thee went;
    Our praise and prayer and anthems
    Before thee we present.

5   In hastening to thy Passion,
    They raised their hymns of praise;
    In reigning 'midst thy glory,
    Our melody we raise.

6   Thou didst accept their praises:
    Accept the prayers we bring,
    Who in all good delightest,
    Thou good and gracious King.

5 ALL HAIL THE POWER OF JESUS' NAME

This hymn should have a broad appeal. Its author, Edward Perronet (1724–92), went through no fewer than four different denominations, passing from Anglicanism by way of Methodism to membership of the Countess of Huntingdon's Connection and ending up an Independent.

Perronet's grandfather was a French Huguenot who had come over to England to escape persecution after the revocation of the Edict of Nantes in 1685. His father was the vicar of Shoreham in Kent for fifty-seven years and was deeply influenced by the Evangelical Revival in the mid eighteenth century. He was a close friend of the Wesleys and earned the title of the 'Archbishop of Methodism'. Edward shared his father's evangelical faith and became an itinerant preacher in the style of John Wesley. In 1757 he published *The Mitre,* a bitter satire on the Church of England which greatly offended the Wesleys who were not prepared to break completely with Anglicanism. He parted company with the Methodists and became minister of the Canterbury chapel of the Countess of Huntingdon's Connection. However, even the Countess became annoyed with the violence of his anti-Anglican feelings and he ended up as the pastor of a small Independent congregation in Canterbury.

Perronet wrote a large number of hymns, but this is the only one which is remembered and used today. It is printed overleaf as it first appeared in the April 1780 issue of the *Gospel Magazine.* It has been called 'The Coronation Hymn' for obvious reasons and its clear purpose is to affirm the kingship of Christ. Much of its imagery is drawn from the Book of Revelation (the morning star and martyrs calling from the altar), and from the Lamentations of Jeremiah (the wormwood and the gall).

As sung today, the hymn differs in several ways from Perronet's original and broadly follows an amended version contained in a selection of hymns which appeared in 1787, edited by Dr John Rippon (1751–1836). A Baptist minister who spent all his working life in London, Rippon omitted the original second verse, changed the wording of the eighth (which has subsequently been further altered by different hands) and added a new last verse:

> O that, with yonder sacred throng,
> We at His feet may fall,
> Join in the everlasting song,
> And crown Him Lord of all!

Rippon also provided titles for the various verses, as follows:

All hail the power of Jesus' name	*Angels*
Crown Him, ye morning stars of light	*The Created Order*
Crown Him, ye martyrs of your God	*Martyrs*
Ye seed of Israel's chosen race	*Converted Jews*
Hail Him, ye heirs of David's line	*The Church, the New Israel*
Sinners, whose love can ne'er forget	*Redeemed Sinners*
Let every tribe and every tongue	*All Mankind*
O that, with yonder sacred throng	*Ourselves*

Three different tunes, all specially written for this hymn, are in regular use today. Anglicans tend to favour the oldest, Miles Lane or Scarborough, composed by William Shrubsole (1760–1806) which appeared in the *Gospel Magazine* for November 1779 with the first verse only of 'All hail the power'. Shrubsole grew up in Canterbury where he was a chorister at the Cathedral and got to know Peronnet. He later became organist at Bangor Cathedral, but was dismissed in 1784 for frequenting Dissenting Conventicles; he ended up at Spa Fields Chapel, London, one of the main places of worship of the Countess of Huntingdon's Connection. Nonconformists have generally preferred to use the jaunty tune Diadem which was written in 1838 by James Ellor, an eighteen-year-old hatmaker who ran the Wesleyan chapel choir in the village of Droylsden near Manchester. More recently, W. H. Ferguson (1874–1950) has provided Ladywell, which appears in several modern hymn-books.

On the Resurrection: The Lord is King

All hail the power of Jesus' Name;
  Let Angels prostrate fall;
Bring forth the royal diadem
  To crown Him Lord of all.

2 Let highborn seraphs tune the lyre,
     And as they tune it, fall
   Before His face Who tunes their choir,
     And crown Him Lord of all.

3 Crown Him, ye morning stars of light,
     Who fix'd this floating ball;
   Now hail the strength of Israel's might,
     And crown Him Lord of all.

4 Crown Him, ye martyrs of your God,
     Who from His altar call;
   Extol the stem-of-Jesse's rod,
     And crown Him Lord of all.

5 Ye seed of Israel's chosen race,
     Ye ransom'd of the fall,
   Hail Him Who saves you by His grace,
     And crown Him Lord of all.

6 Hail Him, ye heirs of David's line,
     Whom David Lord did call,
   The God Incarnate, Man Divine,
     And crown Him Lord of all.

7 Sinners, whose love can ne'er forget
     The wormwood and the gall,
   Go spread your trophies at His feet,
     And crown Him Lord of all.

8 Let every tribe and every tongue
     Before Him prostrate fall,
   And shout in universal song
     The crownèd Lord of all.

6 ALL MY HOPE ON GOD IS FOUNDED

This is a good example of a hymn which has only become really popular because of a particular tune. Until Herbert Howells composed Michael for it in 1930, 'All my hope on God is founded' was sung comparatively little. Since then it has been a favourite, particularly in public school chapels, although it is still not found in as many hymn-books as it ought to be considering the quality of both its words and music and the renewed interest in the theology of hope to which it testifies so strongly.

It is loosely based on a German hymn, '*Meine Hoffnung stehet feste*', by Joachim Neander (1650–80). Neander was born in Bremen, became a Christian pastor following a dramatic conversion after a youth devoted to riotous living, and at the age of twenty-four was appointed headmaster of the Latin School at Dusseldorf. His highly independent and unorthodox views caused some trouble with the authorities and he was forced to sign a declaration that he would not engage in extreme religious fervour. Although he died of consumption at the age of thirty, he left around sixty hymns (including No. 110 in this collection), many of which are still sung by reformed congregations in Germany.

'*Meine Hoffnung Stehet feste*', which appeared in Neander's hymn collection *Alpha and Omega,* published in 1680, was originally intended to be sung as a grace after a meal. It was based on the passage in 1 Timothy 6:17, in which the rich are charged not to 'trust in uncertain riches, but in the living God, who giveth us richly all things to enjoy'.

In the last decade of the nineteenth century, the English poet Robert Bridges (1844–1930) freely adapted Neander's original to create the hymn printed overleaf. Educated at Eton and Corpus

Christi College, Oxford, Bridges studied medicine at St Bartholomew's Hospital, London, and qualified as a doctor. After eight years in practice, however, he retired to the village of Yattendon in Berkshire to devote himself to writing. For many years he was the village choirmaster and it was his frustration at the poor quality of many hymns that led him to assemble a collection of a hundred new hymns, some based on translations and others entirely his own work. These were published as a collection in 1899 under the title the *Yattendon Hymnal*. Several have found their way into modern hymn-books, perhaps the most popular, apart from this one and 'O sacred Head, Sore wounded' (No. 100 in this collection), being 'Thee will I love, my God and King' and 'Happy are they, they that love God'. Bridges became Poet Laureate in 1913.

Originally, 'All my hope' was set to the tune which Joachim Neander had himself written for *'Meine Hoffnung'*. That tune is still used today, but much more popular is Herbert Howells's sprightly Michael, written in response to a request from the director of music at Charterhouse School and named after the composer's son, who had died in infancy. Howells later said that on receiving the request he had written the tune there and then, at the breakfast table where he was opening his mail. There is also a very serviceable Welsh tune, Groeswen by J. Ambrose Lloyd (1815–74). Founder of the Welsh Choral Union of Liverpool, Lloyd was a prolific composer, producing a number of good hymn tunes, a cantata, *The Prayer of Habakkuk*, and a part-song, 'Bloedeuyn Olef', which achieved the status of a classic in his native Wales.

All my hope on God is founded;
  He doth still my trust renew,
Me through change and chance he guideth,
  Only good and only true.
      God unknown,
      He alone
Calls my heart to be his own.

2   Pride of man and earthly glory,
  Sword and crown betray his trust;
What with care and toil he buildeth,
  Tower and temple, fall to dust.
      But God's power,
      Hour by hour,
Is my temple and my tower.

3   God's great goodness aye endureth,
  Deep his wisdom, passing thought:
Splendour, light, and life attend him,
  Beauty springeth out of naught.
      Evermore
      From his store
New-born worlds rise and adore.

4   Daily doth th' Almighty Giver
  Bounteous gifts on us bestow;
His desire our soul delighteth,
  Pleasure leads us where we go.
      Love doth stand
      At his hand;
Joy doth wait on his command.

5   Still from man to God eternal
  Sacrifice of praise be done,
High above all praises praising
  For the gift of Christ his Son.
      Christ doth call
      One and all:
Ye who follow shall not fall.

7 ALL PEOPLE THAT ON EARTH DO DWELL

This simple but majestic paraphrase of Psalm 100 ('Make a joyful noise unto the Lord, all ye lands') has the distinction of being the earliest hymn written in the English language which is still in general use today. It is one of the first of the many metrical versions of the Psalms which were made in the early days of the Reformation and which are particularly associated with the Scots.

Most of the metrical psalms were written by followers of John Calvin who believed that these were the only form of hymn which ought to be sung in churches. This one is the work of William Kethe (?–1594), a Scotsman who, like many Puritans, left Britain during the reign of the Catholic Queen Mary from 1553 to 1558. He went first to Frankfurt and then to the Calvinist stronghold of Geneva, where he helped to translate the Bible into English and to compile a book of metrical psalms. 'All people that on earth do dwell' was first published in Geneva in 1561 in the *Fourscore and Seven Psalms of David*. Later that year the Geneva Psalter, as it was called, was published in London. Kethe's version of Psalm 100 also appeared in the first Scottish Psalter, published in 1564. He returned to Britain and was chaplain to the forces under the Earl of Warwick in 1563 before becoming rector of Childe Okeford in Dorset, where he seems to have remained until his death.

The first four verses of the hymn were written by Kethe. The doxology that forms the fifth verse was sung in the early days of the Methodist movement following the conversion of any member of the congregation. It was also traditionally sung by inhabitants of the fenlands of East Anglia as a thanksgiving at the end of a period of danger of flooding and high tides.

Certain modern hymnals render the third line of the first verse

'Him serve with mirth', following a change that was first made in the Scottish Psalter to bring the hymn more in line with the second verse of Psalm 100, which runs: 'Serve the Lord with gladness'. One cannot help feeling that Kethe was a little severe in his paraphrasing at this point, but he does at least allow us a 'cheerful voice' in the line before.

For a long time the third line of the second verse was thought to begin, 'We are his flock'. This was because when the hymn was first published in England the word 'folk' was spelt in its old English form 'folck'. It was thought to be a misprint for 'flock', and not long afterwards the line was changed. This mistake persisted for nearly three centuries; when efforts were finally made to rectify it and restore 'folk' (which is much closer to the original third verse of the psalm: 'We are his people and the sheep of his pasture'), there was a considerable outcry. The *Daily Mirror*, for example, described it as an abomination when the 1904 edition of *Hymns Ancient and Modern* substituted 'folk' for the time-honoured 'flock'. Most modern hymnals now have the correct 'folk'.

The tune, known as the Old Hundredth, is also from the Geneva Psalter, although it pre-dates Kethe's paraphrase of Psalm 100 and is first found in the French-language edition of 1551, where it accompanies Psalm 134. It is by Louis Bourgeois (1510–61), who was born in Paris and followed Calvin to Geneva, where he was appointed cantor of one of the churches and given the job of providing the music for the metrical psalter then in preparation. In England the tune has always been associated with 'All people that on earth do dwell'. For some time after 1700 it was known as Savoy because of its frequent use by the congregation of a chapel in the area of London off the Strand known by that name.

Psalm C

All people that on earth do dwell,
   Sing to the Lord with cheerful voice;
Him serve with fear, his praise forth tell,
   Come ye before him, and rejoice.

2   The Lord, ye know, is God indeed;
    Without our aid he did us make;
We are his folk, he doth us feed,
    And for his sheep he doth us take.

3   O enter then his gates with praise,
    Approach with joy his courts unto;
Praise, laud, and bless his name always,
    For it is seemly so to do.

4   For why? the Lord our God is good;
    His mercy is for ever sure;
His truth at all times firmly stood,
    And shall from age to age endure.

5   To Father, Son, and Holy Ghost,
    The God whom heaven and earth adore,
From men and from the angel-host
    Be praise and glory evermore.

8 ALL THINGS BRIGHT AND BEAUTIFUL

This much-loved children's hymn is, as far as I am aware, unique in this collection for having been the object of recent censorship in Britain on political grounds. The third verse was banned from use in all schools run by the Inner London Education Authority in 1982 because of its inegalitarian sentiments.

In fact, the intention of the authoress, Cecil Frances Alexander, née Humphreys (1818–95), in penning the offending words was less to reinforce the class distinctions of Victorian Britain than to point to the equality of all men and women before God. But it is understandable that the verse jars on modern ears. Indeed, the hymn as a whole is heard much less often at school assemblies and children's services than it used to be and tends to be dismissed nowadays as a piece of Victorian sentimentality. It is something of a period piece, but its message of praise and wonder at the beauty of creation is still relevant in our conservation-conscious age, and it deserves to be kept in active service and not consigned to the graveyard.

Mrs Alexander, whose prolific output is represented by three other items in this collection (Nos. 58, 66 and 134) was born in Dublin, the daughter of a former army officer who managed the estates of the Earl of Wicklow. She developed an early love of poetry and was also strongly influenced while young by the religious teachings of the leading figures in the Oxford Movement. She was extremely attractive and was courted by two leading clergymen in the Irish Church, Professor William Archer Butler and the Revd William Alexander. Her dilemma as to which of these two suitors she should marry was ended by the death of the former and she married the latter in 1850, when he was a curate. He went on to become, first, Bishop of Derry and Raphoe and, later, Archbishop of Armagh and Primate of all Ireland. Like his wife, he was a talented poet.

Many of Mrs Alexander's religious poems and hymns were written before her marriage. They were nearly all designed for children in the Sunday Schools in which she taught, and were used to illustrate and explain the basic doctrines of Christianity, in particular the meaning of the Apostles' Creed. Her well-known carol, 'Once in Royal David's City', for example, was written to illuminate the phrase 'Born of the Virgin Mary'.

'All things bright and beautiful' was designed to explain to children the meaning of the opening words of the Creed: 'I believe in God the Father Almighty, Maker of heaven and earth.' It was almost certainly written at Markree Castle at Collooney, near Sligo. It first appeared in Frances Humphreys's *Hymns for Little Children*, published in 1848 with a preface by John Keble. The book went into a hundred editions and the profits were devoted to a school for deaf mutes in Londonderry.

The tune generally associated with the hymn – which, though light and lively, has suffered from over-use and rather verges on the trite – is Royal Oak, an adaptation of a traditional English melody by Martin Shaw (1875–1958). Greater use of some of the other tunes to which Mrs Alexander's words have been set might help to convince the sceptics that they are not just sentimental drivel and do still have some life in them. I recommend All Things Bright by William Henry Monk (1823–89), whom we have already come across as the composer of the fine tune Eventide for 'Abide with me', a tune of the same name by Sir Frederick Duseley (1825–89) and Greystone by W. R. Waghorne.

All things bright and beautiful
All creatures great and small,
All things wise and wonderful,
The Lord God made them all.

2   Each little flower that opens,
     Each little bird that sings,
    He made their glowing colours,
     He made their tiny wings.

3   The rich man in his castle,
     The poor man at his gate,
    God made them, high or lowly,
     And ordered their estate.

4   The purple headed mountain,
     The river running by,
    The sunset and the morning,
     That brightens up the sky;

5   The cold wind in the winter,
     The pleasant summer sun,
    The ripe fruits in the garden,
     He made them every one;

6   The tall trees in the greenwood,
     The meadows for our play,
    The rushes by the water,
     To gather every day;

7   He gave us eyes to see them,
     And lips that we may tell
    How great is God Almighty,
     Who has made all things well.

9 ALLELUIA! SING TO JESUS

This communion hymn is much better known among Anglicans than it is among members of other denominations. It was written in 1866 by William Chatterton Dix (1837–98), a devout High Churchman who felt that the Church of England was lacking in Eucharistic hymns.

Dix was born in Bristol, the son of a surgeon with literary leanings who wrote a life of the poet Thomas Chatterton – hence William's second name. After attending Bristol Grammar School he went into business and became manager of a marine insurance company in Glasgow.

In his spare time Dix was a prolific hymn-writer, and published four volumes of his own hymns as well as translating Abyssinian hymns and offices of the Eastern Orthodox Church. Among other hymns by him which are still sung today are 'As with gladness men of old', 'To Thee, O Lord, our hearts we raise', and 'Come unto Me, ye weary, and I will give you rest'.

'Alleluia! sing to Jesus' first appeared in Dix's *Altar Songs*, published in 1867. It was intended to be sung principally at Ascensiontide and has several references to Christ's ascension, most notably in the lines 'Though the cloud from sight received him' and 'Thou within the veil hast entered'. It is also interesting in referring to Christ as the 'bread of angels', picking up the reference in John 6:32 to 'the true bread from heaven' which also features so prominently in 'Guide me, O thou great Jehovah' (No. 48).

For a long time the first verse of the hymn was repeated at the end to give a total of five stanzas. Nowadays only the four verses printed overleaf are sung and the second is sometimes left out.

When Dix's hymn appeared in the appendix to the first edition of

31

Hymns Ancient and Modern in 1868, it was accompanied by a tune specially written for it by Samuel Sebastian Wesley (1810–76) and called Alleluia. This is still the preferred tune in *Hymns Ancient and Modern*, although it is little sung today. For the 1909 edition a new tune called Adoration was composed by B. Luard Selby, but it is not found in any modern hymn-book.

The tune to which the hymn is now nearly always sung, and to which it is admirably suited, is the majestic Hyfrydol by R. H. Prichard (1811–87). Prichard was a loom-tender's assistant in the works of the Welsh Flannel Manufacturing Company in Holywell, North Wales. He was only twenty when he wrote this lovely melody, which is also much used for 'Love divine, all loves excelling' (No. 83) and 'I will sing the wondrous story of the Christ who died for me'.

Redemption by the Precious Blood

Alleluia! sing to Jesus,
  His the sceptre, his the throne;
Alleluia! his the triumph,
  His the victory alone:
Hark! the songs of peaceful Zion
  Thunder like a mighty flood;
Jesus, out of every nation,
  Hath redeemed us by his blood.

2 Alleluia! not as orphans
  Are we left in sorrow now;
Alleluia! he is near us,
  Faith believes, nor questions how;
Though the cloud from sight received him
  When the forty days were o'er,
Shall our hearts forget his promise,
  'I am with you evermore'?

3 Alleluia! bread of angels,
  Thou on earth our food, our stay;
Alleluia! here the sinful
  Flee to thee from day to day:
Intercessor, friend of sinners,
  Earth's Redeemer, plead for me,
Where the songs of all the sinless
  Sweep across the crystal sea.

4 Alleluia! King eternal,
  Thee the Lord of Lords we own;
Alleluia! born of Mary,
  Earth thy footstool, heav'n thy throne:
Thou within the veil hast entered,
  Robed in flesh, our great High Priest;
Thou on earth both priest and victim
  In the Eucharistic feast.

10 AMAZING GRACE

There was a time in the early 1970s when it was almost impossible to listen to the radio for any length of time without hearing the words or melody of this hymn by John Newton (1725–1807). Recorded by the pipes and drums of the Royal Scots Dragoon Guards as a filler on their long-playing record, the tune was 'Top of the Pops' for nine weeks and remained in the charts for some months. Several vocalists subsequently made records of the hymn, which also sold well.

Yet, surprisingly, 'Amazing grace' appears in very few major modern British hymn-books. The situation is quite different in the United States where it has long been popular and is to be found in the main Presbyterian, Baptist, Methodist and Lutheran hymnals.

John Newton was one of the most remarkable figures in the Evangelical Revival that swept through Britain in the eighteenth century. His father was a sailor and his mother died when he was seven. After only two years of schooling, he was sent to sea at the age of eleven. His early life was by his own account godless and dissolute. Flogged for deserting from the navy, at the age of twenty-two he became captain of a ship engaged in the slave trade between Britain, West Africa and the West Indies. Three years later he underwent a dramatic conversion to Christianity, which seems to have started while he was reading Thomas à Kempis's book *The Imitation of Christ* on a voyage across the Atlantic. A violent storm blew up, and Newton spent nine hours manning the pumps and a further seventeen hours at the ship's wheel as the waves crashed around him. Several times he found himself crying aloud to God for protection. The storm eventually abated and Newton later traced the first stirrings of the 'great change' that was to turn him towards evangelical religion to his sense of deliverance after this terrible experience.

Forsaking the slave trade and the seafaring life, he became friendly with John Wesley and George Whitfield, the two leading figures in the Evangelical Revival, and spent nine years training for the Anglican ministry. In 1764 he was ordained and became curate at Olney in Buckinghamshire. There he collaborated with the poet William Cowper, a fellow Evangelical, to produce a collection of hymns which includes 280 of his own compositions, including such favourites as 'Glorious things of thee are spoken' (No. 42) and 'How sweet the name of Jesus sounds' (No. 57). He remained at Olney for sixteen years and then went to London as rector of St Mary Woolnoth where he stayed until his death.

'Amazing grace' first appeared in *Olney Hymns*, which was published in 1779. It reflects Newton's own intense conversion experience and his profound sense that it was only the overwhelming grace of God which had saved one as wretched as himself from eternal damnation. Julian says of it – with some justice – that 'it is far from being a good example of Newton's work'.

Some versions of the hymn contain an additional verse written by John Rees (1828–1900):

> When we've been there ten thousand years,
>   Bright shining as the sun,
> We've no less days to sing God's praise
>   Than when we first begun.

The tune Amazing Grace is based on an American folk melody called Virginia Harmony. It is almost certainly Scottish in origin and was probably brought across the Atlantic by colonists in the eighteenth century.

Faith's Review and Expectation

Amazing grace! how sweet the sound
   That saved a wretch like me!
I once was lost, but now am found,
   Was blind, but now I see.

2   'Twas grace that taught my heart to fear,
   And grace my fears relieved;
How precious did that grace appear
   The hour I first believed.

3   Through many dangers, toils, and snares
   I have already come;
'Tis grace hath brought me safe thus far,
   And grace will lead me home.

4   The Lord has promised good to me,
   His word my hope secures;
He will my shield and portion be
   As long as life endures.

11 AND CAN IT BE; THAT I SHOULD GAIN

This powerful hymn by Charles Wesley (1707–88) has much the same intensely personal message as John Newton's 'Amazing grace'. Both are about the conversion of an individual soul to faith in the atoning death of Christ. But there is also a sense of mystery and universality in this great hymn which lifts it far above the mainstream of 'born again' Christian experience. Wesley's is altogether a nobler and more edifying treatment of the central theme of God's wonderful and limitless grace.

Charles Wesley has rightly been described as 'the prince of English hymn-writers'. More of his hymns are sung today than those of any other hymn-writer and no fewer than ten of them appear in this book. He was born at Epworth in Lincolnshire, where his father Samuel was rector. Charles was the eighteenth child in the family; his brother John, commonly regarded as the founder of Methodism, was four years his senior. Educated at Westminster School, Charles went on to Christ Church, Oxford, where in 1729 he became a tutor. He was ordained in 1735 and joined his brother who was evangelizing in the British colony of Georgia. But Charles found the work there uncongenial and he returned to England where he came under the influence of Peter Boehler, a Moravian missionary, and underwent a conversion to the 'vital religion' of Evangelicalism. For the rest of his life he was an itinerant preacher in Britain.

Opinions vary as to exactly how many hymns Charles Wesley wrote, but his total known output amounted to 8,989 religious poems, of which over 6,000 can properly be classified as hymns. All of them were written after his conversion to 'vital religion' which took place on 21 May 1738. 'And can it be, that I should gain' was one of the first, being composed (together with 'Where shall my wondering soul begin') a matter of hours after he had made the 'great change'. The scriptural passage which he had in mind when he wrote it can be found in Galatians 2:20, 'I live by the faith of the Son of God, who loved me, and gave himself for me.' It was first published in his brother John's *Psalms and Hymns* in 1738 and then in his *Hymns and Sacred Poems* the following year. The *Wesleyan Hymn Book* of 1780 dropped the fifth verse and it has continued to be omitted in subsequent hymn-books.

There is a strong probability that John Wesley sang this hymn on the evening of his own conversion to 'vital religion', which took place in Aldersgate, London, three days after that of his brother Charles. We know that he sang a hymn that evening to the tune Crucifixion by Samuel Akeroyd. In John Wesley's first tune-book, published in 1742 and known as the *Foundery Tune Book*, that melody accompanies 'And can it be', although in later Methodist hymnals it is set to 'Where shall my wandering soul begin'.

From the mid nineteenth century onwards 'And can it be' has generally been sung to Thomas Campbell's soaring tune Sagina. Campbell (1800–1876), who came from Sheffield, published a book of twenty-three hymn tunes in 1825, entitled *The Bouquet*. He gave botanical names to all his tunes; Sagina, the Latin name for the pearlwort, is the only one which is generally sung nowadays.

Free Grace

And can it be, that I should gain
    An interest in the Saviour's blood?
Died He for me, who caused His pain –
    For me, who Him to death pursued?
Amazing love! How can it be
That Thou, my God, shouldst die for me?

2 'Tis mystery all! The Immortal dies:
      Who can explore His strange design?
   In vain the first-born seraph tries
      To sound the depths of love divine.
   'Tis mercy all! let earth adore,
   Let angel minds inquire no more.

3 He left His Father's throne above, –
      So free, so infinite His grace –
   Emptied Himself of all but love,
      And bled for Adam's helpless race:
   'Tis mercy all, immense and free;
   For, O my God, it found out me!

4 Long my imprisoned spirit lay
      Fast bound in sin and nature's night;
   Thine eye diffused a quickening ray, –
      I woke, the dungeon flamed with light;
   My chains fell off, my heart was free,
   I rose, went forth, and followed Thee.

5 Still the small inward voice I hear,
      That whispers all my sins forgiven;
   Still the atoning Blood is near,
      That quenched the wrath of hostile heaven.
   I feel the life His wounds impart;
   I feel my Saviour in my heart.

6 No condemnation now I dread;
      Jesus, and all in Him, is mine!
   Alive in Him, my living Head,
      And clothed in righteousness divine,
   Bold I approach the eternal throne,
   And claim the crown, through Christ my own.

12 AND DID THOSE FEET IN ANCIENT TIME

Does William Blake's mystical poem really constitute a hymn? Compilers of hymn-books have often been understandably coy about including it – in the *English Hymnal*, for example, it for long appeared unnumbered at the very end of the appendix and without a tune. But there is no doubt that, set to Sir Hubert Parry's majestic tune Jerusalem, it has attained the status of a national hymn, if not even a second National Anthem. It is no longer the invariable accompaniment to Women's Institute meetings, but continues to be sung with gusto on the last night of the Proms and is regularly heard in churches and school chapels.

William Blake (1757–1827) was born in London, the son of a hosier. He had no formal schooling but was apprenticed to an engraver. From an early age he was a seer of visions and a dreamer of dreams. Most of his literary works, which were illustrated by his own engravings, had a highly mystical flavour. A constant theme in them is the exaltation of love and imagination against the restrictive codes of conventional morality. But in his later works a new element enters in – the revelation of forgiveness through Christ.

The verses, as set out overleaf, first appeared in the preface to one of Blake's last works, *Milton*, which was written in 1804. Underneath them he wrote, 'Would to God that all the Lord's people were prophets', and gave the biblical source from which this quotation comes – Numbers 11:29. In the work that follows, the seventeenth-century poet is depicted as returning from eternity and entering into Blake to preach the message of Christ crucified and the doctrines of self-sacrifice and forgiveness.

The imagery of the poem is complex. Some of it is borrowed from the Bible, like the phrase 'chariots of fire' which is taken from 2 Kings 2:11, but much is of Blake's own invention. In suggesting that Jesus may have set foot in England, Blake is resurrecting the old legend which told of Christ's wanderings as a young man with St Joseph of Arimathea. The story goes that Joseph was a tin merchant and that Jesus went with him to Cornwall. A verse from Blake's long poem *Jerusalem*, which also dates from 1804, echoes this theme:

> She walks upon our meadows green;
>   The Lamb of God walks by her side:
> And every English child is seen,
>   Children of Jesus and his Bride.

There are two very different interpretations of the main message in 'And did those feet'. One school of thought, strongly represented in the *Handbook to the Church Hymnary*, sees it as a plea for intuition and imagination against scientific rationalism. On this interpretation, the 'dark satanic mills' have nothing to do with factories but represent the cold logical approach of philosophers like Locke and Bacon that Blake so much deplored, while Jerusalem represents the ideal life of freedom.

The other way of interpreting the poem is as a call for the rule of those values of social justice and freedom which will build a new Jerusalem in Britain. Although the language is undeniably mystical and personal, I am myself inclined to regard it as having such a political and social message. That certainly is how it was interpreted by the man who can claim the credit for turning Blake's verses into a hymn. In 1916 Robert Bridges asked the distinguished musician Sir Hubert Parry (1848–1918) if he could write some 'suitable, simple music' to which Blake's verses could be sung at a meeting of the 'Fight for the Right' movement at Queen's Hall.

The tune which Parry provided was also sung at a meeting held in March 1918 in the Albert Hall to celebrate the granting of votes for women. Afterwards, Mrs Millicent Fawcett, one of the leaders of the suffragette movement, suggested to the composer, 'Your "Jerusalem" ought to be made the Women Voters' Hymn,' Parry responded enthusiastically: 'I wish indeed it might become the women voters' hymn. People seem to enjoy singing it. And having the vote ought to diffuse a good deal of joy too. So they would combine happily.' The first hymn-book to include Blake's verses set to Parry's tune was the *Student Hymnal* of 1923.

And did those feet in ancient time
    Walk upon England's mountains green?
And was the holy Lamb of God
    On England's pleasant pastures seen?

2   And did the countenance divine
    Shine forth upon our clouded hills?
And was Jerusalem builded here
    Among those dark satanic mills?

3   Bring me my bow of burning gold!
    Bring me my arrows of desire!
Bring me my spear! O clouds, unfold!
    Bring me my chariot of fire!

4   I will not cease from mental fight,
    Nor shall my sword sleep in my hand,
Till we have built Jerusalem
    In England's green and pleasant land.

13 AS PANTS THE HART FOR COOLING STREAMS

For more than a century after the Reformation the only kind of congregational singing practised in British churches was the chanting of metrical versions of the Psalms. We have already come across one of these in William Kethe's paraphrase of Psalm 100 (No. 7). This is another.

A book containing metrical versions of all 150 Psalms which was published in 1562 may properly be regarded as the first hymn-book of the Church of England. Known as the 'Old Version' (its proper title being *The Whole Booke of Psalmes, collected into English metre*), it was the work of Thomas Sternhold and John Hopkins, two men who came from Gloucestershire. Although it was to last for 134 years as the official book of praise of the Church, nothing in it is still sung today.

In 1696 this psalter was revised by Nahum Tate (1652–1715) and Nicholas Brady (1659–1726). It is from their revision, generally known as Tate and Brady or the 'New Version' and much used by American Episcopalians during the eighteenth century, that this fine paraphrase of Psalm 42 comes. Tate and Brady were also responsible for 'Through all the changing scenes of life' (No. 137) and the well-known Christmas carol, 'While shepherds watched their flocks by night'.

Psalm 42 ('As the hart panteth after the water brooks') has inspired several notable paraphrases. Tate and Brady's version introduces the idea of a hunt which is not found in the original, but is otherwise fairly faithful to it. It is printed below in its entirety, as it first appeared in their revised version of the psalter. In modern hymnals the hymn is greatly reduced in length, often only including verses 1, 2 and 12 of the original and with the following doxology added:

To Father, Son, and Holy Ghost,
    The God whom we adore,
Be glory, as it was, is now,
    And shall be evermore.

Both Tate and Brady were of Irish descent. Tate was the son of a Dublin clergyman called Faithful Teate. He came to England after graduating from Trinity College, Dublin, and changed his name to Tate. He became friendly with the leading English poet, John Dryden, and was a distinguished versifier in his own right, producing the libretto for Henry Purcell's opera, *Dido and Aeneas*. He also rewrote Shakespeare's *King Lear* to give it a happy ending. In 1692 he was made Poet Laureate, but in later life he fell a victim to excessive drinking and ended his days in a debtors' prison.

Brady was also a graduate of Trinity College, Dublin. He is said to have saved his native town of Brandon in County Cork from being burned down by rebel mobs and to have first come to England to petition William III on its behalf. The king subsequently appointed him as a personal chaplain and he ended his career as vicar of Stratford-upon-Avon.

The tune to which this hymn is now universally sung, Martyrdom or All Saints, is by Hugh Wilson and was first published in R. A. Smith's *Sacred Music Sung in St George's Church, Edinburgh* (1825). Wilson (1766–1824) was an Ayrshire shoemaker who later became manager of a mill at Pollokshaws, near Glasgow.

Psalm XI

As pants the hart for cooling streams
    When heated in the chase;
So longs my soul, O God, for thee
    And thy refreshing grace.

2 For thee, my God, the living God,
    My thirsty soul doth pine;
O when shall I behold thy face,
    Thou Majesty divine?

3 Tears are my constant food, while thus
    Insulting foes upbraid,
'Deluded wretch, where's now thy God,
    And where thy promis'd aid?'

4 I sigh whene'er my musing thoughts
    Those happy days present,
When I with troops of pious friends
    Thy temple did frequent;

5 When I advanc'd with songs of praise
    My solemn vows to pay;
And led the joyful sacred throng
    That kept the festal day.

6 Why restless, why cast down, my soul?
    Trust God, and he'll employ
His aid for thee, and change these sighs
    To thankful hymns of joy.

7 My soul's cast down, O God, and thinks
    On thee and Sion still;
From Jordan's banks, from Hermon's heights,
    And Missar's humbler hill.

8   One trouble calls another on
   And, bursting o'er my head,
Fall spouting down, till round my soul
   A roaring sea is spread.

9   But when thy presence, Lord of life,
   Has once dispelled this storm,
To thee I'll midnight anthems sing,
   And all my vows perform

10 God of my strength, how long shall I,
   Like one forgotten, mourn?
Forlorn, forsaken, and expos'd
   To my oppressors' scorn.

11 My heart is pierced as with a sword,
   Whilst thus my foes upbraid,
'Vain boaster, where is now thy God?
   And where his promised aid?'

12 Why restless, why cast down, my soul?
   Hope still; and thou shalt sing
The praise of him who is thy God,
   Thy health's eternal spring.

14 AT THE NAME OF JESUS

This is a hymn that can have a totally different impact depending on the tune to which it is sung. It is set to a wide variety of melodies, some of which make it grand and confident, others quieter and more reflective, and one – John Michael Brierley's Camberwell – which makes it positively swinging.

It is the work of Caroline Maria Noel (1817–77), the first of a remarkable group of sickly Victorian spinsters whom we shall encounter at various points in this book and whose contribution to English hymnody was considerable. She belonged firmly to the Evangelical wing of the Church of England. Her father, Canon Gerard Thomas Noel, for many years vicar of Romsey in Hampshire, was himself a hymn-writer. So was her uncle, the Hon. Baptist Wriothesley Noel, a colourful figure who, after being ordained into the Church of England and appointed a chaplain to Queen Victoria, became a believer in adult baptism and switched to the Baptist Church. His hymns, which were still being sung by Baptists until recently, include the intriguingly entitled 'There's not a bird with lonely nest'.

Caroline wrote her first hymn at the age of seventeen but produced nothing more until she was forty, when illness turned her back to hymn-writing. She hoped that her verse would cheer and comfort others who were sick. She wrote a large number of hymns in the last twenty-five years of her life, which were spent in almost constant pain and sickness. They were published in two volumes, *The Name of Jesus, and Other Verses for the Sick and Lonely* (1861) and *The Name of Jesus, and Other Poems* (published posthumously in 1878). She is buried outside the Abbey Church at Romsey, next to the grave of her father.

'At the name of Jesus' first appeared in the second of her two volumes of hymns and was probably written in the early 1870s. It is based on the passage in Philippians 2:9–11:

> Wherefore God also hath highly exalted him, and given him a name which is above every name; that at the name of Jesus every knee should bow, of things in heaven, and things in earth, and things under the earth; and that every tongue should confess that Jesus Christ is Lord, to the glory of God the Father.

In his book *A Panorama of Christian Hymnody*, Erik Routley has described 'At the name of Jesus' as 'the only objective theological hymn to come from the hand of a nineteenth-century woman writer'. Certainly it is completely free of the strongly personal and sentimental elements which characterize much of the work of Frances Crosby (Nos. 19 and 140 in this collection) and Anna and Susan Warner (Nos. 65 and 69). Caroline Noel wrote it with Ascension Day processions in mind, which may partly explain its length, but it is appropriate for congregational use at any point in the Church's calendar. The hymn is strongly biblically based, drawing clearly (in addition to the text quoted above) on the opening verses of St John's Gospel:

> In the beginning was the Word, and the Word was with God, and the Word was God. The same was in the beginning with God. All things were made by him; and without him was not any thing made that was made. In him was life; and the life was the light of men.

In the Revised Standard Version of the Bible, which appeared shortly before Caroline Noel died, the wording of the passage from Philippians was changed to read 'in the name of Jesus every knee shall bow'. She changed the first line of her hymn to match the new translation, and for many years it appeared in Baptist, Methodist and Presbyterian hymn-books as 'In the name of Jesus'. Nearly all hymnals have now restored the original. The second verse of the hymn is commonly omitted.

As I pointed out earlier, 'At the name of Jesus' has been set to an extraordinarily wide variety of tunes. The Baptists for long used Ashbury by Sir George Clement Martin (1844–1916), and the *English Hymnal* offered either King's Weston by Ralph Vaughan Williams (1872–1958) or *Laus Tibi Domini Christe* from a fourteenth-century

German processional melody. Several tunes have been specially composed for the hymn. They include Evelyns, written by William Henry Monk (1823–89) for the revised edition of *Hymns Ancient and Modern* in 1875, Cuddesdon, written by William Harold Ferguson (1874–1950) for the *Public School Hymnbook*, and *In Nomine Jesu*, written by Arthur Oldham for the third edition of the *Church Hymnary*.

The swinging tune Camberwell, which I mentioned earlier, first appeared in the album *Thirty Twentieth-Century Hymn Tunes*, which was published in 1960. It is in some ways a classic product of that decade: easy, catchy, confident, and without any hidden depths or subtle shades. I was brought up on it in school chapel in the 1960s and have to confess to a great liking for it, although I can see its limitations and can understand why many churches have now returned to Evelyns or Cuddesdon. It certainly made singing this particular hymn fun – a bit too much fun, perhaps.

Every knee shall bow

At the name of Jesus
　　Every knee shall bow,
Every tongue confess him
　　King of glory now;
'Tis the Father's pleasure
　　We should call him Lord,
Who from the beginning
　　Was the mighty word.

2　Mighty and mysterious
　　　In the highest height,
　God from everlasting,
　　　Very light of light:
　In the Father's bosom
　　　With the spirit blest,
　Love, in love eternal,
　　　Rest, in perfect rest.

3　At his voice creation
　　　Sprang at once to sight,
　All the Angel faces,
　　　All the hosts of light,
　Thrones and dominations,
　　　Stars upon their way,
　All the heavenly orders,
　　　In their great array.

4　Humbled for a season,
　　　To receive a name
　From the lips of sinners
　　　Unto whom he came,
　Faithfully he bore it
　　　Spotless to the last,
　Brought it back victorious
　　　When from death he passed:

5   Bore it up triumphant
      With its human light,
   Through all ranks of creatures,
      To the central height,
   To the throne of Godhead,
      To the Father's breast;
   Filled it with the glory
      Of that perfect rest.

6   Name him, brothers, name him,
      With love as strong as death,
   But with awe and wonder,
      And with bated breath;
   He is God the Saviour,
      He is Christ the Lord,
   Ever to be worshipped,
      Trusted, and adored.

7   In your hearts enthrone him;
      There let him subdue
   All that is not holy,
      All that is not true:
   Crown him as your captain
      In temptation's hour;
   Let his will enfold you
      In its light and power.

8   Brothers, this Lord Jesus
      Shall return again,
   With his Father's glory,
      With his Angel train;
   For all wreaths of empire
      Meet upon his brow,
   And our hearts confess him
      King of glory now.

15 AWAKE, MY SOUL, AND WITH THE SUN

This stirring morning hymn was the work of Thomas Ken (1637–1711), one of the most saintly figures in the history of the Church of England.

Left an orphan as a young child, he was brought up by Izaak Walton, the author of *The Compleat Angler*. He was educated at Winchester and New College, Oxford, and ordained at the age of twenty-six. Six years later he returned to his old school as a teacher and chaplain, becoming also a Prebendary of Winchester Cathedral.

Ken later achieved considerable fame as chaplain to King Charles II, whose amorous adventures he found impossible to sanction. On one celebrated occasion Charles found himself in Winchester with his mistress Nell Gwyn and asked Ken to put them up in his house. Ken refused, declaring, 'Not for your kingdom would I allow such an insult on the house of a Royal chaplain.' Despite the snub, the King held no grudge against Ken and appointed him to the bishopric of Bath and Wells in 1685. Later that year he attended at Charles's deathbed. He fell foul of Charles's brother, James II, refusing to sign the Declaration of Indulgence which suspended penal laws against Roman Catholics and Dissenters. As a result he was imprisoned in the Tower of London. Although reinstated in his see by William of Orange after the Glorious Revolution of 1688, he was soon in trouble once again for refusing to take the oath of allegiance to the new monarch. He retired and spent his last days at Longleat House, the home of Lord Weymouth.

'Awake, my soul' was written while Ken was still at Winchester and before he had become embroiled in the world of politics. In 1674 he published a manual of prayers for the boys at the College, and in the 1695 edition of that work this hymn appeared together with hymns to be sung in the evening and at midnight. In the preface to the manual the young scholars were exhorted 'to sing the Morning and Evening hymns in your chamber devoutly', though it was not made clear whether they should also wake themselves up in the middle of the night to sing the midnight hymn. During Ken's own time as a pupil at Winchester, the day began at 5 a.m. with morning prayers and a Latin hymn, *'Iam lucis orto sidere'* ('Now the daylight fills the sky'), which was sung before breakfast. Subsequent generations of boys had cause to thank him for producing something in English for their morning devotions, even if it was on the long side.

The hymn as printed overleaf is as Ken originally wrote it. He produced a revised version in 1709 in which the first two lines of verse 2 were changed to 'Redeem thy mis-spent time that's past,/ And live this day as if thy last', and two new verses were added:

> Let all thy converse be sincere,
> Thy conscience as the noon-day clear;
> Think how all-seeing God thy ways
> And all thy secret thoughts surveys.

> Awake, awake, ye heavenly choir,
> May your devotion me inspire,
> That I like you my age may spend,
> Like you may on my God attend.

Modern hymn-books tend to print a shortened version. The hymn is generally sung to the tune Morning Hymn by François Hippolite Barthelemon (1741–1808). Also known as Hippolytus and Magdalene, it was specially written for 'Awake, my soul' at the request of the chaplain of a female orphan asylum in London and was first published in 1785. Previously the orphans had used the tune Uffingham by Jeremiah Clarke (1670–1707), famous as the composer of the Trumpet Voluntary. The hymn can also be sung to Tallis's Canon, normally associated with Ken's evening hymn, 'All praise to thee, my God, this night' (later changed to 'Glory to thee, my God, this night').

At his own request Ken was buried at sunrise in the churchyard at Frome, Somerset, with his beautiful morning hymn being sung.

Morning Hymn

Awake, my soul, and with the sun
Thy daily stage of duty run,
Shake off dull sloth, and joyful rise
To pay thy morning sacrifice.

2   Thy precious time misspent, redeem,
Each present day thy last esteem,
Improve thy talent with due care,
For the Great Day thyself prepare.

3   By influence of the Light divine
Let thy own light to others shine.
Reflect all heaven's propitious ways
In ardent love, and cheerful praise.

4   Wake, and lift up thyself, my heart,
And with the angels bear thy part,
Who all night long unwearied sing
High praise to the eternal King.

5   All praise to thee who safe hast kept
And hast refreshed me while I slept.
Grant, Lord, when I from death shall wake
I may of endless light partake.

6   Heav'n is, dear Lord, where e'er thou art,
O never then from me depart;
For to my soul 'tis hell to be
But for one moment void of thee.

7   Lord, I my vows to thee renew,
Disperse my sins like morning dew.
Guard my first springs of thought and will
And with thyself my Spirit fill.

8   Direct, control, suggest this day
All I design, or do, or say,
That all my powers with all their might
In thy sole glory may unite.

9   Praise God, from whom all blessings flow,
Praise him, all creatures here below,
Praise him above, ye heavenly host,
Praise Father, Son, and Holy Ghost.

16 BE STILL, MY SOUL

This is a hymn which owes its popularity very largely to a tune which has been borrowed from a symphonic work by a major classical composer. Other examples of equally successful 'hijackings' of the classics include 'Thine be the glory, risen, conquering Son' (No. 135) and 'I vow to thee, my country' (No. 60). But whereas in those two cases the classical melody was associated with the hymn from the beginning, it was nearly a century after the first appearance of 'Be still, my soul' that it was set to the tune from Sibelius's 'Finlandia' to which it is now invariably sung.

The hymn is based on a German original, '*Stille, mein Wille: dein Jesus hilft siegen*', which was written in 1752 by Katharina von Schlegel (1697–?). She is said to have been head of the Evangelical Lutheran nunnery in the city of Cothen, but it seems more likely that she was, in fact, attached to the ducal court there. The translation into English was made in 1855 by Jane Laurie Borthwick (1813–97). The elder daughter of the manager of the North British Insurance Company in Edinburgh, Miss Borthwick was a devout member of the Free Church of Scotland. With her sister Sarah Findlater she published a volume of translations of German hymns under the title *Hymns from the Land of Luther* and it was there that 'Be still, my soul' first appeared.

In her book Miss Borthwick attached the text 'In your patience possess ye your souls' (Luke 21:19) to this hymn. The opening words are based on Psalm 46:10, 'Be still, and know that I am God', while the last two lines of the second verse recall the words of St Mark 4:41, 'What manner of man is this, that even the wind and the sea obey him?'

Altogether Jane Borthwick supplied sixty-nine of the translations which went into *Hymns from the Land of Luther*, while her sister provided fifty-three. She lived for a time in Switzerland and published a further book of translations under the title *Alpine Lyrics* in 1875. Like so many other Victorian spinster hymn-writers she was also a devoted doer of good works, being actively involved in the Edinburgh House of Refuge, the Moravian Mission in Labrador and the Home and Foreign Missions of her own church.

For a long time 'Be still, my soul' was sung to the tune St Helen which was specially composed for it in 1868 by Walter Hately (1843–1907), a leading precentor and choirmaster in the Free Church in Edinburgh. It was first set to the chorale-like melody in Sibelius's symphonic poem *Finlandia* by the Presbyterian Board for Christian Education in the United States in 1933.

Jean Sibelius (1865–1957) was born in Finland and spent nearly all his working life there after studying in Berlin and Vienna. It has been said of his orchestral compositions that 'they seem to have passed over black torrents and desolate moorlands, through pallid sunlight and grim primeval wet greys and blacks, relieved only by brightness, wan and elusive as the northern summer, frostily green as the polar light'.

Finlandia was written in 1899 for a great patriotic demonstration in favour of the freedom of the press at a time when the Finns were struggling against Russian domination. Interestingly, 'Be still, my soul' is not the only well-known British hymn to have a tune from Finland. The popular carol 'Good King Wenceslas' is set to a melody from *Piae Cantiones*, a Finnish tune-book of 1582.

Submission

Be still, my soul; the Lord is on thy side;
    Bear patiently the cross of grief or pain;
Leave to thy God to order and provide;
    In every change he faithful will remain.
Be still, my soul: thy best, thy heavenly Friend
Through thorny ways leads to a joyful end.

2   Be still, my soul: thy God doth undertake
    To guide the future as he has the past.
Thy hope, thy confidence let nothing shake;
    All now mysterious shall be bright at last,
Be still, my soul: the waves and winds still know
His voice who ruled them while he dwelt below.

3   Be still, my soul: when dearest friends depart,
    And all is darkened in the vale of tears,
Then shalt thou better know his love, his heart,
    Who comes to soothe thy sorrow and thy fears.
Be still, my soul; thy Jesus can repay,
From his own fulness, all he takes away.

4   Be still, my soul: the hour is hastening on
    When we shall be for ever with the Lord,
When disappointment, grief and fear are gone,
    Sorrow forgot, love's purest joys restored.
Be still, my soul: when change and tears are past,
All safe and blessèd we shall meet at last.

17 BE THOU MY VISION, O LORD OF MY HEART

Considering the wealth of both poetry and folk music in Celtic Britain, it is surprising that it is only in recent times that some of the religious lyrics from this great and distinctive Christian culture have been translated and fashioned into hymns. Perhaps the most popular hymn derived from a Celtic original, 'I bind unto myself to-day' (No. 58), is less than a hundred years old, while this one first appeared in the early years of this century.

It derives from an eighth-century Irish poem, '*Rob tu mo bhiole, a Comdi cride*', which was translated from the original Gaelic into English in 1905 by Mary Byrne (1880–1931), an expert on the Irish language. In 1912 it was versified by Dr Eleanor Hull (1860–1935), the author of a number of books on the subject of Celtic folklore. The verses were published in her *Poem Book of the Gael* and first appeared as a hymn, in the form printed here, in the *Irish Church Hymnal* of 1919.

It is only very recently that most British hymn-books have included 'Be thou my vision'. It appears in a number of different forms, with particularly significant variations occurring in the last verse. In the *New English Hymnal* this is given as:

> High King of heaven, thou heaven's bright Sun,
> O grant me its joys after vict'ry is won,
> Great Heart of my own heart, whatever befall,
> Still be thou my vision, O Ruler of all.

The third edition of the *Church Hymnary* offers the following alternative:

> High King of heaven, after victory won,
> May I reach heaven's joys, O bright heav'n's Sun!

Heart of my own heart, whatever befall,
Still be my Vision, O Ruler of all.

'Be thou my vision' is universally sung to a traditional Irish air, Slane, which was resurrected in *Joyce's Old Irish Folk Music and Songs*, published in 1920. The same tune is also often used for 'Lord of all hopefulness, Lord of all joy' and for 'Lord of creation, to thee be all praise' (see No. 82). In his book *Hymns for Today Discussed*, Cyril Taylor makes a strong plea for Slane to be reserved for this hymn and not to have its impact weakened through over-use. It is such a strong and powerful tune that I am not sure it can be over-used, but I would certainly agree with him that if it is to be reserved for one hymn alone, then 'Be thou my vision' should be that one.

Be thou my vision, O Lord of my heart,
Naught be all else to me save that thou art;
Be thou my best thought in the day and night,
Waking or sleeping thy presence my light.

2　Be thou my wisdom, be thou my true word,
I ever with thee and thou with me, Lord;
Thou my great Father, and I thy true son;
Thou in me dwelling, and I with thee one.

3　Be thou my breast-plate, my sword for the fight,
Be thou my armour, and be thou my might,
Thou my soul's shelter, and thou my high tower,
Raise thou me heavenward, O Power of my power.

4　Riches I heed not, nor man's empty praise,
Thou mine inheritance through all my days;
Thou, and thou only, the first in my heart,
High King of heaven, my treasure thou art!

5　High King of heaven when battle is done,
Grant heaven's joy to me O bright heaven's sun,
Christ of my own heart, whatever befall,
Still be my vision, O Ruler of all.

18 BLESS'D ARE THE PURE IN HEART

This hymn is an interesting composite. The first and third verses are the work of one of the outstanding figures in the Victorian Church of England, John Keble (1792–1866), while the third and fourth were written by the much less well-known William John Hall (1793–1861).

John Keble was one of the leading figures in the Oxford Movement, which sought to take the Church of England back to its Catholic roots. Indeed, the assize sermon which he preached in the University Church of St Mary the Virgin in Oxford in July 1833 on the theme of national apostasy is generally taken to mark the start of the movement. Unlike many other Tractarians, he remained loyal to the Church of England and did not become a Roman Catholic. Commemorated today in Keble College, Oxford, he was revered in his lifetime as a saintly parish priest.

Keble was born at Fairford, where his father was vicar. After obtaining a double first at Oxford, he became a fellow of Oriel College at the age of eighteen and was ordained six years later. From 1831 to 1841 he was Professor of Poetry at Oxford University, and in 1836 he became vicar of Hursley in Hampshire where he remained for thirty years until his death.

'Bless'd are the pure in heart' comes from a poem which Keble wrote in October 1819 for the feast of the Purification of the Blessed Virgin Mary. It is based on the beatitudes in Matthew 5:8, 'Blessed are the pure in heart; for they shall see God.' The poem was published in Keble's *The Christian Year* (1827), a collection of devout reflections and meditations in verse for all the major festivals and fast days of the Church. The book sold over 108,000 copies in twenty-five years and went into forty-three editions. Although it was not designed as a hymnal, nearly a hundred of its verses were adapted for use as hymns, including the ever popular 'New every morning is the love' (No. 90). The use of Keble's verses in this way played an important part in establishing the proprietyof hymn-singing in the Anglo-Catholic wing of the Church of England.

Keble's original poem ran to seventeen verses. In 1836 William John Hall, a minor canon of St Paul's Cathedral who later became vicar of Tottenham in north-east London, took the first and last of these and added two stanzas of his own to form the hymn with which we are now familiar and which is printed overleaf. He slightly changed the wording of the stanza by Keble which became the third verse of the hymn, substituting 'dwelling' in the third line for the original 'cradle'.

There is a strong case for adding more of Keble's original verses to this hymn, perhaps at the expense of those by Hall which Erik Routley has not unjustly described as 'platitudinous'. Might I suggest that for a start some consideration could be given to including the second verse of the poem:

> Might mortal thought presume
> To guess an angel's lay,
> Such are the notes that echo through
> The courts of Heaven today.

The tune to which the hymn is generally sung is Franconia by W. H. Havergal (1793–1870), which is adapted from a tune in Konig's *Harmonischer Liederschatz* (1748).

The Purification

Bless'd are the pure in heart,
For they shall see our God,
The secret of the Lord is theirs,
Their soul is Christ's abode.

2   The Lord, who left the heavens
Our life and peace to bring,
To dwell in lowliness with men,
Their Pattern and their King;

3   Still to the lowly soul
He doth himself impart,
And for his dwelling and his throne
Chooseth the pure in heart.

4   Lord, we thy presence seek;
May ours this blessing be;
Give us a pure and lowly heart
A temple meet for thee.

19 BLESSÈD ASSURANCE, JESUS IS MINE

This confident evangelical hymn is the work of one of the most prolific hymn-writers of all time, Mrs Frances Jane van Alstyne (1820–1915), better known by her maiden name, Fanny Crosby.

Born in New York, she was totally blind from infancy and went at the age of fourteen to the first special school for the blind established in the United States. In later life she returned to teach there and met her future husband who was also a blind teacher at the school. Fanny Crosby wrote verse from an early age and was encouraged by William Cullen Bryant, the distinguished American poet and hymn-writer. At the age of twenty-four she published her first book of verse, *The Blind Girl and Other Poems*.

Fanny Crosby was converted to Evangelical religion during the singing of Isaac Watts's hymn 'Here, Lord, I give myself away' at a meeting in a Methodist Church in New York. Later she met the great evangelist and composer Ira D. Sankey, who set many of her verses to music.

Altogether Fanny Crosby wrote more than 8,000 hymns and sacred songs. She had regular contracts with a number of evangelical publishers. One firm commissioned her to write three songs a week and for two firms alone she wrote 5,000 hymns. She used 216 different pen names. Among her most popular hymns are 'To God be the glory' (No. 140), 'Safe in the arms of Jesus', 'Rescue the Perishing', 'I am Thine, O Lord; I have heard thy voice', and 'O my Saviour, hear me'.

It has to be admitted that many of her hymns do sound as though they have come off a production line, and lack subtlety and imagination. No one would claim that 'Blessèd assurance' is great poetry but it expresses the heart of the Christian gospel of salvation simply and movingly, even if its language is rather too personal and possessive for many tastes. It has long been popular in Evangelical circles and became the theme song of the Billy Graham evangelistic movement, being used in his 'Hour of Decision' broadcasts. Those who have some doubts about the approach adopted in this kind of evangelistic enterprise have penned a parody of the opening lines:

Blessèd assurance, Jesus is mine:
I had an experience at a quarter to nine.

The tune for 'Blessèd assurance' was the work of Mrs Phoebe Knapp (1839–1908), the wife of J. F. Knapp, founder of the Metropolitan Life Assurance Company of New York and one of the richest men in the city. It may well be that it preceded the words, since the story goes that in 1873 Mrs Knapp played the tune through on a visit to the blind poetess and asked her what it said to her. Fanny Crosby is said to have come up almost instantly with the words of the hymn.

Blessèd assurance, Jesus is mine:
O what a foretaste of glory divine!
Heir of salvation, purchase of God;
Born of His Spirit, washed in His blood.

This is my story, this is my song,
Praising my Saviour all the day long.

2   Perfect submission, perfect delight,
Visions of rapture burst on my sight;
Angels descending, bring from above
Echoes of mercy, whispers of love.

3   Perfect submission, all is at rest,
I in my Saviour am happy and blest;
Watching and waiting, looking above,
Filled with His goodness, lost in His love.

20 BREATHE ON ME, BREATH OF GOD

The idea of breath has always had a central role in Christian theology. The creative function of God has often been conceived of as the action of breathing life into mankind, following the description in Genesis 2:7, 'And the Lord God formed man of the dust of the ground, and breathed into his nostrils the breath of life; and man became a living soul.'

Breath has also long been synonymous in Christian thought with the concept of the Holy Spirit. Both Greek and Latin have the same words for spirit and breath (*pneuma* and *spiritus*). Whereas to a physicist pneumatology means the science of air and gases, to a theologian it means the doctrine and study of the Holy Spirit.

It is this notion of the Holy Spirit as the breath of God breathed on and into his creatures that Edwin Hatch (1835–89) develops in this simple devotional hymn. It first appeared in 1878 in a privately printed pamphlet, *Between Doubt and Prayer*.

Born of Nonconformist parents, Hatch was educated at King Edward the Sixth School, Birmingham, and Pembroke College, Oxford, where he was friendly with several future members of the Pre-Raphaelite brotherhood, including William Morris, Edward Burne-Jones and Algernon Swinburne. As an undergraduate he contributed articles to several magazines and reviews, but instead of following his friends into a literary or artistic career he was ordained into the Church of England and served for a period in a parish in the East End of London.

For most of his adult life Hatch held academic positions. From 1859 to 1867 he was Professor of Classics at Trinity College, Toronto. In 1867 he returned to Oxford as Vice-Principal of St Mary's Hall. He had a brief spell as Rector of Purleigh in Essex before ending his days as University Reader in Ecclesiastical History (1885–9). Despite his academic eminence, Hatch was a man of deep and simple piety, as this hymn shows. It was said of his religion that it was as simple and unaffected as a child's.

'Breathe on me' is sung to a bewildering number of tunes. Perhaps the most effective are Aylesbury (also known as Winksworth, Fetter Lane and Brentford), which was first found in John Chetham's *Book of Psalmody* in 1718 and harmonized by S. S. Wesley (1810–76), and Carlisle by Charles Lockhart (1745–1815). Despite being blind from infancy, Lockhart was a notable church organist in London and was particularly renowned for his training of children's choirs. Other tunes to which the hymn is sung include *Veni Spiritus* by Sir John Stainer (1840–1901), Hampton, which first appeared in 1770 in the *Universal Psalmodist* compiled by Aaron Williams (1731–76), St George by H. J. Gauntlett (1805–76), Boylston by Lowell Mason (1792–1872), a bank clerk in Savannah who founded the Boston Academy of Music, and Trentham by Robert Jackson (1842–1914). The use of this last tune comes in for something of a hammering from Donald Webster in his book, *Our Hymn Tunes, their Choice and Performance* (Edinburgh, 1983). 'One might conclude from it and the way it is sung,' he writes, 'that the breath of God was an anaesthetic, not a "Giver of Life".' My own favourite is Carlisle.

The Breath of the Spirit

Breathe on me, Breath of God,
  Fill me with life anew,
That I may love what thou dost love,
  And do what thou wouldst do.

2   Breathe on me, Breath of God,
       Until my heart is pure,
Until with thee I will one will,
       To do and to endure.

3   Breathe on me, Breath of God,
       Blend all my soul with thine,
Until this earthly part of me
       Glows with thy fire divine.

4   Breathe on me, Breath of God;
       So shall I never die,
But live with thee the perfect life
       Of thine eternity.

21 BRIGHT THE VISION THAT DELIGHTED

This bouncy and breezy hymn dates from 1837, the year of Queen Victoria's accession. It is the work of Richard Mant (1776–1848), a leading divine in the Church in Ireland.

Educated at Winchester and Trinity College, Oxford, Mant was ordained at the age of twenty-six and served as a curate at Buriton, Hampshire, Crawley, Surrey, and in his father's parish in Southampton. After holding livings in Essex, London and Surrey, he moved to Ireland in 1820 as Bishop of Killaloe and Kilfenoragh. In 1823 he was translated to the see of Connor and Down, and in 1833 the see of Dromore was added to his diocese. He wrote a substantial history of the Church in Ireland and two volumes of hymns. The only other one of his hymns which is still sometimes sung today has the following first verse:

> For all thy saints, O Lord,
> Who strove in thee to live,
> Who followed thee, obeyed, adored,
> Our grateful hymn receive.

The seer mentioned in the second line of 'Bright the vision that delighted' is the prophet Isaiah, who lived in the kingdom of Judah during the eighth century B C. The hymn is, in fact, about the vision which he had around the year 740 and which led him to become a prophet. It is based on the account in Isaiah 6:1–4:

In the year that King Uzziah died I saw also the Lord sitting upon a throne, high and lifted up, and his train filled the temple. Above it stood the seraphims: each one had six wings; with twain he covered his feet, and with twain he did fly. And one cried unto another and said, Holy, holy, holy is the Lord of hosts: the whole earth is full of his glory. And the posts of the door moved at the voice of him that cried, and the house was filled with smoke.

The tune normally used for the hymn is known variously as Dresden, Redhead or *Laus Deo*. It was adapted from a German melody in 1853 by Richard Redhead (1820–1901), for thirty years organist at St Mary Magdalene's, Paddington. A strong supporter of the Oxford Movement, he wrote many other hymn tunes including Petra for Rock of ages (No. 113). *'Bright the vision'* is sometimes also sung to the tune *Sanctus* by John Richards (1843–1908), a native of Bangor, North Wales, who is said to have got up regularly in the middle of the night with a good tune in his head and written it down with soap on the bedroom mirror, in the absence of more conventional writing materials.

Hymn commemorative of the 'Thrice Holy'

Bright the vision that delighted
    Once the sight of Judah's seer;
Sweet the countless tongues united
    To entrance the prophet's ear.

2 Round the Lord in glory seated
    Cherubim and Seraphim
Filled his temple, and repeated
    Each to each the alternate hymn:

3 'Lord, thy glory fills the heaven;
    Earth is with its fullness stored;
Unto thee be glory given,
    Holy, Holy, Holy, Lord.'

4 Heaven is still with glory ringing,
    Earth takes up the Angels' cry,
'Holy, Holy, Holy,' singing,
    'Lord of hosts, the Lord most high.'

5 With his seraph train before him,
    With his holy Church below,
Thus conspire we to adore him,
    Bid we thus our anthem flow:

6 'Lord, thy glory fills the heaven;
    Earth is with its fullness stored;
Unto thee be glory given,
    Holy, Holy, Holy, Lord.'

22 BRIGHTEST AND BEST OF THE SONS OF THE MORNING

Strange as it may seem now, this very popular hymn was for a long time excluded from many hymnals on the grounds that it involved the worship of a star. Objections were also raised to the fact that its metre was suggestive of a dance. In fact, it is a straightforward Epiphany hymn, telling the story of the three wise men coming to visit the baby Christ in Bethlehem.

'Brightest and best' was the first hymn written by one of the greatest hymn-writers in the Church of England, Reginald Heber (1783–1826). Born into an aristocratic family in the village of Malpas on the Cheshire–Shropshire border where his father was rector, he was educated at Whitchurch Grammar School and privately in Neasden, North London. He went on to Brasenose College, Oxford, where he won the University prize for Latin verse three years running. He was elected to a fellowship at All Souls College and, after an extensive Grand Tour of Europe, became rector of Hodnet in Shropshire. For his later career, see notes to Hymn No. 41.

Heber spent sixteen years as a parish priest and it was during this period that he wrote most of his fifty-seven hymns, which include such favourites as 'Holy, Holy, Holy! Lord God Almighty' (No. 55). He wrote a hymn for nearly every Sunday and for each solemn day and feast day in the Church of England calendar. 'Brightest and best' was written for the Feast of the Epiphany. It was first published in 1811 in the *Christian Observer,* an Evangelical periodical edited by Zachary Macaulay, the father of the writer and statesman Thomas Babington Macaulay. It was a curious choice for the High Church Heber but he was determined to show that hymn-singing was not just a prerogative of the Evangelical wing of the Church of England.

73

The hymn first appeared between hard covers in his *Hymns written and adapted to the weekly Church Service* (1827).

The phrase 'sons of the morning' which Heber uses to such spectacular effect in the first line of this hymn has its origins in Isaiah 14:12, where it is used to describe Lucifer. The first verse also has echoes of Job 38:7, 'When the morning stars sang together, and all the sons of God shouted for joy'. Edom, referred to in the second line of verse 3, was the mountainous land to the south of Moab, stretching down to the Gulf of Aqaba on the Red Sea. The Edomites were enemies of the Israelites and were spoken of bitterly by many of the Old Testament prophets. As far as I know, there is no particular reason to link Edom with the frankincense and myrrh which were brought by the three wise men to the infant Jesus.

The hymn was originally sung to the tune of an old Scottish ballad called 'Wandering Willie'. Since then it has been set to many different tunes. Perhaps the commonest, and the one I think is most suitable although it seems to have gone out of fashion recently, is Epiphany by Joseph Francis Thrupp (1827–67), vicar of Barrington, Cambridge. It first appeared in his *Psalms and Hymns,* published in 1853, and is sometimes called Epiphany Hymn, possibly to distinguish it from another tune called Epiphany by E. J. Hopkins (1818–1901) to which Heber's hymn has also been sung. Other melodies in contemporary use include Bede, adapted from Handel's *Athaliah* of 1733 by Sir John Goss (1800–1880), Wallog by Walford Davies (1869–1941) and Crudwell by Walter Kendall Stanton.

If I had had more space I would have included as the next hymn in this collection another of Heber's compositions, 'By cool Siloam's shady rill'.

Brightest and best of the sons of the morning,
  Dawn on our darkness and lend us thine aid;
Star of the east, the horizon adorning,
  Guide where our infant Redeemer is laid.

2 Cold on his cradle the dew-drops are shining,
  Low lies his head with the beasts of the stall:
Angels adore him in slumber reclining,
  Maker and Monarch and Saviour of all.

3 Say, shall we yield him, in costly devotion,
  Odours of Edom and offerings divine?
Gems of the mountain and pearls of the ocean,
  Myrrh from the forest or gold from the mine?

4 Vainly we offer each ample oblation,
  Vainly with gifts would his favour secure;
Richer by far is the heart's adoration,
  Dearer to God are the prayers of the poor.

23 CHRIST IS MADE THE SURE FOUNDATION

This is another medieval hymn translated from the Latin by John Mason Neale (1818–66). It is to be found in the oldest extant hymn-books of the Western Church which date from the eleventh century and is part of a regular monastic cycle of praise which probably goes back as far as the seventh century.

The original Latin cycle ran to nine stanzas, the last of which was a doxology. It was generally divided into two parts, the first four verses, which began '*Urbs beata Jerusalem*' and dealt with the heavenly city of Jerusalem, being sung at evensong and mattins, while the last four were sung at lauds, the first service of the daily office normally celebrated at daybreak. Neale kept this division in his translation. He turned the first four stanzas into the hymn 'Blessed city, heavenly Salem' and took 'Christ is made the sure Foundation' from the last four verses, which began '*Angularis fundamentum lapis Christus missus est*'. Neale's two translations first appeared in his *Mediaeval Hymns*, published in 1851. An earlier and freer translation of '*Angularis fundamentum*', which began 'Christ is our corner stone', made in 1837 by John Chandler (1806–76), vicar of Witley in Surrey, is still regularly sung today.

The imagery of the hymn is taken from 1 Peter 2:6, 'Behold I lay in Zion a chief corner stone, elect, precious', and from St Paul's words in Ephesians 2:20 that the household of God is 'built upon the foundation of the apostles and prophets, Jesus Christ himself being the chief corner stone'.

Neale, who was responsible for five of the hymns in this anthology (the others are Nos. 4, 62, 92 and 125), was born in London and educated at Sherborne Grammar School in Dorset and Trinity College, Cambridge. He was briefly fellow and chaplain of Downing

College, Cambridge, and won the University prize for sacred poetry eleven times. After holding a curacy in Guildford, Surrey, he was presented to the living of Crawley in Sussex, but never took up the charge as he was afflicted by a lung complaint and retired for a period to Madeira. In 1846 he was back in Britain as warden of Sackville College, a group of almshouses in East Grinstead, Sussex. There he founded the Society of St Margaret, an order of nursing sisters who tended the sick in local villages, and also an orphanage, a girls' school and an establishment in Aldershot for the reclamation of fallen women.

In his latter years Neale got into increasing trouble with the Church of England authorities for his extreme High Church views and closeness to Roman Catholicism. The only preferment that he was offered was the provostship of St Ninian's Cathedral in Perth, Scotland, but the climate was too cold for him to have lived there. He was increasingly afflicted by ill-health, but none the less he continued to work on long-forgotten books and manuscripts of Greek and Latin hymns and to produce superb translations of their lyrics. Altogether, he translated some 100 hymns.

For a long time 'Christ is made the sure Foundation' was sung to a plainsong melody in keeping with its monastic origins. An alternative was *Urbs Coelestis* by the Revd H. E. Hodson (1842–1917). Hodson's tune, written in 1872 one peaceful evening by the River Dove at Ilam in the Derbyshire Peak District, was later incorporated in his cantata, *The Golden Legend*. Nowadays, Neale's words are generally sung to the stately and measured Westminster Abbey, adapted from an anthem by Henry Purcell (1659–95) and also used for the hymn 'God, whose city's sure foundation' (No. 47).

Angularis fundamentum

Christ is made the sure Foundation,
  Christ the Head and Corner-stone,
Chosen of the Lord, and precious,
  Binding all the Church in one,
Holy Zion's help for ever,
  And her confidence alone.

2 All that dedicated city,
    Dearly loved of God on high,
  In exultant jubilation,
    Pours perpetual melody,
  God the One in Three adoring
    In glad hymns eternally.

3 To this temple, where we call thee,
    Come, O Lord of Hosts, today;
  With thy wonted loving-kindness
    Hear thy servants as they pray;
  And thy fullest benediction
    Shed within its walls alway.

4 Here vouchsafe to all thy servants
    What they ask of thee to gain,
  What they gain from thee for ever
    With the blessèd to retain,
  And hereafter in thy glory
    Evermore with thee to reign.

5 Laud and honour to the Father,
    Laud and honour to the Son;
  Laud and honour to the Spirit;
    Ever three and ever one:
  Consubstantial, co-eternal,
    While unending ages run.

24 CHRIST, WHOSE GLORY FILLS THE SKIES

Charles Wesley (1707–88) wrote this morning hymn shortly after 'And can it be, that I should gain' (No. 11; see notes to that hymn for Wesley's biography). It was first published in a book entitled *Hymns and Spiritual Songs* which he produced with his brother John in 1740. For many years it was wrongly attributed to Augustus Montague Toplady, the author of 'Rock of ages', and, rather surprisingly, it did not appear in its complete form in the *Wesleyan Hymn Book* until 1875.

Like most of Wesley's hymns, it draws strongly on metaphors and images from Scripture. The striking phrase 'Sun of Righteousness', which occurs in the third line of the first verse, is taken from the last book of the Old Testament, Malachi 4:2, 'But unto you that fear my name shall the Sun of Righteousness arise with healing in his wings.' Interestingly, Wesley used the phrase again in his fine poem entitled 'Wrestling with Jacob', which begins 'Come, O thou traveller unknown' and is still to be found in several hymnals, although it is really too personal and devotional for congregational singing.

The fifth line of 'Christ, whose glory fills the skies' echoes St Luke 1:78, 'The dayspring from on high hath visited us to give light to them that sit in darkness and in the shadow of death.' The sixth line follows 2 Peter 1:19, 'We have also a more sure word of prophecy whereunto ye do well that ye take heed, as unto a light that shineth in a dark place, until the day dawn, and the day star arise in your hearts.'

The second and third verses of this hymn are quoted in Chapter 38 of George Eliot's novel *Adam Bede,* which was first published in 1859. There they are put into the mouth of Seth Bede, the hero's brother and a devout Methodist, who sings Wesley's hymn, described as one of his favourites, as he is walking home one Sunday morning.

The hymn was originally sung to the German tune Heidelberg, which first appeared in a book of songs and psalms published in Berlin in 1653. There is some reason to think that it may have been the work of Princess Louisa Henrietta of Brandenburg, though it was later ascribed to Johann Crüger (1598–1662). The tune more often used now is Ratisbon, another German melody, which first appeared in a book of chorales published in Leipzig in 1815 as a setting for the words '*Jesu meines Lebens Leben*'.

A Morning Hymn

Christ, whose glory fills the skies,
Christ, the true, the only Light,
Sun of Righteousness, arise,
Triumph o'er the shades of night:
Day-springs from on high, be near;
Day-star, in my heart appear.

2 Dark and cheerless is the morn
Unaccompanied by thee;
Joyless is the day's return,
Till thy mercy's beams I see;
Till they inward light impart,
Glad my eyes, and warm my heart.

3 Visit then this soul of mine,
Pierce the gloom of sin and grief;
Fill me, Radiancy divine,
Scatter all my unbelief;
More and more thyself display,
Shining to the perfect day.

25 CITY OF GOD, HOW BROAD AND FAR

The theology of this hymn is as broad as its description of the city of God – too broad, indeed, for some people who consider that it is not properly a Christian hymn at all. It was not included in *Hymns Ancient and Modern* until 1950 because earlier editors were unhappy about its doctrinal position.

It is quite understandable that 'City of God' has caused difficulties to some Christians; it avoids any mention of Christ or the Holy Spirit and prefers rather to dwell on such abstract ideals as 'freedom, love, and truth'. Yet there is nothing in it that is incompatible with the Christian religion. The notion of the Kingdom of God as a city is a familiar one in the Bible, especially in the Psalms. It provides the basis for a number of hymns, including the more orthodox 'Christ is made the sure Foundation' (No. 23), 'God, whose city's sure foundation' (No. 47) and 'Glorious things of thee are spoken' (No. 42). There is also a strong stress on the unity of the Church in this hymn, which is reminiscent of that sounded in 'Onward, Christian Soldiers' (No. 105) and 'The Church's one foundation' (No. 124).

The author, Samuel Johnson (1822–82), was an American radical who refused to join any established Christian denomination. He was probably closest to the Unitarians, sharing their refusal to accept the Divinity of Christ or the doctrine of the Trinity. Educated at Harvard, he established his own Free Church at Lynn in Massachusetts in 1853, where he ministered until 1870. He was active in movements of political reform, notably the anti-slavery crusade, and was also a scholar of comparative religion, publishing *Oriental Religions and their relation to Universal Religion*.

'City of God' was written in 1860 on a visit to Nice in the South of France which Johnson made with his friend and fellow Unitarian,

Samuel Longfellow. Longfellow, a brother of the poet Henry Wadsworth Longfellow, also wrote hymns and the two men collaborated in producing a book called *Hymns of the Spirit,* published in 1864. The object of the book, its compilers wrote, was 'to exclude all hymns which by their traditional phraseology or out-of-date thought forms would offend the sensibilities of a cultured liberal Christian'. It was in this volume that 'City of God' first appeared.

It is interesting to note that in the first line of the fourth verse Samuel Johnson uses the same imagery of 'watch-fires' (not found in the Bible) that Mrs Julia Ward Howe was to employ just a year later in her 'Mine eyes have seen the glory of the coming of the Lord' (No. 85).

The tune normally used for this hymn is Richmond, otherwise known as Haweis, or Spa Fields Chapel. It was written by Thomas Haweis (1734–1820) and adapted by Samuel Webbe (1770–1843). Haweis was a curate at St Mary Magdalene, Oxford, and then vicar of Aldwinkle in Northamptonshire before leaving the Church of England to become chaplain to Lady Huntingdon's Chapel in Bath. He originally wrote the tune in 1792 for the hymn 'O Thou, from whom all goodness flows'. It is also used for 'Praise to the Holiest in the height' (No. 109) and 'O Jesu, King most Wonderful'.

The Church, the City of God

City of God, how broad and far
  Outspread thy walls sublime!
The true thy chartered freemen are
  Of every age and clime.

2 One holy Church, one army strong,
    One steadfast, high intent;
One working band, one harvest-song,
    One King omnipotent.

3 How purely hath thy speech come down
    From man's primeval youth!
How grandly hath thine empire grown,
    Of freedom, love, and truth!

4 How gleam thy watch-fires through the night
    With never-fainting ray!
How rise thy towers, serene and bright,
    To meet the dawning day!

5 In vain the surge's angry shock
    In vain the drifting sands:
Unharmed upon the eternal Rock
    The eternal City stands.

26 COME, COME, YE SAINTS

Although the verses below are not found in the hymn-books of any mainstream Christian denomination, they deserve a place in an anthology of the best-loved hymns in the English-speaking world. 'Come, Come, ye Saints' is the favourite hymn of the six million strong Church of Jesus Christ of Latter Day Saints, or Mormons as they are better known.

The hymn is the work of William Clayton (1814–79). Born the eldest of fourteen children in the small Lancashire hamlet of Charock Moss, he was one of the first Englishmen to be converted by the Mormon missionaries who came to Britain in 1837. Like other early British converts, he was baptized in the waters of the River Ribble and became a Mormon missionary in the Manchester area. In 1840 Clayton and his wife sailed from Liverpool to the United States to join the burgeoning Mormon community in Nauvoo, Illinois. By 1842 he had become secretary to Joseph Smith, founder of the Church of Latter Day Saints.

In the spring of 1846 increasing persecution led Smith's successor, Brigham Young, to lead a migration from Nauvoo westwards across the prairies towards the Rocky Mountains. The weather was so cold that the fleeing 'Saints' were able to drive their heavy waggons across the frozen Mississippi. They established a camp at Sugar Creek and from there struck out on the 1,300-mile epic journey which was to take them across the Rockies to the valley of the Great Salt Lake, where they settled and founded the state of Utah.

Clayton was appointed the official clerk of the great trek, which took seventeen months and was accomplished in the most terrible conditions. On 15 April 1846, while camped at Locust Creek in Iowa, he heard that his wife, whom he had left behind in Illinois, had safely given birth to a son. It was after hearing this news that he wrote his song 'All is well' to cheer on his fellow pioneers in their painfully slow passage to the Promised Land they were seeking.

'Come, come, ye Saints' immediately caught on as the marching song of the Mormon trekkers. It became a rule of camp that whenever anyone started singing it, everyone else should join in.

Although the reference in the third verse to finding the place which God has prepared 'far away in the West' specifically ties it to the great Mormon trek across the United States in 1846–7, the hymn has no specifically Mormon theological overtones – apart, perhaps, from its references to 'Saints'. Its central message, 'All is well! All is well!', is a fine expression of Christian assurance in the spirit of Julian of Norwich's famous dictum in her *Revelations of Divine Love:* 'But all shall be well and all shall be well and all manner of thing shall be well.'

Clayton took the tune for his hymn from an old English folk song, 'Good morrow, Gossip Joan', which had been brought over to America and had become especially popular in Virginia. It is a fine rousing melody for a hymn of joy. Perhaps non-Mormons might think of using it in their worship, together with Clayton's words, adapted as may be appropriate.

All is well

Come, come, ye Saints, no toil nor labour fear;
But with joy wend your way,
Though hard to you this journey may appear,
Grace shall be as your day.
'Tis better far for us to strive
Our useless cares from us to drive;
Do this, and joy your hearts will swell –
All is well! All is well!

2   Why should we mourn or think our lot is hard?
      'Tis not so; all is right.
  Why should we think to earn a great reward,
      If we now shun the fight?
    Gird up your loins; fresh courage take;
    Our God will never us forsake;
  And soon we'll have this tale to tell –
      All is well! All is well!

3   We'll find the place which God for us prepared,
      Far away in the West,
  Where none shall come to hurt or make afraid;
      There the Saints will be blessed.
    We'll make the air with music ring,
    Shout praises to our God and King;
  Above the rest these words we'll tell –
      All is well! All is well!

4   And should we die before our journey's through,
      Happy day! all is well!
  We then are free from toil and sorrow, too;
      With the just we shall dwell!
    But if our lives are spared again
    To see the Saints their rest obtain,
  O how we'll make this chorus swell –
      All is well! All is well!

27 COME DOWN, O LOVE DIVINE

Like 'All creatures of our God and King' (No. 3), this hymn is a translation of a medieval poem originally written in Italian. It owes much of its popularity to the tune composed for it in the early years of this century by Ralph Vaughan Williams (1872–1958).

The author of the devotional verses calling for the descent of the Holy Spirit which form the basis of the hymn was Bianco da Siena (c. 1350–1434). Born in the Upper Valdarno region of Tuscany, he spent his boyhood as an apprentice in the wool trade in Siena and at the age of seventeen joined an order of mystics. Although he wrote a number of lyrics and hymns, little more is known about him, other than that he spent the last part of his life in Venice.

Bianco's poem, which began 'Discendi, Amor santo' and ran to eight verses, was little known until 1851 when it was copied by an Italian from an ancient manuscript. Some years after this rediscovery, four of the verses were translated by Dr Richard Littledale (1833–90). They appeared in the form printed overleaf in his People's Hymnal, published in 1867.

Littledale's translation retains much of the spirit of the original Italian verses. In particular it preserves Bianco da Siena's allusion to the monastic vocation, especially in the lines in the third stanza which speak of the vesture of holy charity and the inner clothing of lowliness.

Richard Littledale was a High Churchman who translated many hymns from Latin, Greek and other languages. Educated at Trinity College, Dublin, he was curate first at St Matthew's, Thorpe, Norfolk, and then at St Mary the Virgin, Soho. Although a strong Tractarian, he was strongly opposed to the Roman Catholic Church and by his writing did much to keep many of those influenced by the Oxford Movement within the pale of the Anglican Church.

'Come down, O Love divine' was very little sung in Britain until it was chosen as one of the entries for the *English Hymnal* in 1906. Percy Dearmer, the editor, chose the young and virtually unknown Vaughan Williams to be responsible for the musical side of the new book. On the whole, where existing tunes were lacking or inadequate Vaughan Williams tended to prefer settings of English folk songs to new tunes. But 'Come down, O Love divine' was an exception. He wrote a new tune especially for it which he called Down Ampney, after his birthplace in Gloucestershire. It was one of only four new tunes that he wrote for the hymnal (the others being for 'God be with you till we meet again' (No. 43). 'For all the Saints' (No. 38) and 'Hail thee, Festival Day' (No. 50). Thanks largely to his tune, the hymn has become extremely popular, especially at weddings.

Discendi, amor santo

Come down, O Love divine,
Seek thou this soul of mine,
And visit it with thine own ardour glowing;
O Comforter, draw near,
Within my heart appear,
And kindle it, thy holy flame bestowing.

2   O let it freely burn,
Till earthly passion turn
To dust and ashes in its heat consuming;
And let thy glorious light
Shine ever on my sight,
And clothe me round, the while my path illuming.

3   Let holy charity
Mine outward vesture be,
And lowliness become mine inner clothing;
True lowliness of heart,
Which takes the humbler part,
And o'er its own shortcomings weeps with loathing.

4   And so the yearning strong,
With which the soul will long,
Shall far outpass the power of human telling;
For none can guess its grace,
Till he become the place
Wherein the Holy Spirit makes his dwelling.

28 COME, HOLY GHOST, OUR SOULS INSPIRE

This hymn has had a continuous existence of more than a thousand years, though in its present form it is only 350 years old. The original on which it is closely based is a Latin hymn, *'Veni, Creator Spiritus'*, which probably dates from the ninth century. The original plainsong melody to which it was sung is still used for the English version, giving an added sense of mystery and antiquity to its thrilling invocation to the Holy Spirit.

The precise origins and authorship of *'Veni, Creator Spiritus'* are unclear. It has been variously attributed to the Emperor Charles the Fat, grandson of Charlemagne, Gregory the Great, St Ambrose and Rhabanus Maurus, Archbishop of Mainz in the middle of the ninth century. There is clear evidence that it was sung at Whitsuntide in the tenth century and that it was generally accompanied by much solemnity and ceremonial, including the ringing of bells, the lighting of candles and the use of incense. During the eleventh century, it came to be used at ordination services and during the consecration of bishops. It continues to serve that function in the Church of England today.

The translation which is printed overleaf can be found in most hymnals. It was made by John Cosin (1594–1672) and was first published in his *Collection of Private Devotions in the Practice of the Ancient Church* in 1627. At that time, Cosin was rector of Brancepeth in County Durham. He later became Dean and Master of Peterhouse, Cambridge, but was driven out by the Puritans in 1641. After the Restoration he was successively Dean and Bishop of Durham.

Cosin intended his hymn to be sung every morning at nine in memory of the descent of the Holy Spirit upon the Church. His was not, in fact, the first English translation of *'Veni, Creator Spiritus'* –

the 1549 Prayer Book of the Church of England had contained a rather wooden version in common metre for use at ordinations, which ran to sixteen verses and began 'Come, Holy Ghost, eternal God'. The inclusion of Cosin's version in the 1662 Prayer Book, the only hymn to appear in the volume, has made it the best-known English version, although subsequent translators have produced more accurate renditions of the original Latin. They include John Dryden's 'Creator Spirit, by whose aid', Tate and Brady's 'Come Holy Ghost, Creator come', Robert Bridges's 'Come, O Creator Spirit, come' and J. D. Aylward's 'Creator Spirit, all-divine'. Altogether Julian lists fifty-one different English translations.

The reference in the last line of the first verse to 'sev'nfold gifts' is taken from the frequent references in the Book of Revelation to the seven spirits of God. Seven was a sacred number among the Jews and indicated perfection or completion.

The plainsong melody *Veni Creator* seems to have been associated with this hymn since it was first sung. It may well be even older than the hymn. There is evidence that it was previously attached to an Easter hymn by St Ambrose, which began *'Hic est dies verus Dei'*.

Veni, Creator Spiritus

Come, Holy Ghost, our souls inspire,
And lighten with celestial fire;
Thou the anointing Spirit art,
Who dost thy sev'nfold gifts impart.

2   Thy blessed unction from above
Is comfort, life, and fire of love;
Enable with perpetual light
The dullness of our blinded sight.

3   Anoint and cheer our soilèd face
With the abundance of thy grace:
Keep far our foes, give peace at home;
Where thou art guide no ill can come.

4   Teach us to know the Father, Son,
And thee, of both, to be but One;
That through the ages all along
This may be our endless song:

'Praise to thy eternal merit,
Father, Son, and Holy Spirit.   Amen'.

29 COME, LET US JOIN OUR CHEERFUL SONGS

This joyful hymn is the work of the man who is normally regarded as the father of English hymnody and who must surely vie with Charles Wesley for the title of greatest hymn-writer in the English language.

Isaac Watts (1674–1748) was born in Southampton, the son of an elder in an Independent (Congregational) church. Educated at the local grammar school, he early showed himself a formidable scholar. Not being a member of the Church of England, he was unable to study at either Oxford or Cambridge and he trained instead at one of the Dissenting academies. In 1702 he was appointed minister at Mark Lane Chapel in London, but after ten years his health broke down and for the last thirty-six years of his life he lived as the house-guest of Sir Thomas and Lady Abney, first in Hertfordshire and then in Stoke Newington, North London.

In the words of Erik Routley, 'Watts is the liberator of hymnody in English.' It was he who effectively broke the Calvinist tradition of using only metrical psalms in Christian worship. The story goes that at the age of sixteen he complained to his father that what was sung in church was dull and profitless. His father replied, 'Then write something better.' He immediately took up the challenge and produced the first of nearly 700 hymns, many of which are still in regular use today. Watts broke out of the straitjacket of strict metrical paraphrases of biblical texts and wrote much freer verses in his own words; these lent themselves to more exciting tunes.

'Come, let us join our cheerful songs' was published in Watts's *Hymns and Spiritual Songs* in 1707. He attached it to the scriptural reference 'Revelations 5:11–13'. The verses referred to read:

And I beheld, and I heard the voice of many angels round about the throne and the beasts and the elders: and the number of them was ten thousand times ten thousand, and thousands of thousands; saying with a loud voice, Worthy is the Lamb that was slain to receive power and riches, and wisdom, and strength, and honour, and glory, and blessing. And every creature which is in the heaven and on the earth, and under the earth, and such as are in the sea, and all that are in them, heard I saying, Blessing, and honour, and glory, and power, be unto him that sitteth upon the throne, and unto the Lamb for ever and ever.

The tune almost universally used for this hymn is Nativity, which was written by Henry Lahee (1826–1912). For twenty-seven years organist at Holy Trinity Church, Brompton, he composed several cantatas and numerous glees, madrigals and part-songs. This is his only hymn tune still in regular use.

Christ Jesus, the Lamb of God worshipped by all creation

Come, let us join our cheerful songs
  With angels round the throne;
Ten thousand thousand are their tongues,
  But all their joys are one.

2 'Worthy the Lamb that died,' they cry,
    'To be exalted thus;'
  'Worthy the Lamb,' our lips reply,
    'For he was slain for us.'

3 Jesus is worthy to receive
    Honour and power divine;
  And blessings, more than we can give,
    Be, Lord, for ever thine.

4 Let all that dwell above the sky,
    And air and earth and seas,
  Conspire to lift thy glories high,
    And speak thine endless praise.

5 The whole creation join in one
    To bless the sacred name
  Of him that sits upon the throne,
    And to adore the Lamb.

30 COME, YE FAITHFUL, RAISE THE ANTHEM

This hymn has undergone a variety of transmogrifications and does not appear in the same form in any two major hymnals. It is largely the work of J. M. Neale (1818–66; see notes to hymn No. 23) who adapted it from an earlier hymn by Job Hupton (1762–1849).

Hupton was a blacksmith in Staffordshire until he was converted by one of Lady Huntingdon's ministers, whereupon he became an itinerant preacher. Later on he was a Baptist minister at Claxton, Norfolk. In 1805 the *Gospel Magazine* published a hymn which he had written with the title 'An Hymn of Praise to the Redeemer'. The first of its thirteen verses ran:

> Come, ye saints, and raise an anthem,
>   Cleave the skies with shouts of praise,
> Sing to Him who found a ransom,
>   Th' Ancient of eternal days, –
>   In your nature,
>   Born to suffer in your place.

In 1863 J. M. Neale contributed an article to the *Christian Remembrancer* in which he included a substantially revised version of Hupton's hymn 'as an illustration of the possibility of producing a hymn of merit out of somewhat crude materials'. Neale subsequently further altered his own hymn for the *People's Hymnal* of 1867. The text printed below, which is the one that appears in *Hymns Ancient and Modern*, is in all essentials that of his first re-working of Hupton's original – the third verse is the only one of Hupton's stanzas which did not undergo substantial alteration.

Neale's verses have in themselves been altered by several different hands and the hymn is now found in a bewildering variety of forms.

The *New English Hymnal* has a version substantially similar to that printed below, except that it omits the third verse and begins the fourth verse 'Now on those eternal mountains'. *Hymns for Church and School* has the first three verses as printed here but then gives two new verses, beginning 'Yet this earth he still remembers' and 'Trust him, then, ye fearful pilgrims'. *Hymns for Today's Church* changes the first line to 'Alleluia! raise the anthem', while *Songs of Praise* prints a version which has the following opening verse:

> Come, ye people, raise the anthem,
>> Cleave the sky with shouts of praise;
> Sing to him, the Good Physician,
> Who from death the world doth raise;
> Shepherd, Prophet, Word Incarnate,
>> Him the heart of man obeys.

The tune at least is the same for all these versions. It is the vigorous and effective Neander, also known as Ephesus and *Unser Herrscher*, which is first found set to the German hymn '*Unser Herrscher, Unser König*' in Joachim Neander's collection *Alpha and Omega*, published in Bremen in 1680. For Neander's biographical details, see the notes to No. 6.

> Come, ye faithful, raise the anthem,
>> Cleave the skies with shouts of praise;
> Sing to him who found a ransom,
>> Ancient of eternal Days,
> God of God, the Word incarnate,
>> Whom the heaven of heaven obeys.

2   Ere he raised the lofty mountains,
     Formed the seas, or built the sky,
  Love eternal, free, and boundless,
     Moved the Lord of Life to die,
  Fore-ordained the Prince of Princes
     For the throne of Calvary.

3   There, for us and our redemption,
     See him all his life-blood pour!
  There he wins our full salvation,
     Dies that we may die no more;
  Then, arising, lives for ever,
     Reigning where he was before.

4   High on yon celestial mountains
     Stands his sapphire throne, all bright,
  Midst unending Alleluias
     Bursting from the sons of light;
  Sion's people tell his praises,
     Victor after hard-won fight.

5   Bring your harps, and bring your incense,
     Sweep the string and pour the lay;
  Let the earth proclaim his wonders,
     King of that celestial day;
  He the Lamb once slain is worthy,
     Who was dead, and lives for ay.

6   Laud and honour to the Father,
     Laud and honour to the Son,
  Laud and honour to the Spirit,
     Ever Thee and ever One,
  Consubstantial, co-eternal,
     While unending ages run.

31 COME, YE THANKFUL PEOPLE, COME

This is another favourite hymn which appears in a markedly different version in virtually every major hymn-book. It was written by Henry Alford (1819–71) for use in services to celebrate the harvest and almost certainly remains the most popular of all Harvest Festival hymns today.

Two of Christ's parables are echoed in the hymn: the story of the wheat and the tares in Matthew 13:24–30, and the story in Mark 4:26–9 which tells of the seed which springs up without the sower knowing of it, and which includes the line: 'For the earth bringeth forth of herself; first the blade, then the ear, after that the full corn in the ear.'

Henry Alford was the son of an Anglican clergyman and himself took Holy Orders, becoming Dean of Canterbury Cathedral in 1857. He was a distinguished scholar and wrote numerous books, including an important critical commentary on the Greek New Testament. A strong Evangelical, he wrote several hymns which are still popular today, including 'Ten thousand times ten thousand' (No. 123, the notes on which contain a fuller account of his life).

'Come, ye thankful people, come' was first published in Alford's *Psalms and Hymns* in 1844. The author revised it for his *Poetical Works* published in 1865 and it is this revised version, which also appeared in his *Year of Praise* (1867), that is printed overleaf. It can, I think, reasonably be regarded as the authentic text. The *Church Hymnary* is the only major modern hymnal that I know of which reproduces it without any alterations.

The version of the hymn printed in *Hymns Ancient and Modern* differs very considerably from that printed here. When it was first included in that book in 1861, the compilers made substantial alterations; these were firmly repudiated by the author, but have persisted to this day and can be found in the current 'New Standard' version. For example, the last four lines of the second verse run:

> Ripening with a wondrous power
> Till the final Harvest hour
> Grant, O Lord of Life, that we
> Holy grain and pure may be.

The third and fourth verses of the *Ancient and Modern* version are also completely different from those printed opposite. The *New English Hymnal* prints yet another version of these verses. Its final verse is worthy of quotation:

> Then, thou Church triumphant, come,
> Raise the song of harvest-home;
> All be safely gathered in,
> Free from sorrow, free from sin,
> There for ever purified
> In God's garner to abide;
> Come, ten thousand Angels, come,
> Raise the glorious harvest-home!

The tune which is universally associated with this hymn, St George by Sir George Elvey (1816–93) was actually written for another hymn, 'Hark, the song of Jubilee'. It first appeared in a selection of psalm and hymn tunes published in 1858. Elvey was organist and choirmaster at St George's Chapel, Windsor.

After Harvest

Come, ye thankful people, come,
Raise the song of harvest-home:
All is safely gathered in,
Ere the winter storms begin;
God, our Maker, doth provide
For our wants to be supplied:
Come to God's own temple, come,
Raise the song of harvest-home.

2 All this world is God's own field,
Fruit unto His praise to yield;
Wheat and tares together sown,
Unto joy or sorrow grown;
First the blade, and then the ear,
Then the full corn shall appear:
Lord of harvest, grant that we
Wholesome grain and pure may be.

3 For the Lord our God shall come,
And shall take His harvest home;
From His field shall in that day
All offences purge away;
Give His angels charge at last
In the fire the tares to cast;
But the fruitful ears to store
In His garner evermore.

4 Even so, Lord, quickly come;
Bring Thy final harvest home:
Gather Thou Thy people in,
Free from sorrow, free from sin;
There, for ever purified,
In Thy garner to abide:
Come, with all Thine angels, come,
Raise the glorious harvest-home.

32 CROWN HIM WITH MANY CROWNS

This is yet another hymn that appears in several different versions. The original, printed overleaf, is the work of Matthew Bridges (1800–1893), but it was subsequently altered by Godfrey Thring (1823–1903) and again by Percy Dearmer (1867–1936).

Matthew Bridges (not to be confused with Robert Bridges, the compiler of the *Yattendon Hymnal* and author of hymns Nos. 6 and 100 in this collection) was born in Maldon, Essex. He was brought up as an Anglican, but later became a Roman Catholic. After spending much of his life in Canada, he died in Sidmouth, Devon.

'Crown Him with many crowns' first appeared in Bridges's *Hymns of the Heart* in 1851. The title he gave it comes from Revelation 19:12. In 1874 Godfrey Thring, a Prebendary of Wells Cathedral, wrote a hymn modelled on that of Matthew Bridges with the title 'Crown him with crowns of gold'. Six years later Thring published a composite version which began with Bridges's first verse and continued with stanzas of his own. Subsequently several versions of the hymn appeared which mixed the verses of the two writers. For *Songs of Praise* in 1931 Percy Dearmer made further substantial alterations to produce a version which stressed the social message of the gospel. Its first verse went as follows:

> Crown him upon the throne
> Of justice and of right,
> In him the love of God is shown,
> To shine in human light:
> He reigns, the Son of Man,
> All grace divine is his:
> Pierce through the creeds, his features scan,
> And see him as he is.

Most hymn-books have now reverted to printing Bridges's original version with the sixth verse omitted, although the *Church Hymnary* gives Thring's revision which retains only the first verse of the original and contains the following second verse:

Crown him the Lord of Life
Who triumphed o'er the grave,
And rose victorious in the strife
For those he came to save.
His glories now we sing,
Who died and rose on high;
Who died, eternal life to bring,
And lives that death may die.

Hymns for Church and School contains a different composite version which includes the stanza above and another of Thring's verses:

Crown him the Son of God,
Before the worlds began;
And ye, who tread where he hath trod,
Crown him the Son of Man,
Who every grief hath known
That wrings the human breast,
And takes and bears them for his own,
That all in him may rest.

The expression 'mystic Rose' which occurs in the fifth line of Bridges's original second verse is a medieval title for the Virgin Mary. The next two lines echo Isaiah 11:1–2, 'And there shall come forth a rod out of the stem of Jesse, and a Branch shall grow out of his roots: and the spirit of the Lord shall rest upon him.'

Several melodies are associated with this hymn. The most popular is almost certainly Diademata by Sir George Elvey, whom we have just encountered as the composer of the tune used for 'Come, ye thankful people, come.' Diademata was written for the first appearance of 'Crown Him with many crowns' in *Hymns Ancient and Modern* in 1868. Another tune specially written for the hymn is Corona, composed in 1927 by C. Hylton Stewart (1884–1932).

On his head were many crowns

Crown Him with many crowns,
The Lamb upon His throne;
Hark! How the heav'nly anthem drowns
All music but its own:
Awake, my soul, and sing
Of Him Who died for thee,
And hail Him as thy matchless King
Through all eternity.

2   Crown Him the Virgin's Son,
The God Incarnate born,
Whose arm those crimson trophies won
Which now His brow adorn:
Fruit of the mystic Rose,
As of that Rose the Stem;
The Root whence mercy ever flows,
The Babe of Bethlehem.

3   Crown Him the Lord of love:
Behold His hands and side,
Those wounds yet visible above
In beauty glorified:
No Angel in the sky
Can fully bear that sight,
But downward bends his burning eye
At mysteries so bright.

4   Crown Him the Lord of peace,
    Whose power a sceptre sways
From pole to pole, that wars may cease,
    And all be prayer and praise:
    His reign shall know no end,
    And round His piercèd feet
Fair flowers of Paradise extend
    Their fragrance ever sweet.

5   Crown Him the Lord of years,
    The Potentate of time,
Creator of the rolling spheres,
    Ineffably sublime.
    Glassed in a sea of light,
    Where everlasting waves
Reflect his throne – the Infinite,
    Who lives – and loves – and saves.

6   Crown Him the Lord of heaven,
    One with the Father known,
And the blest Spirit through him given
    From yonder triune throne:
    All hail, Redeemer, hail!
    For thou hast died for me!
Thy praise shall never, never fail
    Throughout eternity.

33 DEAR LORD AND FATHER OF MANKIND

This is indisputably one of the most popular of all hymns in the English language, voted number three in the 1985 BBC 'Songs of Praise' poll and appearing high in American lists of favourite hymns. Yet its author, John Greenleaf Whittier (1807–92), would have been horrified at the thought of it being sung in church, and particularly by the lusty enthusiasm with which it is often tackled in public school chapels. It comes from a long poem which he wrote comparing the heartiness and excitement of much Christian worship with the stimulation found by followers of certain Eastern religions through the use of hallucinogenic drugs.

Whittier was an American Quaker descended from one of the Pilgrim Fathers who arrived in Massachusetts from England in 1638. Brought up on a New England farm, he was an early campaigner against slavery, and in 1835 was elected to the Massachusetts state legislature. He devoted much of his life to writing. Despite his dislike of singing in worship, more than fifty of his poems have been turned into hymns, including 'Immortal love forever full', 'O Brother man, fold to thy heart thy brother' and 'O Lord and master of us all'.

'Dear Lord and Father of mankind' is taken from a poem Whittier wrote in 1872, called 'The Brewing of Soma'. Soma was an intoxicating drink which was almost certainly made from the fungus *Amanita muscaria*, or fly agaric, and used in Vedic rituals by Hindus in India. A few scraps of the fungus were soaked in milk, drunk and then passed through the bladder to produce the soma which had a strongly hallucinogenic effect and was used to induce a state of religious frenzy.

In the latter part of his poem Whittier compared the stirring of the emotions in Christian worship through music, ceremonial and the like with the Indians' use of drugs to achieve religious ecstasy:

> In sensual transports, wild as vain,
> We brew in many a Christian fane
> The heathen Soma still!

It is for these 'foolish ways' that Christians are urged to beg forgiveness from God in the lines that form the beginning of the hymn that we now sing with such gusto. Whittier had a strong dislike of highly emotional religion and of hearty, tub-thumping hymns. His particular *bête noire* was 'Hold the fort, for I am coming' (No. 54). The theme of his poem is the Quaker conviction that God is to be found in silence and stillness, through the inward peace of the worshipper rather than through outward stimulation and sensual excitement.

The last six verses of 'The Brewing of Soma' were turned into a hymn by an English Congregationalist, William Garrett Horder, who included 'Dear Lord and Father of mankind' in his *Congregational Hymns* (1884). He made several alterations to Whittier's original, substituting 'feverish' for 'foolish' in the second line of the first verse and 'pulses of desire' for 'heats of our desire' in the first line of the last verse. Nearly all modern hymnals print Whittier's original words, however, and they appear in the text overleaf.

In the United States the hymn is usually set to the tune Woodland by Nathaniel Gould. In Britain and the Commonwealth it is generally sung to the haunting melody Repton by Sir Hubert Parry (1848–1918). Parry's tune was originally written in 1887 for the contralto aria 'Long since in Egypt's pleasant land' in his oratorio *Judith*. In 1924 Dr George Gilbert Stocks, director of music at Repton School in Derbyshire, set it to 'Dear Lord and Father of mankind' in a supplement of tunes for use in the school chapel. This inspired matching of words and music caught on and is surely one of the main reasons for the great popularity of the hymn today.

The Brewing of Soma

Dear Lord and Father of mankind,
 Forgive our foolish ways!
Re-clothe us in our rightful mind,
In purer lives thy service find,
 In deeper reverence praise.

2 In simple trust like theirs who heard,
  Beside the Syrian sea,
The gracious calling of the Lord,
Let us, like them, without a word
  Rise up and follow thee.

3 O Sabbath rest by Galilee!
  O calm of hills above,
Where Jesus knelt to share with thee
The silence of eternity,
  Interpreted by love!

4 With that deep hush subduing all
  Our words and works that drown
The tender whisper of thy call,
As noiseless let thy blessing fall
  As fell thy manna down.

5 Drop thy still dews of quietness,
  Till all our strivings cease;
Take from our souls the strain and stress,
And let our ordered lives confess
  The beauty of thy peace.

6 Breathe through the heats of our desire
  Thy coolness and thy balm;
Let sense be dumb, let flesh retire;
Speak through the earthquake, wind, and fire,
  O still small voice of calm!

34 ETERNAL FATHER, STRONG TO SAVE

Known throughout the world as the 'sailors' hymn', this stirring plea for God's mercy to all in peril on the sea is regularly sung on board ships great and small.

It is the work of William Whiting (1825–78), the son of a London grocer. Educated at the Winchester Training Institution, a college for teachers, he stayed on in the city to become the first master of the Quiristers of Winchester College, a group of boys who were supposed to sing in the chapel but were in fact little more than unpaid servants to the young gentlemen attending the college. He continued as the Quiristers' tutor for the next thirty-six years.

The story goes that Whiting wrote this hymn for one of the Winchester Quiristers who was about to sail for America. Whether or not that was in fact its origin, we do know that in 1860 he submitted it as a possible entry for the forthcoming *Hymns Ancient and Modern*, in a version which began:

> O Thou Who bidd'st the ocean deep,
> Its own appointed limits keep,
> Thou, Who didst bind the restless wave,
> Eternal father, strong to save.

The compilers of *Hymns Ancient and Modern* revised it for inclusion in the first edition in 1861 and gave it the opening with which we are now familiar. Whiting himself re-wrote the entire hymn in 1869 and it is this amended version which may be regarded as the authoritative text and which appears below. It is found in most hymnals, though not in *Hymns Ancient and Modern* which doggedly sticks to its own version.

Some of the imagery in the hymn seems to have been taken from

John Milton's *Paradise Lost*. The first verse recalls the description in Book 7 of the Almighty bidding 'the deep within appointed bounds [to] be heaven and earth', while the opening of the third verse echoes the line near the beginning of Book 1 which tells of the Holy Spirit 'who Dove-like sat'st brooding on the vast abyss'.

'Eternal Father, strong to save' has been sung on many great naval occasions in the last hundred years. When Churchill and Roosevelt had their secret meeting in the North Atlantic during the Second World War, Churchill chose it to be sung at Divisions aboard HMS Prince of Wales. The fourth verse is always sung at shipboard Sunday services on the Cunard liner QE2 when it is crossing the Atlantic.

The tune universally associated with the hymn, Melita, was written to accompany its first appearance in *Hymns Ancient and Modern* by the Revd John Bacchus Dykes (1823–76), minor canon and precentor of Durham Cathedral. Dykes heard of the proposed new hymn-book by chance and wrote to the music editor, Dr Monk, enclosing some tunes. Seven of them, including Melita, were accepted and used in the first edition, and twenty-four more appeared in subsequent editions. The name Melita is taken from the biblical story of St Paul's journey from Caesarea to Rome. Acts 28:1 records that after a shipwreck Paul and his fellow prisoners were able to swim to the island of Melita, the name by which Malta was then known.

For those at Sea

Eternal Father, strong to save,
Whose arm doth bind the restless wave,
Who bidd'st the mighty ocean deep
Its own appointed limits keep:
　　O hear us, when we cry to thee,
　　For those in peril on the sea.

2　O Saviour, whose almighty word
　　The winds and waves submissive heard,
　　Who walkedst on the foaming deep
　　And calm amidst its rage didst sleep;
　　　　O hear us when we cry to thee
　　　　For those in peril on the sea.

3　O sacred Spirit, who didst brood
　　Upon the chaos dark and rude,
　　Who bad'st its angry tumult cease
　　And gavest light and life and peace:
　　　　O hear us when we cry to thee
　　　　For those in peril on the sea.

4　O Trinity of love and power,
　　Our brethren shield in danger's hour,
　　From rock and tempest, fire and foe,
　　Protect them wheresoe'er they go:
　　　　And ever let there rise to thee
　　　　Glad hymns of praise from land and sea.

35 FATHER, HEAR THE PRAYER
WE OFFER

Commentators have been rather hard on this American Unitarian hymn and it is not difficult to see why. Frank Colquhoun points out in *A Hymn Companion* that it has no specifically Christian content, while Erik Routley dismissed it in his *Hymns Today and Tomorrow* as 'banal'.

Perhaps its most unfortunate feature is the misrepresentation of Psalm 23 which occurs in the second and third verses. The phrases 'green pastures' and 'still waters' are taken from the psalm to suggest a sluggish and slothful quietism which the author wants to contrast with the courage and energy implicit in treading the 'rugged pathway' and smiting the 'living fountains'. But the fact is that the 23rd Psalm is in no sense a hymn of praise to quietism or an incitement to take the easy way.

Having got that quibble out of the way, there is much to appreciate in this little hymn which neatly and effectively describes the Christian calling to a life of difficulty and frustration, even if it does not mention either the example or the saving work of Christ which make the way of the Cross possible to follow.

The author was Mrs Love Maria Willis (1824–1908), the wife of a doctor who lived for almost her entire life in Rochester, New York. In 1859 she wrote a poem for a monthly magazine which began 'Father hear the prayer I offer'. She later re-wrote it in plural form and altered it in other ways, and in 1864 it appeared in the version opposite in a Unitarian book edited by Samuel Johnson (on whom see notes to hymn No. 25) and Samuel Longfellow, entitled *Hymns of the Spirit*.

Apart from its rather inaccurate borrowings from the 23rd Psalm, 'Father, hear the prayer we offer' draws on a number of other biblical passages for its imagery. The last two lines of the third verse, for example, recall Numbers 20:11, 'And Moses lifted up his hand, and with his rod he smote the rock twice: and the water came forth abundantly.'

The hymn is generally sung to Sussex, one of the jaunty traditional English folk tunes which Ralph Vaughan Williams adapted for *The English Hymnal*. Altogether he introduced thirty-five folk melodies into the hymnal, including that known as 'Our Captain Calls' for 'Who would true valour see' (No. 147), a version of 'Tarry Trousers' for 'Fight the good fight' (No. 36), 'Died for Love' for 'There's a friend for little children' and 'The Ploughboy's Dream' for 'O little town of Bethlehem'.

Father, hear the prayer we offer:
  Not for ease that prayer shall be,
But for strength that we may ever
  Live our lives courageously.

2 Not for ever in green pastures
     Do we ask our way to be,
   But the steep and rugged pathway
     May we tread rejoicingly.

3 Not for ever by still waters
     Would we idly rest and stay,
   But would smite the living fountains
     From the rocks along our way.

4 Be our strength in hours of weakness,
     In our wanderings be our guide;
   Through endeavour, failure, danger,
     Father, be thou at our side.

36 FIGHT THE GOOD FIGHT WITH ALL THY MIGHT

Despite its first line, 'Fight the good fight' is not a Christian battle song in the style of 'Onward, Christian soldiers' or 'Soldiers of Christ, Arise'. It is rather an injunction to faithfulness and steadfastness. Each of its stanzas is based firmly on lines from the Epistles. The first echoes 1 Timothy 6:12, 'Fight the good fight of faith, lay hold on eternal life'; the second follows Hebrews 12:1, 'Let us run with patience the race that is set before us'; the third, 1 Peter 5:7, 'Casting all your care upon him, for he careth for you'; and the fourth, Colossians 3:11, 'Christ is all, and in all.'

This hymn, which first appeared in 1863, is the work of the Revd John Samuel Bewley Monsell (1811–75). Born in Ireland and educated at Trinity College, Dublin, he was ordained into the Anglican Church in 1834 and became chaplain to Bishop Mant, the author of 'Bright the vision that delighted' (No. 21). Monsell came to England in 1853 as vicar of Egham in Surrey. In 1870 he moved to the church of St Nicholas, Guildford. While there, he supervised a major rebuilding programme of the church. One day he was inspecting the progress of the work on the roof when he slipped and fell, sustaining injuries from which he died shortly afterwards.

Monsell published more than 300 hymns, of which this one and 'O worship the Lord in the beauty of holiness' (No. 103) are still regularly sung today. He believed that hymns should be more fervent and joyous. 'We are too distant and reserved in our praises,' he wrote, 'we sing not as we should of him who is Chief among ten thousand, the altogether Lovely.'

'Fight the good fight' is sung to a variety of tunes; the most commonly used is almost certainly the bouncy Duke Street, or Honiton, generally attributed to John Hatton (?–1793), a native of St

Helens, Lancashire. The tune first appeared anonymously under the heading 'Addison's Nineteenth Psalm' in a *Select Collection of Psalms and Hymn Tunes* published in Glasgow and Edinburgh in 1793. Other tunes to which the hymn is sometimes sung include the English traditional melody Shepton-Beauchamp, adapted by Vaughan Williams for the *English Hymnal* from the folk song 'Tarry Trousers', which had been collected by Cecil Sharp, Pentecost by William Boyd (1847–1928), Rushford by Henry G. Lee (1887–1962), and Cannock by Walter Kendall Stanton.

The Fight for Faith

Fight the good fight with all thy might,
Christ is thy strength and Christ thy right;
Lay hold on life, and it shall be
Thy joy and crown eternally.

2 Run the straight race through God's good grace,
Lift up thine eyes and seek his face;
Life with its way before thee lies,
Christ is the path and Christ the prize.

3 Cast care aside; upon thy Guide
Lean, and his mercy will provide;
Lean, and the trusting soul shall prove
Christ is its life, and Christ its love.

4 Faint not nor fear, his arms are near;
He changeth not and thou art dear;
Only believe, and thou shalt see
That Christ is all in all to thee.

37 FIRMLY I BELIEVE AND TRULY

Like 'Dear Lord and Father of mankind' (No. 33), originally this was not written to be sung at all. It comes from a long poem, 'The Dream of Gerontius' by John Henry Newman (1801–90). Unlike Whittier, however, I suspect that Newman would be quite happy to know that his verses were being cheerfully sung by church congregations nearly a century after his death.

Newman is the best known of the figures associated with the Oxford Movement in the mid nineteenth century. The son of a rich London banker of Evangelical views, he had a brilliant academic career at Trinity College, Oxford, and was ordained at the age of twenty-three. As a clergyman, he moved from the Evangelical wing of the Church of England to the High Church or Anglo-Catholic wing and became the acknowledged leader of the new Tractarian movement. From 1828 to 1843 he was vicar of St Mary's, Oxford, the University church where John Keble preached his famous service on national apostasy in 1833.

In 1845, after much agonizing, Newman was received into the Roman Catholic Church. He spent a year and a half in Rome and in 1849 he established an English branch of the brotherhood of St Philip Neri in the Birmingham suburb of Edgbaston. In 1879 he was made a cardinal and there are now moves afoot to canonize him.

Newman wrote 'The Dream of Gerontius' in 1865. It is a dramatic monologue recounting the thoughts of an old monk facing death and describing the passage of his soul to the afterlife. In 1900 the poem was turned into an oratorio with music by Sir Edward Elgar. Six years later the compilers of the *English Hymnal* extracted the five verses printed overleaf to form the hymn 'Firmly I believe and truly'. They left out the following verse which in the original poem formed the penultimate stanza of this section:

> And I take with joy whatever
>> Now besets me, pain or fear,
> And with a strong will I sever
>> All the ties which bind me here.

A Latin verse was also omitted which, with minor variations, is repeated three times in the original poem:

> *Sanctus fortis, sanctus Deus,*
>> *De profundis oro te,*
> *Miserere, Judes meus,*
>> *Parce mihi, Domine.*

'Firmly I believe and truly' is not the only hymn to have been taken from 'The Dream of Gerontius'. In 1868, while Newman was still alive, the editors of *Hymns Ancient and Modern* printed a group of verses from a later section of the poem to make the hymn 'Praise to the Holiest in the height' (No. 109).

The most appropriate tune for this hymn is, I think, the sprightly Shipston, yet another of the English traditional melodies which Vaughan Williams selected for the *English Hymnal*. Alternatives include Halton Holgate by William Boyce (1710–79), which is favoured by *Hymns Ancient and Modern*, and the rather muted melody in the minor key, Ottery St Mary by Henry G. Lee (1887–1962) which, rather surprisingly, is the preferred choice of both *Hymns for Church and School* and the *Church Hymnary*.

Sanctus fortis

Firmly I believe and truly
    God is Thee, and God is One;
And I next acknowledge duly
    Manhood taken by the Son.

2 And I trust and hope most fully
    In that Manhood crucified;
And each thought and deed unruly
    Do to death, as he has died.

3 Simply to his grace and wholly
    Light and life and strength belong,
And I love supremely, solely,
    Him the holy, him the strong.

4 And I hold in veneration,
    For the love of him alone,
Holy Church as his creation,
    And her teachings as his own.

5 Adoration aye be given,
    With and through the angelic host,
To the God of earth and heaven,
    Father, Son, and Holy Ghost.

38 FOR ALL THY SAINTS WHO FROM THEIR LABOURS REST

A magnificent processional song of triumph rejoicing in the communion of saints, this hymn is not, thank goodness, sung only on All Saints' Day, to which strictly speaking it belongs.

Its author, William Walsham How (1823–97), was one of the most conscientious and well loved of all Victorian clergymen. Born and educated in Shrewsbury, where his father was a solicitor, he started writing hymns as a young boy for services which he held with his brother and stepsister. As an undergraduate at Wadham College, Oxford, in the early 1840s he was much influenced by the Tractarian movement and he remained a High Churchman for the rest of his life. He was ordained in 1846 and became a curate first at Kidderminster and then at Shrewsbury. Five years later he became rector of Whittington in Shropshire where he remained for twenty-eight years, writing hymns and indulging his passion for ferns and fishing. In 1879 he was appointed suffragen Bishop of London, with particular responsibility for the East End. His work among the poor in the dockland slums earned him the love of thousands, and he was known as the 'omnibus bishop' because he shunned a private carriage and preferred to travel by public transport.

How turned down several offers of bishoprics, but in 1889 he felt compelled to become the first bishop of the new industrial diocese of Wakefield in West Yorkshire. Shortly after his translation there, he was offered the much more attractive see of Durham but he declined it to stay with the factory and mill workers of the West Riding.

Like most of his fifty-four hymns, 'For all Thy saints' was written while How was rector of Whittington. It appeared as a processional hymn for All Saints' Day in Earl Nelson's *Hymn for a Saint's Day and Other Hymns* (1864). Seven years later in *Church Hymns*, a collection published by the Society for the Propagation of Christian Knowledge and edited by How and another Shropshire rector, John Ellerton (on whom see notes to hymn No. 126), the first line was changed to 'For all the saints' and so it has remained in most hymnals ever since. The original version, which is printed below, ran to eleven verses. The third, fourth and fifth are omitted from all modern hymn-books.

For many years the hymn was sung to the tune entitled For All the Saints, specially written for it in 1869 by Sir Joseph Barnby (1838–96), a noted Victorian composer who was director of music at Eton and later principal of the Guildhall School of Music. In 1906 Ralph Vaughan Williams composed a new tune which he called *Sine Nomine* for the hymn's appearance in the *English Hymnal;* this is now almost universally used.

The Procession of Faith

For all Thy saints who from their labours rest,
Who Thee by faith before the world confessed,
Thy Name, O Jesus, be for ever blest. Alleluia!

2 Thou wast their Rock, their Fortress, and their Might;
Thou, Lord, their Captain in the well-fought fight;
Thou, in the darkness drear, their one true Light. Alleluia!

3 For the Apostles' glorious company,
Who bearing forth the Cross o'er land and sea,
Shook all the mighty world, we sing to thee: Alleluia!

4 For the Evangelists, by whose pure word,
Like fourfold stream, the garden of the Lord,
Is fair and fruitful, be Thy name adored. Alleluia!

5 For Martyrs, who with rapture-kindled eye,
 Saw the bright crown descending from the sky,
 And, seeing, grasped it, thee we glorify. Alleluia!

6 O may Thy soldiers, faithful, true, and bold,
 Fight as the saints who nobly fought of old,
 And win, with them, the victor's crown of gold. Alleluia!

7 O blest communion, fellowship divine!
 We feebly struggle, they in glory shine;
 Yet all are one in Thee, for all are Thine. Alleluia!

8 And when the strife is fierce, the warfare long,
 Steals on the ear the distant triumph song,
 And hearts are brave again, and arms are strong. Alleluia!

9 The golden evening brightens in the west;
 Soon, soon to faithful warriors cometh rest;
 Sweet is the calm of Paradise the blest. Alleluia!

10 But, lo! there breaks a yet more glorious day;
 The saints triumphant rise in bright array;
 The King of Glory passes on His way. Alleluia!

11 From earth's wide bounds, from ocean's farthest coast,
 Through gates of pearl streams in the countless host,
 Singing to Father, Son, and Holy Ghost. Alleluia!

39 FOR THE BEAUTY OF THE EARTH

This is an interesting example of a hymn that has undergone alterations for doctrinal reasons. In its original form it was too Catholic in
its theology and too inclined to stress the sacrificial element in the
communion service for a number of hymn-book compilers, and the
language has been watered down in various ways.

Its author, Folliott Sandford Pierpoint (1835–1917), was a devout
Tractarian. Born in Bath and educated at the grammar school there
and then at Queens' College, Cambridge, he spent most of his life as
a classics master at the Somersetshire College. After retiring he lived
in various places in the West Country. He published three collections
of poems.

'For the beauty of the earth' was written about 1863 and first
published in the Revd Orby Shipley's *Lyra Eucharistica* (1864) in the
form printed overleaf. It was designed for use as a communion
hymn and took its refrain from the post-communion prayer in the
Book of Common Prayer which begins: 'O Lord and heavenly
Father, we thy humble servants entirely desire thy fatherly goodness
mercifully to accept this our sacrifice of praise and thanksgiving.'

Partly because they were worried about its theological implications, and also to make the hymn suitable for general use and not
simply restricted to communion services, the compilers of *Hymns
Ancient and Modern* changed the refrain to:

> Lord of all, to Thee we raise
> This our grateful hymn of praise.

They also changed the last line of the fourth verse from 'For all
gentle thoughts and mild' to 'Pleasures pure and undefiled', and
dropped the last three verses of the hymn which they regarded as

rather too Catholic in their language for an Anglican hymnal. This practice was followed by Nonconformist hymn-books. In the words of the companion to the *Baptist Church Hymnal*, 'It has been shortened and edited, the omitted verses emphasizing a view of the Eucharist we do not share.'

In fact, a growing convergence of views on the importance and significance of the Eucharist has meant that there is now much less variation than there used to be in the way this hymn is presented in different hymn-books. The 'New Standard' edition of *Hymns Ancient and Modern* has restored the original refrain and, while omitting the third verse, prints the sixth, substituting 'Church' for 'Bride' in its first line. This alteration is also made in the *New English Hymnal,* which breaks with the High Church traditions of its predecessors and drops the seventh and eighth verses. The Presbyterian *Church Hymnary* also happily prints Pierpoint's original refrain.

No two hymn-books that I have consulted offer the same tune for this hymn. To my mind the most appropriate is England's Lane, adapted by Geoffrey Shaw (1879–1943) from a traditional English melody for the English Hymnal. Alternatives are the similar-sounding but slightly boring and predictable Dix by Conrad Kocher (1786–1872), Incarnation by Henry Smart (1813–79), St Brannock by E. J. Hopkins (1818–1901), St Ninian by W. H. Monk (1823–89), Ratisbon by J. Crüger (1598–1662), Moseley by John Joubert (1927–   ), *Lucerna Laudoniae* by David Evans (1874–1948) and Noricum by F. James (1858–1922).

The Sacrifice of Praise

For the beauty of the earth,
 For the beauty of the skies,
For the love which from our birth
 Over and around us lies:
  Christ our God, to thee we raise
  This our sacrifice of praise.

2 For the beauty of each hour
  Of the day and of the night,
 Hill and vale, and tree and flower,
  Sun and moon and stars of light:

3 For the joy of ear and eye,
  For the heart and brain's delight,
 For the mystic harmony
  Linking sense to sound and sight:

4 For the joy of human love,
  Brother, sister, parent, child,
 Friends on earth, and friends above,
  For all gentle thoughts and mild:

5 For each perfect gift of thine
  To our race so freely given,
 Graces human and divine,
  Flowers of earth and buds of heaven:

6 For thy Bride that evermore
  Lifteth holy hands above,
 Offering up on every shore
  This pure sacrifice of love:

7 For the Martyrs' crown of light,
  For thy Prophets' eagle eye,
 For thy bold Confessors' might,
  For the lips of infancy:

8 For thy Virgins' robes of snow,
  For thy Maiden-mother mild,
 For thyself, with hearts aglow,
  Jesu, Victim undefiled:

40 FORTH IN THY NAME, O LORD, I GO

Considering the important role that work occupies in most lives, there are surprisingly few hymns on the subject and on how the Christian should approach it. John Keble's 'New every morning is the love' (No. 90) has the important message that 'the trivial round, the common task, will furnish all we ought to ask', and George Herbert's *Teach me, my God and King* (No. 120) reminds us that:

> A servant with this clause
> Makes drudgery divine;
> Who sweeps a room, as for thy laws,
> Makes that and th'action fine.

These verses by Charles Wesley (1707–88; see notes to hymn No. 11) perhaps provide the most comprehensive treatment of the subject.

Wesley wrote the hymn in 1749 and it was first published in his *Hymns and Sacred Poems* in the same year. In most hymn-books it appears in the 'Morning' section but it does not really have to be sung at the beginning of the day, a fact which the *English Hymnal* long acknowledged with a discreet note to the effect that it is 'suitable also for mid-day services'. All hymn-books substitute the phrase 'thy good and perfect will' for 'thy acceptable will' in the last line of the second verse, a change which was made partly for musical and partly for theological reasons. It is also quite common practice for the third verse printed opposite to be omitted. Indeed, John Wesley left it out when he included his brother's hymn in the *Wesleyan Hymn Book* of 1780.

The tune almost always used for this hymn is Angel's Song, or Song 34, by Orlando Gibbons (1583–1625), the famous madrigal composer who was organist of the Chapel Royal and Westminster Abbey. It was one of a set of tunes which he wrote for George Wither's *Hymns and Songs of the Church,* published in 1623. In that book it was set to the hymn 'Thus Angels sung, and thus sing we', hence its title. Another of Wesley's hymns, 'O, for a heart to praise my God', is often sung to Gibbons's Song 67, or St Matthias, which comes from the same collection.

Forth in thy name, O Lord, I go,
  My daily labour to pursue;
Thee, only thee, resolved to know,
  In all I think or speak or do.

2 The task thy wisdom hath assigned
  O let me cheerfully fulfil,
In all my works thy presence find,
  And prove thy acceptable will.

3 Preserve me from my calling's snare,
  And hide my simple heart above,
Above the thorns of choking care,
  The gilded baits of worldly love.

4 Thee may I set at my right hand,
  Whose eyes my inmost substance see,
And labour on at thy command,
  And offer all my works to thee.

5 Give me to bear thy easy yoke,
  And every moment watch and pray,
And still to things eternal look,
  And hasten to thy glorious day;

6 For thee delightfully employ
  What'er thy bounteous grace hath given,
And run my course with even joy,
  And closely walk with thee to heaven.

41 FROM GREENLAND'S ICY MOUNTAINS

This hymn has been dropped by all modern hymn-books and it is included in this collection largely as a period piece. It belongs to that large category of missionary hymns which formed a substantial section in Victorian and early twentieth-century hymnals but which have now all but disappeared from view, and on the whole rightly so. Its sentiments on heathens in far-off lands are quite unacceptable today when we ourselves live in a largely heathen country and when we have come to appreciate much of value in the ancient religions of Africa and Asia. Yet it has a poetic intensity and vigour that is hard to deny, and I trust its appearance here will not cause offence.

The imperialism and racial overtones implicit in the hymn come strangely from the pen of one so innocent and saintly as Reginald Heber (1783–1826). Poor Heber seems to have had a knack of causing offence with his hymns. We have already noted that his *Brightest and best of the sons of the morning* (No. 22 – see notes to that hymn for details of Heber's early life) was for long excluded from hymn-books on the grounds that it worshipped a star.

From Greenland's icy mountains was written while Heber was rector of Hodnet in Shropshire. It was penned in great haste in 1819 for his father-in-law, Dr Shipley, who was Dean of St Asaph. The Dean had to preach at the Whit Sunday service at Wrexham Parish Church and a Royal Letter issued by the Prince Regent had called for alms to be collected in all parish churches on that day for missionary work. The day before he was due to preach, Dr Shipley asked his son-in-law, who was staying with him at the time, for a suitable hymn. Heber immediately sat down at a table in the Dean's front room and composed the first three verses of this hymn. Dr Shipley was delighted, but Heber felt that the hymn was not quite complete and returned to the study to add a fourth verse. The whole process of composition took just twenty minutes. The following day the hymn was sung at Wrexham to the tune of a popular ballad, 'Twas when the seas were roaring', and was a great success. A local printer sold thousands of copies and the hymn was published in the *Evangelical Magazine* of July 1821.

The manuscript of the hymn shows that Heber initially wrote 'savage' in the seventh line of the second verse. His alteration to 'heathen' gave Rudyard Kipling the inspiration for his poem 'The 'Eathen', published in 1896:

> The 'eathen in 'is blindness bows down to wood and stone,
> 'E don't obey no orders, unless they is 'is own;
> 'E keeps 'is side-arms awful: 'e leaves them all about,
> An' then comes up the Regiment an' pokes the 'eathen out.

Heber later altered 'Ceylon's isle' to 'Java's isle', presumably so that the accent should fall in the right place. Four years after writing the hymn, he was himself to settle in 'India's coral strand' when he was appointed Bishop of Calcutta. But his time there was brief. One hot afternoon in April 1826, after preaching on the evils of the caste system before a large congregation at Trichinopoly, he went to cool off in the local swimming pool. He was later found drowned there, having had a stroke. He was just forty-three when he died and he was buried at the Anglican Church in Trichinopoly.

In early days the hymn was sung to an Indian air. Later this was replaced by the melody Greenland, specially composed for it in 1828 by Thomas Clark (1775–1859), leader of psalmody at the Wesleyan chapel and later at the Unitarian church at Canterbury. It was also sung to Crüger and Aurelia (see notes to Nos. 51 and 124).

From Greenland's icy mountains,
  From India's coral strand,
Where Afric's sunny fountains
  Roll down their golden sand,
From many an ancient river,
  From many a palmy plain,
They call us to deliver
  Their land from error's chain.

2 What though the spicy breezes
    Blow soft o'er Ceylon's isle,
  Though every prospect pleases
    And only man is vile,
  In vain with lavish kindness
    The gifts of God are strown,
  The heathen in his blindness
    Bows down to wood and stone.

3 Can we, whose souls are lighted
    With wisdom from on high,
  Can we to men benighted
    The lamp of life deny?
  Salvation! Oh, salvation!
    The joyful sound proclaim,
  Till each remotest nation
    Has learn'd Messiah's name.

4 Waft, waft, ye winds, His story,
    And you, ye waters, roll,
  Till, like a sea of glory,
    It spreads from pole to pole;
  Till o'er our ransom'd nature
    The Lamb for sinners slain,
  Redeemer, King, Creator,
    In bliss returns to reign.

42 GLORIOUS THINGS OF THEE ARE SPOKEN

This is another much-loved hymn written by John Newton (1725–1807), the ne'er-do-well slave trader turned fervent 'born again' Christian whose life story is told in the notes accompanying 'Amazing grace' (No. 10).

Newton attached to this hymn the biblical reference Isaiah 33:20–21. This reads:

Look upon Zion, the city of our solemnities: thine eyes shall see Jerusalem a quiet habitation, a tabernacle that shall not be taken down; not one of the stakes thereof shall ever be removed, neither shall any of the cords thereof be broken. But there the glorious Lord will be unto us a place of broad rivers and streams; wherein shall no galley with oars, neither shall any gallant ship pass thereby.

The hymn takes its first line from the third verse of Psalm 87: 'Glorious things are spoken of thee, O city of God.' The seventh line of the first verse is based on Isaiah 26:1, 'We have a strong city; salvation will God appoint for walls and bulwarks', and the first line of the second verse echoes Psalm 46, verse 4, 'There is a river, the streams whereof shall make glad the city of God.' There are other biblical references in the hymn, notably to the Book of Revelation.

'Glorious things of thee are spoken' is printed overleaf as it first appeared in *Olney Hymns,* which John Newton and his friend William Cowper produced in 1779. The fourth verse has been dropped in all modern hymn-books and several also omit the third verse which is rarely sung nowadays. Where that verse does appear, the fifth line has almost invariably been changed to 'Thus they march, the pillar leading', and the seventh to 'Daily on the manna feeding'.

Some hymn-books have altered the first line of the last verse to read 'Saviour, since of Zion's city'. This apparently small change in wording makes a major difference to the meaning. Newton was a strict Calvinist who believed that no man could be certain whether he belonged to the elect who had been chosen by God to dwell in the eternal city. Modern theology tends towards a more confident view of mankind's chances of salvation.

The tune still first and foremost associated with this hymn is, I suppose, Austria, which was written by Franz Josef Haydn (1732–1809) for the Hapsburg emperor Francis II. The hymn was first performed on the emperor's birthday in 1797. It is said to have been a particular favourite of Haydn's and the story goes that it was the last piece of music that the composer ever played on his piano. It was first used as a hymn tune in England in 1805. Later it was taken up as the music for the German national anthem, '*Deutschland! Deutschland! über alles*'. The German emperor, Kaiser Wilhelm II, is said to have been very startled when, during a visit to his godmother, Queen Victoria, at Windsor Castle, he found himself singing the words of Newton's hymn to it.

A more flowing and less bombastic alternative to Austria is Abbot's Leigh by Cyril Taylor (b. 1907; see notes to hymn No. 82). His tune became familiar largely through the medium of the wireless: it was printed in leaflet form in 1941, and appeared in *Hymns Ancient and Modern* in 1950.

Zion, or the City of God

Glorious things of thee are spoken,
  Zion, city of our God!
He whose word cannot be broken
  Formed thee for his own abode:
On the Rock of Ages founded,
  What can shake thy sure repose?
With salvation's walls surrounded,
  Thou may'st smile at all thy foes.

2 See, the streams of living waters,
  Springing from eternal love,
Well supply thy sons and daughters,
  And all fear of want remove:
Who can faint while such a river
  Ever flows their thirst to assuage?
Grace, which like the Lord the Giver,
  Never fails from age to age.

3 Round each habitation hov'ring,
  See the cloud and fire appear
For a glory and a cov'ring,
  Showing that the Lord is near.
Thus deriving from their banner
  Light by night and shade by day;
Safe they feed upon the manna
  Which he gives them when they pray.

4 Bless'd inhabitants of Zion,
  Wash'd in the Redeemer's blood!
Jesus, whom their hopes rely on,
  Makes them kings and priests to God.
'Tis his love his people raises
  Over self to reign as King,
And, as priests, his solemn praises
  Each for a thank-offering brings.

5   Saviour, if of Zion's city
    I, through grace, a member am,
Let the world deride or pity,
    I will glory in thy name:
Fading is the worldling's pleasure,
    All his boasted pomp and show;
Solid joys and lasting treasure
    None but Zion's children know.

43 GOD BE WITH YOU TILL WE MEET AGAIN

This is an unashamedly sentimental hymn and, such things being out of fashion nowadays, it fails to make an appearance in any of the modern hymn-books I have consulted, except for *Hymns for Church and School* which prints a modern version very different from the original given overleaf. Traditionally sung at partings and farewells, it never failed to bring a lump to the throat. I personally very much regret its loss from our current stock of hymns. I can think of nothing more appropriate or moving to sing at times of parting from old friends.

The author, Dr Jeremiah Eames Rankin (1828–1904), was a Congregational minister and President of Howard University, Washington, DC. He wrote this hymn in 1882, basing it on the etymology of the word 'goodbye' which is a shortened form of 'God be with you'.

The hymn was first sung at the First Congregational Church in Washington where Rankin was minister, and it was immensely popular. He himself attributed its popularity largely to the tune to which it was sung, which had been composed by William Gould Tomer (1832–96). Rankin had sent the first verse of the hymn to two composers, one nationally known and the other the unknown Tomer, a former soldier in the Civil War and clerk in the US Treasury Department who had taken up schoolteaching.

Tomer's tune, also known as God be with You, was for long favoured by British Nonconformists, but Anglicans have largely rejected it in favour of Ralph Vaughan Williams's Randolph. The latter is undoubtedly more sophisticated, but I have to say that I prefer Tomer's melody despite the fact that one critic has dismissed it as 'a tedious maudlin tune'. Its sentimentality goes well with Rankin's words.

As I mentioned above, *Hymns for Church and School,* the successor
to the old *Public School Hymn Book,* contains a version of this hymn.
It is the very last entry in the book and is headed as appropriate for a
farewell. Several schools use it at end-of-term services. Sung to
Randolph and with new words by Donald Hughes (1911–67), a
former headmaster of Rydal School, Colwyn Bay, it bears little
resemblance to the Rankin–Tomer original although the opening
and closing lines of each verse are the same. Its language is less
personal and more challenging, but its underlying message is equally
moving and reassuring. It is probably too much to ask for the resurrection of the original hymn today, but it would be good to see this
modern version in more hymn-books. I am indebted to Mrs Mary
Hughes, the author's sister-in-law, for allowing me to quote it. The
first and last verses run as follows:

> God be with you till we meet again,
>   May he through the days direct you;
>   May he in life's storms protect you;
> God be with you till we meet again.
>
> God be with you till we meet again;
>   May he go through life beside you,
>   And through death in safety guide you;
> God be with you till we meet again.

At a Farewell

God be with you till we meet again;
  By his counsels guide, uphold you,
  With his sheep securely fold you:
God be with you till we meet again.

2 God be with you till we meet again;
  'Neath his wings protecting hide you,
  Daily manna still provide you:
God be with you till we meet again.

3 God be with you till we meet again;
  When life's perils thick confound you,
  Put his arms unfailing round you:
God be with you till we meet again.

4 God be with you till we meet again;
  Keep love's banner floating o'er you,
  Smite death's threatening wave before you:
God be with you till we meet again.

44 GOD IS WORKING HIS PURPOSE OUT

Several of the hymns in this collection were first written for school-boys to sing. We have already encountered Thomas Ken's fine morning hymn for the scholars of Winchester, 'Awake, my soul, and with the sun' (No. 15) and we will later meet '"Lift up your hearts!" We lift them, Lord, to thee' (No. 79) which Henry Montagu Butler penned for the pupils of Harrow. This hymn was written for the boys of Britain's most famous public school, Eton.

The author, Arthur Campbell Ainger (1841–1919), was the son of the vicar of Hampstead. He was educated at Eton and returned to teach there after a brief spell as an undergraduate at Cambridge, where he gained first class honours in the classical tripos. He remained at the school as an assistant master for thirty-seven years and was much liked by his pupils. He is reported to have 'preserved admirable and friendly discipline by means of a dry and ready irony, which was never harsh or unamiable. He set no punishments, and his justice, courtesy, and unruffled good humour won the respect and admiration of the boys.'

Ainger wrote a large number of poems and hymns. He was also responsible for a collection of Eton songs, a book of reminiscences about the school, an English–Latin verse dictionary and a learned treatise on the game of Fives.

'God is working his purpose out' was written in 1894 and dedicated to Archbishop Benson, a former master at Rugby and headmaster of Wellington College, who was Archbishop of Canterbury from 1882 until his death in 1896. The last line of each verse echoes the words of Habakkuk 3:14, 'For the earth shall be filled with the knowledge of the glory of the Lord, as the waters cover the sea.'

When the hymn was first published in leaflet form it was set to the tune Benson which had been specially composed for it by Miss Millicent D. Kingham (1866–1927), organist at St Andrew's, Hertford. That tune is still given in *Hymns for Church and School,* although the *Public School Hymn Book* used its own specially commissioned tune, Alveston. Most other modern hymn-books set Ainger's hymn to Purpose by Martin Shaw (1875–1958).

God is working his purpose out as year succeeds to year;
God is working his purpose out and the time is drawing near;
Nearer and nearer draws the time, the time that shall surely be,
When the earth shall be filled with the glory of God as the waters
    cover the sea.

2   From utmost east to utmost west where'er man's foot hath trod,
By the mouth of many messengers goes forth the voice of God,
'Give ear to me, ye continents, ye isles, give ear to me,
That the earth may be filled with the glory of God as the waters
    cover the sea.'

3   What can we do to work God's work, to prosper and increase
The brotherhood of all mankind, the reign of the Prince of Peace?
What can we do to hasten the time, the time that shall surely be,
When the earth shall be filled with the glory of God as the waters
    cover the sea?

4   March we forth in the strength of God with the banner of Christ
    unfurled.
That the light of the glorious gospel of truth may shine throughout
    the world;
Fight we the fight with sorrow and sin, to set their captives free.
That the earth may be filled with the glory of God as the waters
    cover the sea.

5   All we can do is nothing worth unless God blesses the deed;
Vainly we hope for the harvest-tide till God gives life to the seed;
Yet nearer and nearer draws the time, the time that shall surely be,
When the earth shall be filled with the glory of God as the waters
    cover the sea.

45 GOD MOVES IN A MYSTERIOUS WAY

A hymn of vivid poetic imagery which conveys perhaps better than any other the mystery and impenetrability of God, this is the work of William Cowper (1731–1800), who produced some of the finest religious verse in the English language despite a life spent in acute mental torment.

Cowper came of a distinguished literary and ecclesiastical family. His father was a chaplain to George II and his mother was a descendant of John Donne, the metaphysical poet and Dean of St Paul's. He went to Westminster School, where he showed considerable promise as a versifier in both Latin and English, and then read for the Bar. However, from the age of twenty-one he began to be affected by severe bouts of melancholia. These continued, with increasing severity, for the rest of his life. He was committed to a lunatic asylum in the early 1760s and was never again capable of uninterrupted work.

The one anchor in Cowper's stormy and unhappy life was his strong Evangelical faith, the result of a conversion while he was a patient in a private lunatic asylum run by a convinced Evangelical. In 1767, at the invitation of John Newton (on whom see notes to hymn No. 10), he went to live at Olney in Buckinghamshire, where he was looked after by a clergyman's widow, Mrs Unwin, and did what he could to assist in the life of the parish.

Together Cowper and Newton wrote hymns to be sung at the weekly prayer meetings held in Olney church. They also collaborated on a hymn-book which was published in 1779, with 67 entries by Cowper and 280 by Newton. But what Cowper's contributions lacked in quantity they more than make up for in quality; they comprise some of the gems of English hymnody, including 'O for a closer walk with God' (No. 93), 'Hark my Soul! It is the Lord' and 'Jesus, where'er thy people meet'.

'God moves in a mysterious way' was written in the early 1770s when Cowper was in an almost permanent state of depression, alleviated by occasional periods of calm. The biblical text he attached to it was from Jesus' words to Simon Peter in John 13:7, 'What I do thou knowest not now; but thou shalt know hereafter.' There is a story that he wrote the hymn after being saved from a suicide attempt, but this is apocryphal. Although its language at times suggests a certain anguish, its overall theme is of resounding Christian hope. That is certainly how it has been taken by generations of Christians to whom it has given encouragement. It is reported that when, during the 1840s, a Lancashire mill-owner told his workers that the depression in trade would cause the closure of the works, they roused their spirits by singing 'Ye fearful saints, fresh courage take', led by a young girl. The last verse has a particularly strong message of assurance for those who are perplexed, as surely we all are at times, by the seeming irrationality and arbitrariness of God's ways.

Cowper's verses opposite first appeared in print in July 1774 in an appendage to a collection of letters by John Newton on religious subjects. They were also published in the same month in the *Gospel Magazine*. When the hymn appeared three years later in that same journal, the second verse was omitted and the following verse was added at the end:

> When midnight shades are all withdrawn
> The opening day shall rise,
> Whose ever calm and cloudless morn
> Shall know no low'ring skies.

The tunes most commonly used for the hymn both come from the Scottish Psalter; Dundee comes from the 1615 edition and London New from that of 1635.

Light shining out of darkness

God moves in a mysterious way
  His wonders to perform;
He plants his footsteps in the sea,
  And rides upon the storm.

2 Deep in unfathomable mines
  Of never-failing skill
He treasures up his bright designs,
  And works his sovereign will.

3 Ye fearful saints, fresh courage take;
  The clouds ye so much dread
Are big with mercy, and will break
  In blessings on your head.

4 Judge not the Lord by feeble sense,
  But trust him for his grace:
Behind a frowning providence
  He hides a smiling face.

5 His purposes will ripen fast,
  Unfolding every hour;
The bud may have a bitter taste,
  But sweet will be the flower.

6 Blind unbelief is sure to err,
  And scan his work in vain;
God is his own interpreter,
  And he will make it plain.

46 GOD SAVE OUR GRACIOUS QUEEN

Should our National Anthem properly be regarded as a hymn? It is a supplication addressed to the Almighty and it appears in virtually every major hymn-book, which seem reasons enough to include it in this collection.

Its origins and authorship are obscure. The anthem first appeared in the form printed overleaf (except for the substitution of 'King' for 'Queen' and 'him' for 'her' in appropriate places) in the *Gentleman's Magazine* for October 1745, where it was described as having been sung in several London playhouses. This was at the time of the Jacobite rising of Bonnie Prince Charlie and it seems likely that 'God save the King' was sung by Hanoverian loyalists. The first two verses had appeared in a slightly modified form two or three years earlier in a publication called *Harmonia Anglicana*. The words have often been attributed to Henry Carey (?–1743), the poet who was responsible for both the words and music of the popular song 'Sally in our Alley', but this attribution cannot be proved.

There is, however, strong evidence to suggest that the origins of the anthem may go back to the seventeenth century. Several authorities attribute the tune to Dr John Bull (?–1628), organist at Antwerp Cathedral. A French song, '*Grand Dieu sauvez le roi*', uncannily similar in language, structure and metre to the British National Anthem, was sung at the court of Louis XIV in 1686. Two years later a very similar chorus in Latin was sung at the court of King James II. It may well be that it was these Latin words that Henry Carey translated to form the National Anthem with which we are now familiar. It also seems to have been translated and used in Jacobite circles in the early eighteenth century.

The verses opposite have spawned numerous offspring and imitators. The best known is the one written by an American Unitarian minister, Charles T. Brooks (1813–83) and first published in 1836. Still much sung in the United States, its first verse reads:

God bless our native land!
Firm may she ever stand
   Through storm and night!
When the wild tempests rave,
Ruler of wind and wave,
Father eternal save
   Us by thy might!

The distinctly xenophobic and bellicose character of the second verse of the British National Anthem has long caused unease and it is normally omitted from modern hymnals. The 'New Standard' edition of *Hymns Ancient and Modern* offers as a substitute the following verse written in 1836 by William Edward Hickson (1803–70), a London boot manufacturer turned social reformer who produced an 'alternative' National Anthem of a more pacific and Christian character (which may be found in its entirety in the second edition of the *Church Hymnary*):

Nor on this land alone –
But be Thy mercies known
   From shore to shore.
Lord, make the nations see
All men should brothers be,
One league, one family,
One, the world o'er.

God save our gracious Queen,
Long live our noble Queen,
   God save the Queen.
Send her victorious,
Happy and glorious,
Long to reign over us:
   God save the Queen.

2   O Lord our God, arise,
Scatter our enemies,
   And make them fall;
Confound their politics,
Frustrate their knavish tricks;
On thee our hopes we fix:
   God save us all.

3   Thy choicest gifts in store
On her be pleased to pour,
   Long may she reign.
May she defend our laws,
And ever give us cause
To sing with heart and voice,
   God save the Queen.

47 GOD, WHOSE CITY'S SURE FOUNDATION

This is our first wholly twentieth-century hymn. 'Be thou my vision, O Lord of my heart' (No. 17) can only partially be counted in that category since it was translated from a poem around 1,200 years old!

The author of the verses overleaf, Dr Cyril Alington (1872–1955), was one of the most gifted hymn-writers of the last hundred years. His other compositions include 'Lord of beauty, thine the splendour', 'Good Christian men, rejoice and sing!', 'Ye that know the Lord is gracious' and 'Lord, thou hast brought us to our journey's end'. Had there been more space, I would certainly have included them in this book.

The son of an Anglican clergyman, Alington himself took orders shortly after leaving Oxford. He went to teach at Eton and at the early age of twenty-eight was appointed headmaster of Shrewsbury School. Eight years later he became headmaster of Eton. After seventeen years in that post he moved to Durham as Dean of the cathedral. He remained there until he was seventy-five, introducing services for the Miners' Gala and bringing the cathedral much more into the life of the city. Altogether he wrote nearly forty books, including many on religious subjects and two of an autobiographical nature, *A Schoolmaster's Apology* and *A Dean's Apology*.

'God, whose city's sure foundation' was written for the Friends of Durham Cathedral and contributed to the historical edition of *Hymns Ancient and Modern,* where it was headed 'Saints, martyrs, and doctors of the Church of England'. Strangely, it does not appear in the 'New Standard' edition of that hymn-book. It is, however, included in the *New English Hymnal* where it is marked for use on 8 November, the day on which the Anglican Church commemorates the saints of England. *Hymns for Church and School* widens the scope for its use by changing the first line of the second verse to 'Here before us through the ages'.

'God, whose city's sure foundation' is generally sung to the tune Westminster Abbey, an arrangement of the Alleluias at the end of Henry Purcell's anthem 'O God, Thou art my God'. It was turned into a hymn tune by E. Hawkins and is also used for J. M. Neale's 'Christ is made the sure Foundation' (No. 23). *Hymns for Church and School* offers as an alternative Wolvesey by E. T. Sweeting (1863–1930).

Saints, martyrs and doctors of the Church of England

God, whose city's sure foundation
   Stands upon his holy hill,
By his mighty inspiration
   Chose of old and chooseth still
Men of every race and nation
   His good pleasure to fulfil.

2 Here in England through the ages,
   While the Christian years went by,
Saints, confessors, martyrs, sages,
   Strong to live and strong to die,
Wrote their names upon the pages
   Of God's blessed company.

3 Some there were like lamps of learning
   Shining in a faithless night,
Some on fire with love, and burning
   With a flaming zeal for right,
Some by simple goodness turning
   Souls from darkness unto light.

4 As we now with high thanksgiving
   Their triumphant names record,
Grant that we, like them, believing
   In the promise of thy word,
May, like them, in all good living
   Praise and magnify the Lord.

© *Hymns Ancient and Modern*

48 GUIDE ME, O THOU GREAT JEHOVAH

A favourite with football crowds and church congregations alike, this rousing Welsh hymn was voted ninth in the BBC 'Songs of Praise' poll. Surprisingly, it is the only hymn from the Land of Song to have achieved wide popularity in English.

The Welsh original from which it is translated, *'Arglwydd, arwain trwy'r anialwch'*, was written in 1745 by William Williams (1717–91) and ran to five verses. Williams, who came from Llandovery in Carmarthenshire, trained for the medical profession, but decided to enter the Church in 1738 after hearing a sermon by Howell Harris, the leader of the Evangelical Revival in Wales. He was ordained a deacon in the established Anglican Church by the Bishop of St David's but three years later left to become a preacher in the Welsh Calvinistic Methodist connection. He started writing hymns at Harris's suggestion. Altogether he wrote some 800 hymns and travelled almost 100,000 miles on foot and horseback during more than forty years as an itinerant minister.

In 1771 the first, third and fifth verses of Williams's hymn were translated into English by Peter Williams (no relation of the author) and published in his *Hymns on Various Subjects*. His translation of the first verse was included in a four-verse English version of the hymn which William Williams himself published the following year as a leaflet entitled *A favourite hymn sung by Lady Huntingdon's Young Collegians*. This version, which appears overleaf, was made up of translations of the first, third and fourth verses of the original Welsh hymn together with a new English verse added by the author.

Most hymn-books use this version with the fourth stanza omitted, but some, including *Hymns Ancient and Modern*, substitute 'Redeemer' for 'Jehovah' in the first line. The last line of the first verse is sometimes rendered as 'Feed me now and evermore' or 'Feed me till my want is o'er'. The hymn has been re-written a number of times, notably by John Keble who in 1857 produced a version beginning 'Guide us, thou whose name is Saviour'.

The imagery of the hymn is taken from the biblical story of the Israelites' journey from Egypt to the Promised Land. The 'bread of heaven' comes from Exodus 16:4, 'Then said the Lord unto Moses, Behold, I will rain bread from heaven for you.' The 'crystal fountain' comes from Exodus 17:5, 'Behold, I will stand before thee upon the rock in Horeb; and thou shalt smite the rock, and there shall come water out of it, that the people may drink.' The 'fire and cloudy pillar' is found in Exodus 13:21, 'And the Lord went before them by day and night: he took not away the pillar of the cloud by day, nor the pillar of fire by night, from before the people.'

The tune Cwm Rhondda, which must be one of the best known and certainly one of the most lustily sung of all hymn tunes, is surprisingly recent in origin. It was composed for a Welsh song festival in 1905 by John Hughes (1873–1932), an official of the Great Western Railway and precentor of Salem Baptist Church in Ponty-pridd. Legend has it that he originally wrote it in chalk on a piece of tarpaulin, but more likely is his wife's recollection that he wrote it one Sunday morning while in the Salem chapel. What is certain is that its popularity was greatly boosted by its frequent use in the trenches of Flanders in the First World War, where it was sung so melodiously by Welsh soldiers that German troops took it up. Hughes originally called the tune Rhondda after the great mining valley in South Wales, but had to add the word cwm, or valley, to its title after discovering that there was already a tune called Rhondda.

Praying for Strength

Guide me, O thou great Jehovah,
    Pilgrim through this barren land;
I am weak, but thou art mighty;
    Hold me with thy powerful hand;
      Bread of heaven, bread of heaven,
    Feed me till I want no more.

2   Open now the crystal fountain,
    Whence the healing stream doth flow;
Let the fire and cloudy pillar
    Lead me all my journey through;
      Strong Deliv'rer, Strong Deliv'rer,
    Be thou still my strength and shield.

3   When I tread the verge of Jordan,
    Bid my anxious fears subside;
Death of deaths, and hell's destruction,
    Land me safe on Canaan's side;
      Songs of praises, songs of praises,
    I will ever give to thee.

4   Musing on my habitation,
    Musing on my heav'nly home,
Fills my soul with holy longings:
    Come, my Jesus, quickly come;
      Vanity is all I see;
    Lord, I long to be with Thee!

49 HAIL THE DAY THAT SEES HIM RISE

Another ever-popular hymn by Charles Wesley (1707–88; see notes to hymn No. 11), this has been substantially re-written. Indeed, not one verse of the original survives unscathed in the version that is now so widely sung at Ascension Day services.

The hymn as Wesley wrote it is printed overleaf. It was first published in *Hymns and Sacred Poems* in 1739. It gives a vivid description of the Ascension of Christ and a clear explanation of what Christians believe its significance to be. The view of heaven presented in verses seven, eight and nine may seem a little too definitely located 'up there' for modern tastes, but there can be no denying the poetry of the lines, somewhat muted in the version we sing now, 'High above yon azure height' and 'Following thee beyond the skies'.

The second verse quotes almost verbatim from Psalm 24, verse 7: 'Lift up your heads, O ye gates; And be lift up, ye everlasting doors; And the King of glory shall come in.'

The curious reference in the seventh verse to Christ being 'taken from our head' comes from 2 Kings 2:5, 'Knowest thou that the Lord will take away thy master from thy head today?', while the eighth verse shows Wesley's strong liturgical sense and echoes the collect for Ascension Day in the Book of Common Prayer:

Grant, we beseech thee, Almighty God, that like as we do believe thy only begotten Son our Lord Jesus Christ to have ascended into the heavens; so we may also in heart and mind thither ascend; and with him continually dwell.

In 1820 Wesley's hymn was substantially altered by Thomas Cotterill (1779–1823), vicar of Lane End, Staffordshire, and later perpetual curate of St Paul's, Sheffield. The general effect of his revision was to tone down the ecstatic and emotional language of the original.

His version appears in a number of modern hymn-books, including the *New English Hymnal*. It begins as follows:

> Hail the day that sees him rise
> > Alleluya!
> Glorious to his native skies;
> > Alleluya!
> Christ, awhile to mortals given,
> > Alleluya!
> Enters now the highest heaven!
> > Alleluya!

The practice of adding 'Alleluya' to the end of every line dates from 1852. In 1861 the compilers of *Hymns Ancient and Modern* further altered the hymn and their version appears in a number of contemporary hymnals, including the 'New Standard' edition of *Hymns Ancient and Modern*. It begins:

> Hail the day that sees him rise,
> > Alleluia!
> To his throne above the skies;
> > Alleluia!
> Christ, the Lamb for sinners given,
> > Alleluia!
> Enters now the highest heaven.
> > Alleluia!

The most commonly used tune for this hymn is the joyful and exuberant Ascension, composed in 1861 by W. H. Monk (1823–89) for *Hymns Ancient and Modern*, of which he was musical editor. An alternative is Llanfair by Robert Williams (1781–1821).

Hymn for Ascension Day

Hail the day that sees him rise,
Ravished from our wishful eyes!
Christ, awhile to mortals given,
Reascends his native heaven.

2   There the pompous triumph waits:
'Lift your heads, eternal gates;
Wide unfold the radiant scene;
Take the King of glory in!'

3   Circled round with angel-powers,
Their triumphant Lord, and ours,
Conqueror over death and sin:
'Take the King of glory in!'

4   Him though highest heaven receives,
Still he loves the earth he leaves;
Though returning to his throne,
Still he calls mankind his own.

5   See! he lifts his hands above.
See! he shows the prints of love.
Hark! his gracious lips bestow
Blessings on his Church below.

6   Still for us his death he pleads;
Prevalent he intercedes;
Near himself prepares our place,
Harbinger of human race.

7   Master, (will we ever say,)
Taken from our head today,
See thy faithful servants, see,
Ever gazing up to Thee.

8   Grant, though parted from our sight,
    High above yon azure height,
    Grant our hearts may thither rise,
    Following thee beyond the skies.

9   Ever upward let us move,
    Wafted on the wings of love,
    Looking when our Lord shall come,
    Longing, gasping after home.

10   There we shall with thee remain,
    Partners of thy endless reign,
    There thy face unclouded see,
    Find our heaven of heavens in thee.

50 HAIL THEE, FESTIVAL DAY

There are at least four different versions of this exciting medieval processional hymn, each for use on one of the major festivals in the Christian calendar. The Whit Sunday one, which is printed overleaf, is the most widely sung nowadays, appearing in the hymn-books of a number of different denominations and not simply in those of a High Anglican persuasion, as it once did.

The original Latin hymn from which it is translated begins:

> *Salve, festa dies toto venerabilis aevo,*
> *Qua Deus de coelo gratia fulsit humo.*

It is first found in the Sarum use in a missal dating from the middle of the thirteenth century and a processional of *c.* 1360. It also occurs in the York Processional of 1530. The first line of the hymn is taken from a poem by Venatius Fortunatus (*c.* 530–609), an Italian who moved to France and became Bishop of Poitiers. His poem provides the original of the Easter Day version of the hymn,

> *Hail thee, Festival Day! blest day that art hallowed for ever;*
> *Day wherein Christ arose, breaking the kingdom of death.*

There are other versions of the hymn for Ascension Day – 'Day when our God ascends high in the heavens to reign'; and for a Dedication Festival – 'Day when the Church, Christ's bride, is to her bridegroom espoused'. There is also a version for Corpus Christi, but this is not found in any twentieth-century hymnal.

The fine translation of the Whitsun verses here was made by George Gabriel Scott Gillett (1873–1948) for the *English Hymnal* in 1906. Educated at Westminster School and Keble College, Oxford, Gillett was ordained in 1898 and served as a curate in London and

Brighton before becoming domestic chaplain to Earl Beauchamp and Viscount Halifax. He later worked in South Africa and ended his working life as editorial secretary to the Society for the Propagation of the Gospel.

This hymn takes much of its imagery from the account in Acts 2, of the coming of the Holy Spirit to the disciples at Pentecost. But it expands on that account to introduce such richly poetic phrases as the 'sevenfold mystical dowry' – a reference to the seven sacraments of baptism, confirmation, eucharist, penance, matrimony, holy order and anointing of the sick. The first line of the sixth verse is borrowed from the collect for peace in the Book of Common Prayer which begins: 'O God, who art the author of peace and lover of concord'.

All the Festival Day hymns owe much of their modern popularity to the vigorous unison tune *Salve, Festa Dies* which Ralph Vaughan Williams (1872–1958) composed for their appearance in the *English Hymnal* in 1906.

Salve, festa dies

Hail thee, Festival Day! blest day that art hallowed for ever;
Day wherein God from heaven shone on the world with his grace.

2 Lo! in the likeness of fire, on them that await his appearing,
   He whom the Lord foretold, suddenly, swiftly, descends.

3 Forth from the Father he comes with his sevenfold mystical dowry,
   Pouring on human souls infinite riches of God.

4 Hark! in a hundred tongues Christ's own, his chosen Apostles,
   Preach to a hundred tribes Christ and his wonderful works.

5 Praise to the Spirit of life, all praise to the Fount of our being,
   Light that dost lighten all, Life that in all dost abide.

6 God who art Giver of all good gifts and Lover of concord,
   Pour thy balm on our souls, order our ways in thy peace.

7 God Almighty, who fillest the heaven, the earth and the ocean,
   Guard us from harm without, cleanse us from evil within.

8 Kindle our lips with the live bright coal from the hands of the
      Seraph;
   Shine in our minds with thy light; burn in our hearts with thy
      love.

From the English Hymnal, *by permission of Oxford University Press*

159

51 HAIL TO THE LORD'S ANOINTED

There can be few hymn-writers who have suffered imprisonment on account of their radical political views, but on two occasions that was the fate of the author of this hymn, James Montgomery (1771–1854).

Montgomery was brought up a Moravian. This relatively small religious sect, which had close links with the Lutheran Church and to which John Wesley owed his conversion, had been founded in 1722 by Count Nicholas Ludwig von Zinzendorf as a revival of the fifteenth-century Bohemian Brethren. Montgomery's father was an Irish peasant who became a Moravian pastor and settled in Irvine, Ayrshire. Shortly after James's birth there his parents went out as missionaries to the slaves on the sugar plantations in the West Indies. They died within a few years and James was sent away to be educated at the Moravian seminary at Fulneck in Yorkshire.

He was originally attracted to the Moravian ministry, but did not pursue the idea and instead became a shopkeeper at Mirfield, near Huddersfield. Then in 1792 he moved to Sheffield and became assistant to Joseph Gales, a well-known printer and bookseller. Gales was proprietor of the *Sheffield Register*, famous for its extreme political radicalism, and it was this periodical that Montgomery took over when he was just twenty-three, after Gales had been forced to flee the country. Montgomery changed the title to the *Sheffield Iris* but did not temper the paper's forceful political line. Among the controversial causes which he championed was the teaching of writing in the Sunday School syllabus, a practice that many in authority felt would instil dangerous ideas into working-class youth. He was also a strong opponent of slavery and of the use of child climbing-boys by chimney sweeps. His strong support for the democratic principles of the French Revolution led him to be regarded as a dangerous Jacobin and he was imprisoned in 1795 for writing an enthusiastic account of the release of innocent prisoners during the storming of the Bastille. An equally sympathetic account of a reform riot in Sheffield led to a second spell of imprisonment a few years later.

In 1814 Montgomery became a member of the Wesleyan Society. Later in life he became a communicant member of the Anglican Church. An important influence on his switch to Anglicanism, and on his career as a hymn-writer, was the Revd Thomas Cotterill, perpetual curate of St Paul's Church in Sheffield, whom we have just come across as the reviser of Charles Wesley's hymn, 'Hail the day that sees him rise' (No. 49). In the absence of any Anglican hymn-books at this time, Montgomery helped Cotterill to produce a hymnal for use in his church. Some members of the congregation who objected to learning a lot of new hymns and who felt hymn-singing to be a Dissenting and distinctly un-Anglican practice dredged up an ancient Church law that prohibited the singing in churches of hymns of 'human composure', as opposed to versions of psalms and scriptures. They took their case to the Church courts where the ancient law was upheld, and it looked briefly as though the practice of hymn-singing might have to end in the Established Church. However, the Archbishop of York had the law repealed and from 1821 hymns were officially legitimate in the Church of England.

Altogether Montgomery wrote more than 400 hymns, several of which were written for Cotterill's hymn-book and all of which appeared in a collected volume in 1853. Erik Routley has written:

His work is good, sound, hard-wearing stuff with a touch of the genuinely inspired here and there that makes us able to regard him as the typical English hymn-writer. Without any question on the verdict of posterity, Montgomery was the greatest of Christian lay hymn-writers.

One of his great strengths was undoubtedly his association with several different denominations, which freed him from the narrowness which afflicts some other early nineteenth-century hymn-writers.

According to Julian's *Dictionary of Hymnology*, a quarter of Montgomery's vast output was still in regular use at the end of the last century. Nowadays most hymnals carry at least half a dozen of his hymns. Among those which continue to be sung are 'Stand up, and bless the Lord' (No. 116), 'For ever with the Lord', 'Songs of praise the Angels sang', 'Lift up your heads, ye gates of brass', 'According to thy gracious word', 'Prayer is the soul's sincere desire' and the ever-popular carol, 'Angels from the Realms of Glory'. Strangely, this last hymn attracted no attention at all when it appeared in the *Sheffield Iris*, where Montgomery first published several of his hymns, and it was only when it was included in one of his later collections that it began to be sung in churches.

'Hail to the Lord's Anointed', which is printed here in its full original form, was written for and sung in a Christmas Ode at a Moravian settlement in 1821. The following April, Montgomery recited the hymn at the close of an address in the Wesleyan Chapel in Liverpool. In the congregation was the distinguished Methodist theologian Dr Adam Clarke, who asked for the manuscript and printed it in his own commentary beside the 72nd Psalm. In June it appeared in the *Evangelical Magazine* and later in Montgomery's *Songs of Zion*.

The hymn is closely based on Psalm 72 ('Give the king thy judgments, O God'). The start of the second stanza echoes the fourth verse of the psalm: 'He shall judge the poor of the people, He shall save the children of the needy', and the beginning of the fourth stanza closely parallels verses 6 and 7: 'He shall come down like rain upon the mown grass: As showers that water the earth.' The memorable and evocative phrases, 'Arabia's desert ranger' and 'the Ethiopian stranger' in verse 5, are derived, rather loosely from lines 10 and 11 of the psalm: 'The kings of Tarshish and of the isles shall bring presents: The kings of Sheba and Seba shall offer gifts.' Modern hymn-books print a much shortened version of the original hymn, often including only the first, fourth, sixth and eighth verses.

The tune almost always used for 'Hail to the Lord's Anointed' is Crüger, an adaptation by W. H. Monk (see hymn No. 2) of a tune by Johann Crüger (1598–1662) which was originally published in 1640. Crüger was for forty years cantor at the Cathedral of St Nicholas in Berlin.

Psalm lxxii

Hail to the Lord's Anointed!
  Great David's greater Son;
Hail, in the time appointed,
  His reign on earth begun!
He comes to break oppression,
  To set the captive free,
To take away transgression,
  And rule in equity.

2 He comes in succour speedy
    To those who suffer wrong;
  To help the poor and needy,
    And bid the weak be strong;
  To give them songs for sighing,
    Their darkness turn to light,
  Whose souls, condemned and dying
    Were precious in his sight.

3 By such shall he be fearéd
    While sun and moon endure;
  Beloved, obeyed, reveréd;
    For he shall judge the poor
  Through changing generations,
    With justice, mercy, truth,
  While stars maintain their stations,
    Or moons renew their youth.

4 He shall come down like showers
    Upon the fruitful earth,
  And love, joy, hope, like flowers
    Spring in his path to birth:
  Before him on the mountains,
    Shall Peace, the herald, go;
  And righteousness, in fountains
    From hill to valley flow.

5 Arabia's desert ranger
  To him shall bow the knee,
The Ethiopian stranger
  His glory come to see:
With offerings of devotion,
  Ships from the isles shall meet,
To pour the wealth of ocean
  In tribute at his feet.

6 Kings shall bow down before him,
  And gold and silver bring;
All nations shall adore him,
  His praise all people sing:
For he shall have dominion
  O'er river, sea and shore,
Far as the eagle's pinion
  Or dove's light wing can soar.

7 For him shall prayer unceasing
  And daily vows ascend;
His kingdom still increasing,
  A kingdom without end:
The mountain dews shall nourish
  A seed in weakness sown,
Whose fruit shall spread and flourish,
  And shake like Lebanon.

8 O'er every foe victorious,
  He on his throne shall rest,
From age to age more glorious,
  All-blessing and all-blest;
The tide of time shall never
  His covenant remove;
His name shall stand for ever;
  That name to us is Love.

52 HARK THE GLAD SOUND! THE SAVIOUR COMES

While many of James Montgomery's hymns first saw the light of day in the pages of a radical newspaper, those of Philip Doddridge (1702–51) had a more orthodox début, being first heard in the Northampton chapel where he was minister. Doddridge wrote most of his 370 hymns to ram home the message of his sermons. They were generally sung at the end of the service and based on the biblical text from which he had just preached.

Doddridge was the youngest of the twenty children of an oil merchant and came of staunch Puritan stock. He was interested in religion from his earliest days, and before he could read he learnt Old Testament history from pictures on Dutch tiles in his parents' house. In 1729 he opened a Dissenting academy in Market Harborough on the advice of Isaac Watts. The following year he became pastor of the Congregational chapel at Castle Hill, Northampton, while continuing to run the academy, which trained 120 candidates for the ministry.

Doddridge wrote several books, including *The Progress of Religion in the Soul* which was instrumental in the conversion of William Wilberforce to Evangelical religion. He suffered from consumption and died in Lisbon where he had gone in the hope of finding some relief in the warm climate. His hymns were not published until after his death.

'Hark, the glad sound' was written in December 1735 to accompany an Advent sermon on the text of Luke 4:18–19, in which Christ reads from the prophet Isaiah in the synagogue at Nazareth:

The spirit of the Lord is upon me, because he hath anointed me to preach the gospel to the poor; He hath sent me to heal the broken-hearted, to preach deliverance to the captives, and recovering of sight to the blind, to set at liberty them that are bruised, to preach the acceptable year of the Lord.

It is hardly surprising that modern hymn-books omit the original fourth verse of this Advent hymn, with its inelegant references to 'thick films of vice' and 'the eyeballs of the blind'. But it is surely a pity that the second and sixth verses have also disappeared. The latter provides one of the all too rare references in English hymnody to the year of Jubilee, that wiping of the slate clean which occurred every fifty years in ancient Israel when slaves were freed, all debts were cancelled and the land allowed to lie fallow. Interestingly, a different version of that verse is still sung in Scotland, where an amended version of Doddridge's hymn is given in the *Church Hymnary* as Paraphrase 39:

> The sacred year has now revolved,
>   Accepted of the Lord,
> When heaven's high promise is fulfilled
>   And Israel is restored.

Another of Doddridge's hymns, 'O God of Bethel, by whose hand', continues to be very popular in Scotland and would undoubtedly have found a place in this volume had there been more space.

In 1854 'Hark the glad sound' was sung to the tune of the Old Hundredth on board the flagship of the American fleet which had been sent to secure Japan's abandonment of neutrality and the opening up of trading and diplomatic relations with the United States. Whether the Japanese did in fact look upon the US Navy as their 'Saviour promised long' when they heard it being sung as the fleet approached is not recorded. The hymn is now generally sung to the tune Bristol, which is first found in Ravenscroft's Psalter of 1621.

Hark, the glad sound! the Saviour comes,
    The Saviour promised long!
Let every heart prepare a throne,
    And every voice a song.

2 On him the Spirit largely pour'd
    Exerts its sacred fire:
Wisdom and might, and zeal and love
    His holy breast inspire.

3 He comes the prisoners to release
    In Satan's bondage held;
The gates of brass before him burst,
    The iron fetters yield.

4 He comes from the thick films of vice
    To purge the mental ray,
And on the eyeballs of the blind
    To pour celestial day.

5 He comes the broken heart to bind,
    The bleeding soul to cure,
And with the treasures of his grace
    To enrich the humble poor.

6 The silver trumpets publish loud
    The Jub'lee of the Lord;
Our debts are all remitted now,
    Our heritage restored.

7 Our glad hosannas, Prince of peace,
    Thy welcome shall proclaim,
And heaven's eternal arches ring
    With thy beloved name!

53 HILLS OF THE NORTH, REJOICE

This is another Victorian missionary hymn with something of the flavour of 'From Greenland's icy mountains' (No. 41). But unlike Heber's effort, it has not been consigned to the scrap-heap and appears in most modern hymn-books, albeit in a fairly emasculated form.

It is the work of Charles Edward Oakley (1832–65). Educated at Oxford, he took Holy Orders in 1855 and became rector of Wickwar in Gloucestershire, while at the same time acting as an examiner in jurisprudence and civil law at his old university. In 1863 Oakley became rector of St Paul's, Covent Garden, the fine Inigo Jones church which stands at the western end of the old vegetable market, now a covered shopping piazza.

This was apparently the only hymn which Oakley wrote in his short life. It first appeared as an Advent or Epiphany hymn in Bishop T. V. French's *Hymns adapted to the Christian Seasons*, and then in the *Hymnal Companion* of 1870.

'Hills of the North, rejoice' is in the 'Songs of Praise' Top Hundred and appears in its original version, as overleaf, in the book *Your Favourite Songs of Praise* (1986). Other hymn-books all have watered-down versions – quite understandably in view of the language of verse 3 in particular, with its shades of 'the heathen in his blindness', although it is counterbalanced with the message of verse 4 which speaks with a new relevance to our own age, when California might be said to be the temple of materialism and secularism.

Hymns for Church and School sticks quite closely to the original text, only feeling it necessary to provide the following substitute for verse 3:

> Lands of the East arise,
>   Yours is the first bright dawn:
> Open the seeing eyes,
>   Greet you the world's true morn.
> The God of all, whom you would know
> And seek on high, seeks you below.

Both the *New English Hymnal* and the 'New Standard' edition of *Hymns Ancient and Modern* print the heavily revised version produced by the editors of *English Praise* in 1975. I personally find the surgery that they have performed a bit too drastic. This is how they render the first two verses:

> Hills of the North, rejoice,
>   Echoing songs arise,
> Hail with united voice
>   Him who made earth and skies:
> He comes in righteousness and love,
> He brings salvation from above.
>
> Isles of the Southern seas,
>   Sing to the listening earth,
> Carry on every breeze
>   Hope of a world's new birth:
> In Christ shall all be made anew,
> His word is sure, His promise true.

(*From* English Praise, *by permission of Oxford University Press*)

Whether watered down or original full-flavoured, the hymn is almost always sung to Martin Shaw's vigorous tune, Little Cornard.

Hills of the North, rejoice:
  Rivers and mountain-spring,
Hark to the advent voice!
  Valley and lowland, sing!
Though absent long, your Lord is nigh,
  He judgment brings, and victory.

2 Isles of the Southern seas,
    Deep in your coral caves
  Pent be each warring breeze,
    Lulled be your restless waves:
  He comes to reign with boundless sway,
    And make your wastes His great highway.

3 Lands of the East, awake!
    Soon shall your sons be free,
  The sleep of ages break,
    And rise to liberty:
  On your far hills, long cold and grey,
    Has dawned the everlasting day.

4 Shores of the utmost West,
    Ye that have waited long,
  Unvisited, unblest,
    Break forth to swelling song;
  High raise the note, that Jesus died,
    Yet lives and reigns – the Crucified!

5 Shout while ye journey home!
    Songs be in every mouth! –
  Lo, from the North we come,
    From East, and West, and South:
  City of God, the bond are free;
    We come to live and reign in thee.

54 HO, MY COMRADES, SEE THE SIGNAL

Despite the fact that it had the honour of being the very first entry in Ira Sankey's classic *Sacred Songs and Solos*, this rousing Gospel song is absent from virtually every modern hymn-book. Many of my readers will no doubt feel that so it ought to remain and will share John Greenleaf Whittier's strong distaste for its vulgarity and heartiness (see notes on hymn No. 33). It finds a place in this collection not just because it is a supreme example of its genre, with all the faults as well as the strengths to be found in the Gospel songs of nineteenth-century America, but also because I happen to find it a stirring and uplifting expression of an important part of the Christian gospel.

'Hold the Fort' as it is generally known, has its origin in a message waved from mountain to mountain by General Sherman just before his famous march to the sea, at the height of the US Civil War in 1864, to relieve the besieged Unionist forces who were holding a supply depot at Altoona Pass in Georgia which was surrounded by Southern troops. As hope was running out, the besieged garrison commander saw far away across a valley the message spelt out in semaphore flags, 'Hold the fort; I am coming, W. T. Sherman'. The story of Sherman's message was related by Major Whittle at a Sunday School meeting in Rockford, Illinois, in May 1870. One of those present at the meeting, Philip Bliss, was inspired to write both the words and music of this song.

Bliss (1838–76), who was born in a remote forest area of north Pennsylvania, had a natural instinct for music. He became a close friend and associate of the famous American evangelists, Dwight Moody and Ira Sankey. The day after hearing of Sherman's message, Bliss was speaking at a YMCA meeting in Chicago. He walked over to the blackboard and wrote out the chorus of this hymn. He had worked out the verses the previous evening, and a few days later he had the whole song published in sheet form with the biblical text attached: 'That which ye have hold fast till I come' (Revelation 2:25).

'Hold the Fort' effectively became the theme song of the evangelistic meetings held in Britain during the 1870s by Moody and Sankey. In his memoirs Sankey recalls the great Baptist preacher, C. H. Spurgeon, asking him to sing it in his tabernacle in 1879 to accompany a sermon on the army; the chorus could be heard in adjacent streets. At a meeting to mark the end of an earlier Moody and Sankey crusade in London the great philanthropist and Evangelical statesman Lord Shaftesbury said, 'If Mr Sankey has done no more than teach the people to sing "Hold the Fort" he has conferred an inestimable blessing on the British Empire.'

Bliss had a particular talent for writing hymns based on topical events. After a shipwreck in Cleveland Harbor caused by the extinguishing of the lower lights in the lighthouse during a storm, he wrote some verses, long found in the Methodist hymn-book, which begin:

> Brightly beams our Father's mercy
>   From his lighthouse evermore;
> But to us He gives the keeping
>   Of the lights along the shore.
>
> Let the lower lights be burning,
>   Send a gleam across the wave;
> Some poor fainting, struggling seaman
>   You may rescue, you may save.

Among his other hymns which achieved considerable popularity in Britain were 'Man of Sorrows! what a name' and 'Whosoever heareth! Shout, shout the sound'. He died tragically at the age of thirty-eight when the train in which he and his wife were returning from spending Christmas in Pennsylvania caught fire. Although he at first escaped, his wife was trapped in the carriage and in his efforts to save her he was burned to death.

Hold the Fort

Ho, my comrades! see the signal
    Waving in the sky!
Reinforcements now appearing,
    Victory is nigh!
'Hold the fort, for I am coming,'
    Jesus signals still,
Wave the answer back to heaven,
    'By thy grace we will.'

2   See the mighty host advancing,
    Satan leading on:
Mighty men around us falling,
    Courage almost gone!

3   See the glorious banner waving!
    Hear the trumpet blow!
In our Leader's name we'll triumph
    Over every foe.

4   Fierce and long the battle rages,
    But our help is near:
Onwards comes our great Commander,
    Cheer, my comrades, cheer!

55 HOLY, HOLY, HOLY! LORD GOD ALMIGHTY

The great Victorian Poet Laureate, Alfred, Lord Tennyson, regarded this as the finest hymn in the English language. It is not difficult to see why. With a fine economy of words, while yet containing an abundance of memorable images and pleasing poetic phrases, it clearly and adoringly expresses the complex Christian doctrine of the Trinity.

It is one of the hymns that Reginald Heber (1783–1826) wrote while he was vicar of Hodnet in Shropshire for the solemn days, feast days and ordinary Sundays in the Church of England calendar (see note to hymn No. 22). 'Holy, Holy, Holy' was written to be sung at Hodnet on Trinity Sunday. It was first published shortly after Heber's death in *A Selection of Psalms and Hymns for the Parish Church of Banbury*.

The hymn is based on part of the passage from Revelation 4:8–11 which forms the Epistle for Trinity Sunday in the Book of Common Prayer, and which begins: 'Holy, holy, Lord Almighty, which was, and is, and is to come.' Nowadays its use is no longer restricted to Trinity Sunday, nor is it always treated as a morning hymn despite the second line of the first verse. In an effort to adapt it to any time of the day, various alterations have been made to that line, among them 'Gratefully adoring our song shall rise to thee' and 'Morning, noon and night, our song shall rise to thee', but most hymn-books are happy to stick to the original.

Heber was fastidious in his approach to hymn-writing. He once said, 'I avoid all fulsome, indecorous or erotic language to HIM whom no unclean lips dare approach.' Given this care and sensitivity, it is particularly ironic that, as we have seen, two of his best-known hymns, 'Brightest and best of the sons of the morning' and 'From

174

Greenland's icy mountains', should have caused offence to different generations of hymn-book compilers and been banished from their collections. This, perhaps the most widely used of all his hymns, has happily never faced such a ban, although it has suffered the indignity of being parodied. Soldiers in the First World War sang:

> Raining, raining, raining,
>   Always bloodywell raining,
> Raining in the morning,
>   And raining in the night.
>
> Marching, marching, marching,
>   Always bloodywell marching,
> Marching all the morning
>   And marching all the night.
>
> Grousing, grousing, grousing
>   Always bloodywell grousing
> Grousing at the rations,
>   And grousing at the pay.
>
> Marching, marching, marching
>   Always bloodywell marching;
> When the war is over,
>   We'll damn well march no more.

The tune for 'Holy, Holy, Holy', which is singularly well fitted for a marching song, was written by the Revd John Bacchus Dykes (1823–76) for the original edition of *Hymns Ancient and Modern* in 1861. It has similarities to the German tune *Wachet auf*, but was probably inspired by the tune Trinity by John Hopkins to which Heber's hymn was set in 1850. Dykes called his tune Nicaea – it was at the first Council of Nicaea in 325 that the doctrine of the Trinity was first clearly defined in the face of the heresy of Arianism.

Holy , Holy, Holy! Lord God Almighty!
  Early in the morning our song shall rise to thee:
Holy, Holy, Holy! merciful and mighty!
  God in Three Persons, blessèd Trinity!

2   Holy, Holy, Holy! all the saints adore thee,
      Casting down their golden crowns around the glassy sea,
    Cherubim and Seraphim falling down before thee,
      Which wert, and art, and evermore shalt be.

3   Holy, Holy, Holy! though the darkness hide thee,
      Though the eye of sinful man thy glory may not see,
    Only thou art holy; there is none beside thee,
      Perfect in power, in love, and purity.

3   Holy, Holy, Holy! Lord God Almighty!
      All thy works shall praise thy name in earth and sky and sea;
    Holy, Holy, Holy! merciful and mighty!
      God in Three Persons, blessèd Trinity!

56 HOW LOVELY ON THE MOUNTAINS ARE THE FEET OF HIM

There is a problem about including contemporary hymns and choruses in a collection such as this, since it is difficult to know whether they will withstand the test of time and take their place among the classics of earlier periods.

'Our God reigns', the title by which it is generally known, is undoubtedly among the most popular contemporary hymns not only in the United States and in Britain, where it is No. 20 in the BBC 'Songs of Praise' Top Twenty, but also throughout the world, having been translated into at least twenty different languages.

Both the words and music are the work of Leonard Smith (b. 1942) who was born in Philadelphia, Pennsylvania, studied at Mount St Mary Seminary, Emmitsburg, Maryland, and now works as a carpenter in Clarksboro, New Jersey. So far he has written over 130 scriptural songs of praise and worship. He publishes all his work himself, using the imprint New Jerusalem Music.

The words of the first verse of this particular hymn came to Smith late one night in 1974 when, worried about family and work troubles, he was reading Isaiah, chapter 52. He was particularly struck by the message of the seventh verse:

How beautiful on the mountains are the feet of him that bringeth good tidings, that publisheth peace; that bringeth good tidings of good, that publisheth salvation; that saith unto Zion, Thy God reigneth!

Although his one-verse song was rejected by every publisher to whom he sent it (hence his decision to publish his work himself) it rapidly won favour among many friends and church groups, and by

1977 four different versions were in circulation with extra verses added by people in Australia, California and England. Over a period of eight months during the following year, Smith composed another four stanzas to add to his original first verse and together they constitute the authorized version of the hymn which is printed opposite. Another so-called 'popular version' is current in the United Kingdom, with three added verses; Smith says he would like to suppress it if he could.

In a letter to me Smith writes, 'I think carpentry has helped with my song-writing. I want to write spiritual songs that are not "churchy" sounding. I want to write spiritual songs that other carpenters will want to sing, "earthy" spiritual songs with inspired melodies and lyrics.'

Critics who find spiritual songs such as these altogether too 'earthy' and trite often complain about the vain repetition of the same words in their choruses. But there is nothing new about this – indeed it has very respectable precedents in Old Testament times. If we are to believe the Norwegian scholar Sigmund Mowinckel, there was in ancient Israel an enthronement festival every year at which psalms were sung celebrating Yahweh's kingship and reign over his people. The Hebrew equivalent of 'Our God reigns' must have been sung over and over again at these services.

The verse from Isaiah which inspired Leonard Smith has also provided the inspiration for a number of English hymn-writers in earlier centuries, among them Isaac Watts who wrote a hymn beginning, 'How beautiful the feet of those', Benjamin Gough ('How beauteous on the mountains') and John Mason ('Fair are the feet which bring the news' – later altered by John Keble to 'How beautiful the feet that bring').

Our God reigns

How lovely on the mountains are the feet of Him
Who brings good news, good news;
Announcing peace, proclaiming news of happiness:
Our God reigns, our God reigns!
    Our God reigns! (*four times*)

2 He had no stately form. He had no majesty,
That we should be drawn to Him.
He was despised and we took no account of Him.
Yet now He reigns with the Most High.
    Now He reigns! (*three times*)
    With the Most High!

3 It was our sin and guilt that bruised and wounded Him,
It was our sin that brought Him down.
When we like sheep had gone astray, our Shepherd came
And on his shoulders bore our shame.
    On His shoulders (*three times*)
    He bore our shame.

4 Meek as a lamb that's led out to the slaughterhouse,
Dumb as a sheep before its shearer,
His life ran down upon the ground like pouring rain
That we might be born again.
    That we might be (*three times*)
    Born again.

5 Out of the tomb He came with grace and majesty,
He is alive. He is alive.
God loves us so – see here His hands, His feet, His side,
Yes, we know. He is alive.
    He is alive! (*four times*)

57 HOW SWEET THE NAME OF JESUS SOUNDS

This is another ever-popular hymn by John Newton (1725–1807; see notes to hymn No. 10). It was first published in the *Olney Hymnbook* of 1779 and is based on the Song of Solomon 1:3 'Thy name is as ointment poured forth.'

For doctrinal reasons, several changes have been made to the original version printed overleaf. The fourth verse is generally, and surely rightly, omitted. It harps a little over much on sin, reflecting Newton's own strict Calvinistic position. Towards the end of his life he wrote: 'My memory is nearly gone, but I remember two things, that I am a great sinner and Jesus is a great Saviour.' Many hymn-book compilers have also been unhappy about the reference in the first line of verse 5 to Christ as 'husband'. They have felt, quite reasonably, that Christ's bride is the Church as a whole rather than the individual, and that the expression 'husband' is unsuited to congregational use even though it fits with the mood of the Song of Solomon. Various substitutions have been made, the most common being 'brother' which occurs in *Hymns Ancient and Modern,* the *New English Hymnal* and *Hymns for Church and School.*

Thomas Cotterill (on whom see notes to hymn No. 49) was unhappy about the somewhat cloying flavour of the hymn's opening line and substituted 'blest' for 'sweet' when he included it in the eighth edition of his *Selection of Psalms and Hymns* in 1819. This alteration has not, however, been followed in any subsequent hymn-books.

There is another well-known Evangelical hymn which pursues very much the same theme as Newton's. It is by Frederick Whitfield (1829–1904), vicar of St Mary's, Hastings:

> There is a name I love to hear,
>   I love to sing its worth;
> It sounds like music in mine ear,
>   The sweetest name on earth.
> Oh, how I love Jesus,
>   Oh, how I love Jesus,
> Oh, how I love Jesus,
>   Because he first loved me!

The tune universally used for Newton's hymn is by Alexander Robert Reinagle (1799–1877) who was of Austrian extraction and was organist of St Peter's in the East, Oxford. It first appeared in 1836 in a publication entitled *Psalm Tunes for the Voice and Pianoforte* as a setting for Psalm 118, and is known either as St Peter or Christchurch.

The name of Jesus

How sweet the name of Jesus sounds
    In a believer's ear!
It soothes his sorrows, heals his wounds,
    And drives away his fear.

2   It makes the wounded spirit whole,
      And calms the troubled breast;
'Tis manna to the hungry soul,
      And to the weary rest.

3   Dear name! the rock on which I build,
      My shield and hiding-place,
My never-failing treasury filled
      With boundless stores of grace.

4   By thee my prayers acceptance gain,
      Although with sin defiled;
Satan accuses me in vain,
      And I am owned a child.

5   Jesus! my Shepherd, Husband, Friend,
      My Prophet, Priest, and King,
My Lord, my Life, my Way, my End,
      Accept the praise I bring.

6   Weak is the effort of my heart,
      And cold my warmest thought;
But when I see thee as thou art,
      I'll praise thee as I ought.

7   Till then I would thy love proclaim
      With every fleeting breath;
And may the music of thy name
      Refresh my soul in death.

58 I BIND UNTO MYSELF TODAY

This beautiful hymn, which is traditionally attributed to St Patrick (372–466), shows very clearly the blending of pagan mythology with Christian teaching in the Celtic Church. It combines the functions of incantation, war-song and credal statement. Against 'Satan's spells and wiles' and 'the wizard's evil craft' are invoked not only the power of Christ, the wisdom of God and the 'strong name of the Trinity', but also the forces of nature, 'the virtues of the star-lit heaven' and the 'whiteness of the moon at even'. The whole hymn is given a tremendous force and unity by the notion of 'binding' which is so characteristic of Celtic art, with its intricate knots and interlacing patterns.

The original Gaelic poem on which the hymn is based is known as St Patrick's Lorica, or Breastplate. A lorica was a spiritual coat or breastplate which not only charmed away disease or danger but secured a place in heaven for those who wore it day and night. The word came to be applied to spiritual poems such as this one, which characteristically had three distinct parts: the invocation of the Trinity and the Angels; the enumeration of various parts of the body to be safeguarded; and a list of dangers from which immunity was being sought. The second of these elements is not as clearly marked in this poem as it is, for example, in that other lorica which has been turned into a popular hymn:

> God be in my head and in my understanding:
> God be in my eyes, and in my looking;
> God be in my mouth, and in my speaking;
> God be in my heart, and in my thinking;
> God be at my end, and at my departing.

But it is there in the eighth verse where Christ's presence in every part of the body is carefully invoked.

Legend has it that St Patrick composed his lorica shortly after landing in Ireland in 432 to spread the Christian faith there. He is said to have sung it as he made his way to Tara to confront Leogaire, or Leary, the pagan High King of Ireland, who was in the midst of one of his regular triennial conventions with his vassal kings. Patrick and his followers halted at the Hill of Slane near the River Boyne, ten miles from Tara, and lit a great fire to celebrate the eve of the Christian festival of Easter. The High King, who was celebrating a pagan festival, was furious when he saw the Christians' fire in the distance and sent men out to destroy it. However, his soldiers drew back when they got near the flames, fearing that Patrick might cast a spell on them. Seeing the chariots of the king's forces drawn up before him, the saint recited the twentieth psalm, with its seventh verse: 'Some trust in chariots, and some in horses, but we will remember the name of the Lord our God', and then launched into his lorica. It is sometimes also known as 'The Deer's Cry' because King Leogaire's men are said to have mistaken Patrick and his followers for deer in the darkness surrounding the fire.

Whether or not St Patrick himself actually wrote the lorica, it is a supreme expression of that sense of the holiness and wholeness of nature that marked Celtic Christianity and which was summed up in another statement attributed to the saint: 'Our God is the God of Heaven and Earth, of sea and river, sun and moon and stars, of the lofty mountain and lowly valley.' The fourth verse could almost be the theme song of the Greens and certainly has a new relevance in our belatedly ecology-conscious age.

The translation printed overleaf, the best-known of several that have been made of St Patrick's Breastplate, is the work of Mrs Cecil Frances Alexander (1818–95; see notes to hymn No. 8). Erik Routley has described it in his *Panorama of Christian Hymnody* as 'easily her finest piece of hymnic literature ... (she) makes of it a credal recitation, entirely appropriate to the ancient rites of baptism, and supremely appropriate to the celebrations of Holy Saturday, or Easter eve, which was associated in the early Church with baptism and confirmation.'

Mrs Alexander made her translation for use on St Patrick's Day in 1889 at the request of H. H. Dickinson, Dean of the Chapel Royal at Dublin Castle, who was preparing a new and enlarged edition of the *Irish Church Hymnal*. He later recalled:

> I wrote to her suggesting that she should fill a gap in our Irish Church Hymnal by giving us a metrical version of St Patrick's "Lorica" and I sent her a carefully collated copy of the best prose translations of it. Within a week she sent me that exquisitely beautiful as well as faithful version which appears in the appendix to our Church Hymnal.

The hymn soon found its way into hymn-books where it was set to an arrangement of the traditional Irish melody St Patrick by Sir Charles Villiers Stanford (1852–1924). This is universally used for the main part of the hymn, which is now often shortened, with the third, sixth and seventh verses being generally omitted. The eighth verse, 'Christ be with me', is sung to one of three traditional Irish melodies: an unnamed tune from Donegal which Stanford adapted for *Hymns Ancient and Modern;* Deirdre, which was preferred by the compilers of the *English Hymnal;* or Clonmacnoise, which is found in the *Church Hymnary.*

A translation of St Patrick's Breastplate which is closer to the original in form and words than Mrs Alexander's better-known version was made by Robert Alexander Stewart Macalister (1870– 1950) for the revised version of the *Church Hymnary* in 1927. Macalister came from Dublin and held the chair in Celtic Archaeology at University College there. His version, which can be found in the *Church Hymnary,* begins:

> Today I arise
> Invoking the Blessed Trinity,
> Confessing the Blessed Unity,
> Creator of all the things that be.

St Patrick's Breastplate

I bind unto myself to-day
   The strong name of the Trinity,
By invocation of the same
   The Three in One and One in Three.

2   I bind this day to me for ever
      By power of faith, Christ's incarnation;
His baptism in Jordan river,
   His death on Cross for my salvation;
His bursting from the spicèd tomb,
   His riding up the heavenly way,
His coming at the day of doom
   I bind unto myself to-day.

3   I bind unto myself the power
      Of the great love of Cherubim;
The sweet 'Well done' in judgment hour,
   The service of the Seraphim,
Confessors' faith, Apostles' word,
   The Patriarchs' prayers, the prophets' scrolls,
All good deeds done unto the Lord
   And purity of virgin souls.

4   I bind unto myself to-day
      The virtues of the star-lit heaven,
The glorious sun's life-giving ray,
   The whiteness of the moon at even,
The flashing of the lightning free,
   The whirling wind's tempestuous shocks,
The stable earth, the deep salt sea
   Around the old eternal rocks.

5   I bind unto myself to-day
      The power of God to hold and lead,
His eye to watch, his might to stay,
   His ear to hearken to my need.

The wisdom of my God to teach,
    His hand to guide, his shield to ward;
The word of God to give me speech,
    His heavenly host to be my guard.

6   Against the demon snares of sin,
        The vice that gives temptation force,
    The natural lusts that war within,
        The hostile men that mar my course;
    Or few or many, far or nigh,
        In every place and in all hours,
    Against their fierce hostility
        I bind to me those holy powers.

7   Against all satan's spells and wiles,
        Against false words of heresy,
    Against the knowledge that defiles,
        Against the heart's idolatry,
    Against the wizard's evil craft,
        Against the death-wound and the burning,
    The choking wave, the poisoned shaft,
        Protect me, Christ, till thy returning.

8   Christ be with me, Christ within me,
        Christ behind me, Christ before me,
    Christ beside me, Christ to win me,
        Christ to comfort and restore me.
    Christ beneath me, Christ above me,
        Christ in quiet, Christ in danger,
    Christ in hearts of all that love me,
        Christ in mouth of friend and stranger.

9   I bind unto myself the name,
        The strong name of the Trinity,
    By invocation of the same,
        The Three in One and One in Three.
    Of whom all nature hath creation,
        Eternal Father, Spirit, Word:
    Praise to the Lord of my salvation,
        Salvation is of Christ the Lord.

59 I DANCED IN THE MORNING

Of the thousands of spiritual songs and choruses which have been written in the last thirty years, few have been as widely taken up and sung in churches as this infectiously joyful and catchy hymn by Sydney Carter. I call it a hymn for so it has effectively become through its use in services of worship by many different denominations. The author himself more properly describes it as a carol, 'a dancing kind of song, the life of which is in the dance as much as in the verbal statement'.

Sydney Carter was born in Camden Town, London, in 1915 and educated at Christ's Hospital and Balliol College, Oxford. He became a schoolmaster and during the Second World War served in the Friends' Ambulance Unit. He attributed his later career as a folksong writer and performer, which he combined with teaching and lecturing, to the two years he spent in Greece with the Unit during the war.

'Lord of the Dance', as it is generally called, was written in 1963 in the early days of the folk-song revival in Britain. Many of the other songs which Carter wrote at this time had a radical social and political message, and to some extent this song is a protest against the immobility and stuffiness of traditional church services. But it has a much more positive message as well. In his book *Green Print for Song* (1974), the author writes of it:

Scriptures and creeds may come to seem incredible, but faith will still go dancing on. I see Christ as the incarnation of that piper who is calling us. He dances that shape and pattern which is at the heart of our reality. By Christ I mean not only Jesus: in other times and places, other planets, there may be other Lords of the Dance. But Jesus is the one I know first and best. I sing of the dancing pattern in the life and words of Jesus.

In portraying Christ as the Lord of the Dance, Carter was, in fact, returning to a strong theme in medieval popular theology, expressed in the carol 'Tomorrow shall be my dancing day' in which Christ is represented as coming into the world 'to call my true love to my dance'. More directly, he was influenced by the Shaker movement of the eighteenth century. The Shakers, who began as a Quaker group in the north-west of England and then moved to America in 1774, expressed their joyful assurance of salvation and belief in the imminence of Christ's second coming by singing and dancing. Carter used the tune of this Shaker song, 'Simple Gifts', for his own carol:

> 'Tis the gift to be simple, 'tis the gift to be free,
> 'Tis the gift to come down where we ought to be,
> And when we find ourselves in the place just right
> 'Twill be in the valley of love and delight.
>
> When true simplicity is gained
> To bow and to bend we shan't be ashamed;
> To turn, turn, will be our delight
> 'Til by turning, turning we come round right.

Although they have not achieved the same popularity as 'Lord of the Dance', some of Sydney Carter's other spiritual songs appear in contemporary hymn-books. Perhaps the best-known are 'When I need a neighbour', 'The Devil wore a crucifix', 'It was on a Friday morning' and 'One more step along the world I go'.

Lord of the Dance

I danced in the morning
  When the world was begun,
And I danced in the moon
  And the stars and the sun,
And I came down from heaven
  And I danced on the earth;
At Bethlehem
  I had my birth:

Dance, then, wherever you may be;
I am the Lord of the Dance, said he,
And I'll lead you all, wherever you may be,
And I'll lead you all in the dance, said he.

2   I danced for the scribe
  And the pharisee,
But they would not dance
  And they wouldn't follow me;
I danced for the fishermen,
  For James and John;
They came with me
  And the dance went on:

3   I danced on the Sabbath
  And I cured the lame:
The holy people
  Said it was a shame.
They whipped and they stripped
  And they hung me high,
And they left me there
  On a cross to die:

4   I danced on a Friday
     When the sky turned black;
  It's hard to dance
     With the devil on your back.
  They buried my body
     And they thought I'd gone;
  But I am the dance
     And I still go on:

5   They cut me down
     And I leapt up high;
  I am the life
     That'll never, never die;
  I'll live in you
     If you'll live in me:
  I am the Lord
     Of the Dance, said he:

60 I VOW TO THEE, MY COUNTRY

This is the hymn to which film directors invariably turn when they want to evoke the atmosphere of a vanished England ruled by patriotic public school values. It tends to be heard in the distance over shots of playing fields on which flannelled fools 'play up, play up and play the game'.

The circumstances in which it was written could certainly have come straight out of the pages of the *Boys' Own Paper*. Its author, Cecil Spring-Rice (1859–1918), was a distinguished member of the British diplomatic corps. After beginning his career as a clerk in the Foreign Office, he served in Teheran, Cairo and Petrograd. In 1908 he went to Stockholm as minister to Sweden. While there he wrote a poem, *'Urbs Dei'*, which explored the theme that a Christian is a citizen of two countries, his own and the heavenly kingdom.

In 1912 Spring-Rice was sent as Ambassador to Washington. While there he did much to coax the United States out of its neutrality in the First World War. He was naturally somewhat peeved when, following President Woodrow Wilson's decision to enter the war against Germany, he was recalled from Washington at the end of 1917 and replaced by a member of the War Cabinet. On the eve of his departure on 12 January 1918, he re-cast the poem he had written in Stockholm. The second verse he kept much as it was, but the first he altered significantly. In his original poem it had been belligerently patriotic, glorifying war, but the experience of the previous four years had much altered Spring-Rice's attitudes. He sent the verses to an American friend with an accompanying note that read: 'The greatest object of all – at the most terrific cost and the most tremendous sacrifice – will, I hope, at last be permanently established, Peace.'

The phrase 'The love that asks no question' has often been criticized for suggesting a blind, uncritical patriotism – 'my country, right or wrong'. But that is not how Spring-Rice visualized it. He was thinking rather in terms of the Christian notion of sacrifice, as he pointed out in a speech in Ottawa a few days after completing the revision of his poem: 'The Cross is a sign of patience under suffering, but not patience under wrong. The Cross is the banner under which we fight – the Cross of St George, the Cross of St Andrew, the Cross of St Patrick; different in form, in colour, in history, yes, but the same spirit, the spirit of sacrifice.'

Cecil Spring-Rice died suddenly only a month after re-writing his hymn and while he was still in Ottawa on the first leg of his journey home to Britain. He was just fifty-eight. His daughter had earlier been sent to St Paul's Girls School in London where she was in the same class as Imogen Holst, daughter of the director of music at the school, Gustav Holst (1874–1934). It was almost certainly through this connection that Holst learned of Spring-Rice's poem and came to set to it the melody he had written early in 1917 for the 'Jupiter' movement of his orchestral suite, *The Planets*. He named the hymn tune Thaxted, after the Essex village where he had a cottage and where he had written much of the suite.

'I vow to thee, my country' was first included in a hymn-book in 1925, when it appeared in *Songs of Praise*. In July 1981 it was chosen by Lady Diana Spencer for her marriage to the Prince of Wales at St Paul's Cathedral. There were predictions then that her choice would do for the hymn what the wedding of the Queen and Prince Philip had done for 'The Lord's my Shepherd', but – as far as I know – brides have not been clamouring for it.

The Two Fatherlands

I vow to thee, my country – all earthly things above –
Entire and whole and perfect, the service of my love:
The love that asks no question, the love that stands the test,
That lays upon the altar the dearest and the best;
The love that never falters, the love that pays the price,
The love that makes undaunted the final sacrifice.

2   And there's another country, I've heard of long ago,
Most dear to them that love her, most great to them that know;
We may not count her armies, we may not see her King;
Her fortress is a faithful heart, her pride is suffering;
And soul by soul and silently her shining bounds increase,
And her ways are ways of gentleness and all her paths are Peace.

61 IMMORTAL, INVISIBLE, GOD
ONLY WISE

A particular favourite of the Queen, this hymn was sung, together with 'Praise, my soul, the King of heaven' and 'Now thank we all our God', at the service at the Chapel Royal, Windsor Castle, on 21 April 1986 to mark Her Majesty's sixtieth birthday. Surprisingly, it is only comparatively recently that it has gained wide popularity. It did not, for example, appear in *Hymns Ancient and Modern* until 1950.

Its author, the Revd Walter Chalmers Smith (1824–1908), was born in Aberdeen and educated at the grammar school and university in that city and at New College, Edinburgh. He was ordained in 1850 to the charge of the Scottish Church in Chadwell Street, Islington, North London, and subsequently was minister of Free Church congregations in Milnathort, Glasgow and Edinburgh. The culmination of his career was the moderatorship of the Free Church of Scotland in 1893.

Smith wrote several hymns, which appeared in his *Hymns of Christ and the Christian Life* in 1876. It was in that collection that 'Immortal, invisible' first appeared. The hymn is based on 1 Timothy 1:17: 'Now unto the King eternal, immortal, invisible, the only wise God, be honour and glory for ever and ever.' The reference to 'the Ancient of Days' in the third line of the first verse comes from Daniel 7:9, while the third line of the second verse echoes Psalm 36, verse 6: 'Thy righteousness is like the great mountains.' The last line of the penultimate verse is based on 2 Corinthians 3:15–16, 'Even unto this day, when Moses is read, the veil is upon their heart. Nevertheless when it shall turn to the Lord, the veil shall be taken away.'

In 1884 Garrett Horder included Smith's hymn in his *Congregational Hymns,* omitting the last two lines of verses 4 and 5 to give a new hybrid final verse:

> Great Father of Glory, pure Father of Light,
> Thine angels adore thee, all veiling their sight;
> All laud we would render: O help us to see
> 'Tis only the splendour of light hideth thee.

It is Horder's version of the hymn which is found in all modern hymn-books.

The majestic tune, St Denio or Joanna, is based on a Welsh folk song, *'Can Mlynedd i'nawr'*. It first appeared as a hymn tune in a Welsh collection published in 1839.

God, All in All

> Immortal, invisible, God only wise,
> In light inaccessible hid from our eyes,
> Most blessèd, most glorious, the Ancient of Days,
> Almighty, victorious, thy great name we praise.

2   Unresting, unhasting, and silent as light,
    Nor wanting, nor wasting, thou rulest in might –
    Thy justice like mountains high-soaring above
    Thy clouds which are fountains of goodness and love.

3   To all life thou givest, to both great and small;
    In all life thou livest, the true life of all;
    We blossom and flourish as leaves on the tree,
    And wither and perish; but naught changeth thee.

4   Great Father of Glory, pure Father of Light,
    Thine angels adore thee, all veiling their sight;
    But of all thy rich graces this grace, Lord, impart –
    Take the veil from our faces, the vile from our heart.

5   All laud we would render; O help us to see
    'Tis only the splendour of light hideth thee,
    And so let thy glory, almighty, impart,
    Through Christ in his story, thy Christ to the heart.

62 JERUSALEM THE GOLDEN

This sweet – perhaps even over-sweet – evocation of the joys of the Heavenly City of Zion comes somewhat unexpectedly from a satirical medieval poem which was largely concerned with lampooning the corrupt condition of Church and state in twelfth-century Europe.

De Contemptu Mundi, or *Hora Novissima* as it is also sometimes known from its opening line, '*Hora novissima, tempora pessima sunt: vigilemus!',* was the work of St Bernard of Cluny (born *c.* 1100). Although both his parents were English, Bernard was born and grew up in Morlaix in Brittany and spent most of his life as a monk in the great abbey at Cluny. He dedicated his poem, which was written around 1140, to the abbot, Peter the Venerable.

Like so many other medieval lyrics which have found their way into the hymn-books, we owe 'Jerusalem the golden' to J. M. Neale (1818–66; see notes to hymn No. 23). After reading all 2,966 lines of St Bernard's poem in the original Latin, Neale wrote: 'The greater part is a bitter satire on the fearful corruptions of the age. But as a contrast to the misery and pollution of the earth, the poem opens with a description of the peace and glory of heaven, of such rare beauty as not easily to be matched by any medieval composition on the same theme.'

Neale first translated some of the verses of St Bernard's poem in 1849. Nine years later he published *The Rhythm of Bernard de Morlaix, Monk of Cluny, on the Celestial Country,* a translation of 218 lines from the *Hora Novissima.* His translation of sixteen verses from near the beginning of the poem, which portray the glories of heaven as a contrast to the evils of the world, has yielded four separate hymns: 'Jerusalem the golden', 'Brief life is here our portion', 'The world is

197

very evil' and 'For thee, O dear, dear country'. 'Jerusalem the golden', translated from verses which began *'Urbs Sion aurea'*, has been by far the most popular, although the others also richly repay reading and singing.

The fourth verse was substantially altered in 1860 by the compilers of *Hymns Ancient and Modern*. Their revision has been adopted in many modern hymn-books, though not in the *New English Hymnal*. It is certainly easier to sing than Neale's original, but loses much of its force and assurance. It reads:

> O sweet and blessed country,
>   The home of God's elect!
> O sweet and blessed country
>   That eager hearts expect!
> Jesu, in mercy bring us
>   To that dear land of rest;
> Who art, with God the Father
>   And spirit ever blest.

The majestic melody Aurelia which Samuel Sebastian Wesley wrote for this hymn is seldom, if ever, used for it now (see note to hymn No. 124). The preferred tune, known variously as Ewing, Argyle, Bernard or St Bede's, was written in 1853 by Lieut.-Colonel Alexander Ewing (1830–95) for another of Neale's hymns derived from *De Contemptu Mundi,* 'For thee, O dear, dear country'. Its attachment to 'Jerusalem the golden' probably dates from the first edition of *Hymns Ancient and Modern*. Ewing was trained for the law, but went into the army and served with distinction in the Crimean War and in China with General Gordon. Remarkably, he seems never to have written a note of music apart from this tune.

Urbs Sion aurea

Jerusalem the golden,
  With milk and honey blessed,
Beneath thy contemplation
  Sink heart and voice oppressed.
I know not, O I know not
  What joys await us there,
What radiancy of glory,
  What light beyond compare.

2 They stand, those halls of Zion,
    Conjubilant with song,
  And bright with many an angel,
    And all the martyr throng;
  The Prince is ever in them,
    The daylight is serene:
  The pastures of the blessèd
    Are decked in glorious sheen.

3 There is the throne of David,
    And there, from care released,
  The shout of them that triumph,
    The song of them that feast;
  And they who, with their Leader,
    Have conquered in the fight,
  For ever and for ever
    Are clad in robes of white.

4 O sweet and blessed country,
    Shall I ever see thy face?
  O sweet and blessed country,
    Shall I ever win thy grace?
  Exult, O dust and ashes,
    The Lord shall be thy part:
  His only his for ever
    Thou shalt be, and thou art.

63 JESU, GOOD ABOVE ALL OTHER

The author of this much-loved hymn, the Revd Percy Dearmer (1867–1936), was one of the leading figures in twentieth-century British hymnody. As editor both of the *English Hymnal* which first appeared in 1906 and of *Songs of Praise* which came out in 1925, he was responsible for introducing to English congregations many American hymns, translations of medieval and European lyrics, and verses by such great religious poets as George Herbert, John Donne and Henry Vaughan. He also wrote a number of hymns himself, of which this is the best known.

Percy Dearmer was educated at Westminster School and Christ Church, Oxford. Ordained in 1891, he served as curate in a number of London parishes before becoming vicar of St Mary's, Primrose Hill, in 1901. He remained there for fourteen years. During the First World War he served abroad. From 1919 until his death he was Professor of Ecclesiastical Art at King's College, London. In 1931 he was made a canon of Westminster Abbey.

'Jesu, good above all other' is closely based on a hymn by J. M. Neale (1818–66; see notes to hymn No. 23) which began:

> Jesus, kind above all other,
> Gentle Child of gentle Mother,
> In the stable born our Brother,
> Whom the angelic hosts adore.

Dearmer's hymn first appeared in 1906 when it was included in the first edition of the *English Hymnal* in the form printed opposite. The author subsequently changed the last line of the third verse to 'Keep us to thy presence near'. In virtually all modern hymn-books, the first line now appears as 'Jesus, good above all other'.

Dearmer wrote his hymn (which was particularly intended for children) with the fourteenth-century German carol tune, *Quem Pastores Laudavere*, in mind. It continues to be sung to that beautiful melody.

Perseverance

Jesu, good above all other,
Gentle Child of gentle Mother,
In a stable born our Brother,
  Give us grace to persevere.

2 Jesus, cradled in a manger,
For us facing every danger,
Living as a homeless stranger,
  Make we thee our King most dear.

3 Jesus, for thy people dying,
Risen Master, death defying,
Lord in heaven, thy grace supplying,
  Keep us by thine altar near.

4 Jesu, who our sorrows bearest,
All our thoughts and hopes thou sharest,
Thou to man the truth declarest;
  Help us all thy truth to hear.

5 Lord, in all our doings guide us,
Pride and hate shall ne'er divide us;
We'll go on with thee beside us,
  And with joy we'll persevere!

64 JESU, LOVER OF MY SOUL

There are several different accounts of the circumstances which prompted Charles Wesley (1707–88; see notes to hymn No. 11) to write this powerful appeal for the Saviour's protection. One story has it that he was moved by a narrow escape from death during a storm while crossing the Atlantic, another that he was sitting at his desk when a small bird, which was being pursued by a hawk, flew in through the open window. The safety of the bird in his study supposedly inspired him to write of the safety to be found in Christ's haven.

In his book *My Life and Sacred Songs,* Ira Sankey maintains that Wesley wrote the hymn while on an open-air preaching tour in County Down, Ireland. After being attacked by a gang who disliked his doctrines he sought refuge in a farmhouse. When the mob arrived at the door he escaped through a rear window and hid under a hedge. According to Sankey, it was in that hiding-place, with the cries of his pursuers in his ears, that he wrote the hymn.

All three stories are almost certainly apocryphal, but whatever the events that inspired it, 'Jesu, lover of my soul', which was written around 1740, is undoubtedly one of Wesley's greatest hymns. Curiously, his brother John omitted it from the Methodist collection of 1780. It has not been without its critics. The great Liberal statesman W. E. Gladstone commented, 'It has no unity, no cohesion, no procession and no special force'; he took particular exception to the second line, maintaining that 'the familiarity of a hymn ought not to go beyond that of Scripture. St John undoubtedly lay on the bosom of his Lord. But he alone; and we are not all St Johns.' Others have objected to the notion of grace conveyed by the second line of the last verse. *Hymns Ancient and Modern* substitutes 'Grace to cleanse from every sin' and also changes 'nearer' to 'gathering' in the third line of the first verse. The third verse printed here is omitted in all modern hymn-books.

But if the hymn has had its detractors, it has also had many admirers. Henry Ward Beecher, the great nineteenth-century American theologian, said, 'I would rather have written that hymn than to have the fame of all the kings that ever sat upon the earth . . . It will go on singing until the trump brings forth the angel band; and then I think it will mount up on some lip to the very presence of God.' Dr George Duffield, the author of 'Stand up! stand up for Jesus' (No. 117), described it as 'the hymn of the ages'. Ira Sankey, who recalls that it was sung as the body of his fellow evangelist Dwight Moody was lowered into the grave, tells a moving story about an incident in the American Civil War. A Confederate soldier had aimed his rifle and was about to shoot through the heart of a Unionist sentry when he was stopped short by hearing his intended victim singing the words, 'Cover my defenceless head with the shadow of thy wing.' Nearly thirty years later the Confederate veteran recognized the voice of the man whose life he had spared singing the same hymn on an excursion steamer on the Potomac river. He went up and told him how and why his life had been spared.

At first Wesley's hymn was sung to the tune Hotham by M. Madan, and later to Hollingside by J. B. Dykes (1823–76), to which it is still set in some hymnals. But now it is almost invariably sung to the haunting melody in the minor key by Joseph Parry (1841–1903) entitled Aberystwyth. Parry, who came from Merthyr Tydfil, was an ironmaster who turned professional musician. He wrote one hymn tune every Sunday for a number of years, Aberystwyth being composed in the seaside town of that name in 1879.

In Temptation

Jesu, lover of my soul,
   Let me to thy bosom fly,
While the nearer waters roll,
   While the tempest still is high;
Hide me, O my Saviour, hide,
   Till the storm of life is past;
Safe into the haven guide,
   O receive my soul at last.

2 Other refuge have I none,
   Hangs my helpless soul on thee;
Leave, ah! leave me not alone,
   Still support and comfort me:
All my trust on thee is stayed,
   All my help from thee I bring;
Cover my defenceless head
   With the shadow of thy wing.

3 Wilt thou not regard my call?
   Wilt thou not accept my prayer?
Lo! I sink, I faint, I fall!
   Lo, on thee I cast my care!
Reach me out thy gracious hand!
   While I of thy strength receive,
Hoping against hope I stand,
   Dying, and behold I live.

4   Thou, O Christ, art all I want;
     More than all in thee I find;
  Raise the fallen, cheer the faint,
     Heal the sick, and lead the blind.
  Just and holy is thy name;
     I am all unrighteousness:
  False and full of sin I am;
     Thou art full of truth and grace.

5   Plenteous grace with thee is found,
     Grace to cover all my sin;
  Let the healing streams abound,
     Make and keep me pure within:
  Thou of life the fountain art;
     Freely let me take of thee;
  Spring thou up within my heart,
     Rise to all eternity.

65 JESUS BIDS US SHINE

This classic Victorian children's hymn still finds a place in several modern hymn-books despite being dismissed by some as a dated piece of sentimental piety.

It is the work of Miss Susan Warner (1819–85), who was born and grew up in New York. Her father was, in the words of the *Companion to the Church Hymnary*, 'a lawyer of high character who fell into undeserved misfortune'. In order to help the meagre family fortunes, Susan and her younger sister Anna, who were both deeply religious, sought to earn money by story-writing and became the chief family breadwinners. Susan's first book, *The Wide, Wide World*, published in 1850 under the pseudonym of Elizabeth Wetherell, was second only to *Uncle Tom's Cabin* in popularity among mid-nineteenth-century American novels. She wrote numerous other novels, all with an improving flavour, and a large number of books based on stories in the Bible.

Despite the apparent crash in their father's fortunes, Susan and Anna Warner lived for most of their lives in a large mansion on Constitution Island in the Hudson River. Every Sunday afternoon cadets from the nearby West Point Military Academy were rowed over to the island by a servant to take part in Bible classes run by the Warner sisters, which were followed by tea and gingerbread. Susan was subsequently buried at West Point.

'Jesus bids us shine' first appeared anonymously in a book called *The Little Corporal* published in Chicago in 1868 and went on to achieve enormous popularity on both sides of the Atlantic. Like her sister Anna's equally popular *Jesus loves me! this I know* (No. 69), Susan Warner's hymn has tended to come under attack in recent years for its simplistic piety and sentimentalism. But it still seems to

206

me to be a valid restatement in language that all can understand of Christ's enormously challenging and difficult command to the crowd who had flocked to hear the Sermon on the Mount: 'Let your light so shine before men that they may see your good works and give glory to your Father who is in Heaven' (Matthew 5:16). The idea of 'you in your small corner and me in mine' is admittedly potentially misleading in its individualistic implications – as the third verse of the hymn reminds us, shining our lights should be a corporate rather than just an individual activity. But overall I find little with which to quarrel in the message of this hymn. Indeed, it strikes me that the comparison of the light which Christ asks us to shine to a candle is singularly apt. Unlike the predictable beam of an electric light, a candle can falter and flicker – just as we do in our attempts to follow the Christian way. It casts shadows and is not of a uniform brightness. But its light is warm and comforting, not harsh and glaring like that of a fluorescent tube.

The tune Lumetto to which this hymn is always sung was written specially for it by David Evans (1874–1948), Professor of Music at the University of Wales. Born in Resolven in Wales under the name Edward Arthur, he wrote a number of hymn tunes, of which at least one other, *Lucerna Laudoniae,* is still used today (see note to hymn No. 39).

Jesus bids us shine
   With a pure, clear light,
Like a little candle
   Burning in the night.
In this world is darkness;
   So let us shine.
You in your small corner,
   And I in mine.

2   Jesus bids us shine,
   First of all for Him;
Well He sees and knows it,
   If our light grows dim:
He looks down from heaven
   To see us shine,
You in your small corner,
   And I in mine.

3   Jesus bids us shine,
   Then, for all around;
Many kinds of darkness
   In the world are found –
Sin, and want, and sorrow;
   So we must shine,
You in your small corner,
   And I in mine.

66 JESUS CALLS US: O'ER THE TUMULT

This is another hymn from the prolific pen of Mrs Cecil Frances Alexander (1818–95; see notes to hymn No. 8). It was written for St Andrew's Day (30 November) and is based on the story of Christ's calling of his first disciples in Matthew 4:18–20:

As Jesus walked by the Sea of Galilee, he saw two brothers, Simon who is called Peter and Andrew his brother, casting a net into the sea, for they were fishermen. And he said to them, 'Follow me and I will make you fishers of men.' Immediately they left their nets and followed him.

The message of this simple and moving hymn is essentially the same as that of the second verse of 'Dear Lord and Father of mankind' (No. 33), which tells of the same episode in the Gospels:

> In simple trust like theirs who heard,
> Beside the Syrian sea,
> The gracious calling of the Lord,
> Let us, like them, without a word
> Rise up and follow thee.

'Jesus calls us: o'er the tumult' first appeared in 1852 in *Hymns for Public Worship*, published by the Society for the Propagation of Christian Knowledge. Mrs Alexander revised the hymn slightly in 1881, changing the third line of the first verse to 'Day by day his voice is sounding' and the third line of the fifth verse to 'Give our hearts to thy obedience'. Most modern hymn-books print this revised version and some have other minor variations in the text.

The first line of the second verse is sometimes changed to 'As of old apostles heard it' to make the hymn suitable for singing at all times of the year, and not just on St Andrew's Day. But this seems to me an unnecessary alteration. Although 'Jesus calls us' has a special association with St Andrew's Day and therefore a special significance for Scots, it is really quite suitable as it stands for use at any time of the year. Its theme of the universality and insistence of Christ's call is certainly not restricted in its applicability to 30 November.

The most appropriate tune for this hymn is surely St Andrew, which was composed in 1875 by Edward Henry Thorne (1834–1916) for *Hymns Ancient and Modern*. Thorne was educated at St George's Chapel, Windsor, under Sir George Elvey, the composer of Diademata (see notes to hymn No. 32). He became assistant organist to Elvey at the remarkably early age of twelve and went on to serve as organist at a number of parish churches in London and the South of England and also at Chichester Cathedral. He wrote a large amount of music for the organ as well as anthems and part-songs. Other tunes to which 'Jesus calls us' is sometimes sung are Wraysbury by Edward John Hopkins (1818–1901), organist of the Temple Church, and *Omni Die* from Corner's *Gesangbuch* of 1631.

Jesus calls us: o'er the tumult
  Of our life's wild restless sea
  Day by day his sweet voice soundeth,
Saying, 'Christian, follow me':

2 As of old Saint Andrew heard it
      By the Galilean lake,
    Turned from home and toil and kindred,
      Leaving all for his dear sake.

3 Jesus calls us from the worship
      Of the vain world's golden store,
    From each idol that would keep us,
      Saying, 'Christian, love me more.'

4 In our joys and in our sorrows,
      Days of toil and hours of ease,
    Still he calls, in cares and pleasures,
      'Christian, love me more than these.'

5 Jesus calls us: by thy mercies,
      Saviour, may we hear thy call,
    Give our hearts to thine obedience,
      Serve and love thee best of all.

67 JESUS CHRIST IS RISEN TODAY

This, perhaps the most popular and commonly sung of all Easter hymns, has undergone a number of very radical changes. The version which is sung today bears little resemblance to the original English text printed below which dates from the early eighteenth century.

The hymn is based on a fourteenth-century Latin hymn, '*Surrexit Christus Hodie*', by an unknown Bohemian author. It first appeared in English in a fairly literal translation in a collection of divine songs and hymns published in 1708 under the title *Lyra Davidica*. This is the version which is printed overleaf.

The modern form of the hymn dates from 1749, when the following version appeared in Arnold's *Compleat Psalmodist*:

> Jesus Christ is risen today, Hallelujah.
> Our triumphal holy day;
> Who did once, upon the Cross,
> Suffer to redeem our loss.
>
> Hymns of praise let us sing
> Unto Christ our heavenly King,
> Who endured the Cross and grave,
> Sinners to redeem and save.
>
> But the pain that he endured
> Our salvation has procured;
> Now above the sky he's King,
> While the Angels ever sing.

As can be seen, only the first verse of the above bears any relation to the original. The second and third verses in fact depart completely from the Latin text. A supplement to Tate and Brady's *New Version of the Psalms* published in 1816 included the hymn in virtually the same form that it had appeared in 1749. Three small changes were made – 'then' was inserted into the middle of the first line of the second verse to make it scan better, the first line of the third verse was changed to 'But the pains which he endured', and the first word of the last line was changed to 'where'.

Most modern hymn-books use the 1816 version of the hymn. Some change 'pain' to 'anguish' in the first line of the third verse, and the third line of this verse is usually rendered nowadays as 'Now beyond our sight he's king'; presumably to avoid the suggestion that heaven is 'up there' in the sky. Charles Wesley added a doxology which is found in some hymn-books:

> Sing we to our God above
> Praise eternal as His love;
> Praise Him, all ye heavenly host,
> Father, Son, and Holy Ghost.

Amidst all this change, it is at least reassuring to know that the tune Salisbury or Easter Hymn to which the hymn is always sung has remained the same since its first appearance in the *Lyra Davidica*. Its authorship is unknown.

Surrexit Christus hodie

Jesus Christ is risen today, Halle-Halle-lujah.
Our triumphant holy day!
Who so lately on the cross
Suffer'd to redeem our loss;

2   Haste ye females from your fright,
Take to Galilee your flight.
To His sad disciples say
Jesus Christ is risen today.

3   In our Paschal joy and feast
Let our Lord of Life be blest
Let the Holy Trine be praised
And thankful hearts to Heaven be raised.

68 JESUS LIVES! NO LONGER NOW

This joyful and confident Easter hymn is based on Jesus' words in St John's Gospel, 14:19, 'Because I live, you shall live also.' It comes from a German original by Christian Furchtegott Gellert (1715–69).

The son of a country clergyman, Gellert was born in Saxony and studied at Meissen and Leipzig with the intention of going into the Lutheran ministry. But feeling too shy to be a preacher, he instead became a lecturer in poetry and eloquence at Leipzig University and later Professor of Philosophy there. He numbered among his pupils Goethe and Lessing, and was a much-loved tutor and lecturer. He wrote and published fifty-four hymns, as well as volumes of poems, essays, tales and fables. His remains were buried in a vault in St John's Church, Leipzig, beside the tomb of J. S. Bach.

Gellert's hymn, *'Jesus lebt, mit Ihm auch ich'*, first appeared in a collection of spiritual odes and songs published in Leipzig in 1751. It was translated into English by Frances Elizabeth Cox (1812–97) and was first published in the form printed here in her *Sacred Hymns from the German* (1841), headed by the text: 'He that raised up Christ from the dead shall also quicken your mortal bodies' (Romans 8:11). Frances Cox, who came from Oxford, translated a total of fifty-six hymns from German into English which were published in two volumes.

In 1851 the hymn was recast, with the author's approval, for inclusion in Rorison's *Hymns and Anthems*. It is this revised version which is sung nowadays. It is usually sung to the tune St Albinus, which was written in 1852 by Henry John Gauntlett (1805–75) for another Easter hymn, 'Angels to our Jubilee', and runs as follows:

Jesus lives! thy terrors now
 Can, O death, no more appal us:
Jesus lives! by this we know
 Thou, O grave, canst not enthral us. *Alleluia!*

Jesus lives! henceforth is death
 But the gate of life immortal:
This shall calm our trembling breath,
When we pass its gloomy portal. *Alleluia!*

Jesus lives! for us he died:
 Then, alone to Jesus living,
Pure in heart may we abide,
 Glory to our Saviour giving. *Alleluia!*

Jesus lives! our hearts know well
 Naught from us his love shall sever;
Life nor death nor powers of hell
 Tear us from his keeping ever. *Alleluia!*

Jesus lives! to him the throne
 Over all the world is given:
May we go where he is gone,
 Rest and reign with him in heaven. *Alleluia!*

Easter Hymn

Jesus lives! no longer now
 Can thy terrors, Death, appal me;
Jesus lives! by this I know
 From the grave He will recall me;
Brighter scenes at death commence;
This shall be my confidence.

2   Jesus lives! to Him the Throne
      High o'er heaven and earth is given;
   I may go where He is gone,
      Live and reign with Him in heaven;
   God through Christ forgives offence;
   This shall be my confidence.

3   Jesus lives! who now despairs,
      Spurns the Word which God hath spoken
   Grace to all that Word declares,
      Grace whereby sin's yoke is broken:
   Christ rejects not penitence;
   This shall be my confidence.

4   Jesus lives! for me He died;
      Hence will I, to Jesus living,
   Pure in heart and act abide,
      Praise to Him and glory giving;
   Freely God doth aid dispense;
   This shall be my confidence.

5   Jesus lives! my heart knows well
      Nought from me His Love shall sever;
   Life, nor death, nor powers of hell,
      Part me now from Christ for ever:
   God will be a sure Defence;
   This shall be my confidence.

6   Jesus lives! henceforth is death
      Entrance-gate of life immortal;
   This shall calm my trembling breath,
      When I pass its gloomy portal:
   Faith shall cry, as fails each sense,
   Lord, Thou art my Confidence.

69 JESUS LOVES ME! THIS I KNOW

This children's hymn has recently been the subject of considerable controversy – not, as one might expect, because of its words, but rather as a result of its having been given a new tune which is not to everyone's taste.

It was written by Anna Bartlett Warner (1820–1915), whose elder sister, Susan, we have already come across as the author of 'Jesus bids us shine' (No. 65). Under the pseudonym of Amy Lothrop, Anna wrote a number of novels, and under her own name she edited *Hymns of the Church Militant* (1858) and *Wayfaring Hymns, Original and Translated* (1869). Another of her hymns, 'The world looks very beautiful', was until recently to be found in a number of British and American hymn-books.

'Jesus loves me! this I know' first appeared in *Say and Seal* (1859), a novel on which the Warner sisters collaborated. It rapidly achieved immense popularity as a Sunday School and missionary hymn. Ira Sankey tells of a missionary in India who heard a young Hindu boy singing it in the street. He soon gathered an audience who asked him who Jesus was and what was the Bible. The boy, who had picked up the song at missionary school, told them: 'The Bible is the book from God, they say, to teach us how to get to heaven; and Jesus is the name of the Divine Redeemer that came into the world to save us from our sins; that is what the missionaries say.' His hearers were uncertain about this explanation, but they liked the song and asked him to sing some more. 'And so the little boy went on,' the missionary recalled, 'a heathen himself, and singing to the heathen –

about Jesus and his love. "That is preaching the Gospel by proxy," I said to myself, as I turned my pony and went away, well satisfied to leave my little proxy to tell his interested audience all he himself knew, and sing them over and over that sweet song of salvation.'

Such a simplistic and sentimental hymn as this one undoubtedly is might well be expected to be out of favour now, and it certainly is with some hymnologists. In his book *Solid Joys and Lasting Treasures*, published in 1985, Tyler Whittle describes it as 'a mawkish, infinitely popular hymn of the era'. But it still does duty in Sunday Schools and children's assemblies up and down the land and is to be found in a number of contemporary hymn-books.

Increasingly, and especially in Scotland, 'Jesus loves me! this I know' is now sung to the tune of an old Gaelic lullaby, *Mo Churachan*, which tells of a woman who left her baby lying in a field. There have been many protests about the imposition of this tune, particularly from older Church members who remember from their youth the original rather sugary tune, written by William Batchelder Bradbury (1816–68). A native of Maine, Bradbury turned out a large number of Sunday School tunes, including Woodworth which is still used for Charlotte Elliott's hymn 'Just as I am, without one plea' (No. 72). He also wrote a very popular sacred cantata, *Esther*.

Jesus loves me! this I know,
For the Bible tells me so;
Little ones to Him belong;
They are weak, but He is strong.
Yes! Jesus loves me!
The Bible tells me so.

2   Jesus loves me! He who died
Heaven's gate to open wide;
He will wash away my sin,
Let His little child come in.

3   Jesus loves me! He will stay
Close beside me all the way;
Then His little child will take
Up to heaven, for His dear sake.

70 JESUS SHALL REIGN WHERE'ER THE SUN

This majestic paraphrase of Psalm 72 is by Isaac Watts (1674–1748; see notes to hymn No. 29). Like James Montgomery's 'Hail to the Lord's Anointed' (No. 51), it transforms the Hebrew psalm into a Christian hymn by applying to Christ words which were almost certainly originally intended to refer to King Solomon. The first verse of 'Jesus shall reign' takes up the theme of the fifth, seventh and eighth verses of the psalm, which proclaimed of the Israelite king:

> They shall fear thee as long as the sun and moon endure, throughout all generations.
> In his days shall the righteous flourish; and abundance of peace so long as the moon endureth.
> He shall have dominion also from sea to sea, and from the river unto the ends of the earth.

Not only did Watts Christianize the great sacred poems of the Jews, but he also anglicized them. In some of his other paraphrases he changed the names of Judah and Israel to England and Scotland, and the names of Old Testament kings to those of British monarchs. His paraphrase of Psalm 147, 'Praise ye the Lord: for it is good to sing praises unto our God', began:

> O Britain; praise thy mighty God,
> And make his honours known abroad;
> He bid the ocean round thee flow;
> Not bars of brass could guard thee so.

'Jesus shall reign' first appeared in Watts's *Psalms of David Imitated in the Language of the New Testament and applied to the Christian State and Worship* which was published in 1719 and contained paraphrases of 138 of the 150 psalms in the Bible. Verses 2, 3, 4 and 7 are now generally omitted, although a few hymnals still print verse 4 with the first line changed to 'To him shall endless pray'r be made'.

This hymn is often regarded as the first proper missionary hymn and it has been sung in many far-off lands. On Whit Sunday, 1862, for example, it was sung by thousands of South Sea Islanders at a service to mark the adoption of a Christian form of government. An observer noted: 'Who so much as they could realize the full meaning of the poet's words? They had been rescued from heathenism and cannibalism and they were that day met for the first time under a Christian constitution, under a Christian king, and with Christ Himself reigning in the hearts of most of those present.'

Several tunes are associated with the hymn, including Galilee, which appeared in the revised edition of *Hymns Ancient and Modern* and had been written for it by Philip Armes (1836–1908), cathedral organist at Chichester and Durham; Warrington, by Ralph Harrison (1748–1810), a Presbyterian minister from Lancashire; Rimington by F. Duckworth (1862–1941); Duke Street by John Hatton (d. 1793); and Truro, which comes from *Psalmodia Evangelica* (1789). My own preference lies between the warm and easily flowing Warrington and the affirmative Truro.

Christ's Kingdom among the Gentiles

Jesus shall reign where'er the sun
Does his successive journeys run;
His kingdom stretch from shore to shore,
Till moons shall wax and wane no more.

2   Behold the Islands with their Kings,
And Europe her best tribute brings;
From North to South the Princes meet
To pay their homage at his feet.

3   There Persia glorious to behold,
    There India stands in Eastern Gold;
    And barbarous nations at his word
    Submit and bow and own their Lord.

4   For him shall endless pray'r be made,
    And praises throng to crown his head;
    His name like sweet perfume shall rise
    With every morning sacrifice;

5   People and realms of every tongue
    Dwell on his love with sweetest song;
    And infant-voices shall proclaim
    Their early blessings on his name.

6   Blessings abound where'er he reigns,
    The prisoner leaps to lose his chains,
    The weary find eternal rest,
    And all the sons of want are blest.

7   Where he displays his healing power
    Death and the curse are known no more;
    In him the tribes of Adam boast
    More blessings than their father lost.

8   Let every creature rise and bring
    Peculiar honours to our king;
    Angels descend with songs again,
    And earth repeat the long *Amen.*

71 JUDGE ETERNAL, THRONED IN SPLENDOUR

With the welcome re-assertion of the social teachings of the Gospel
that has taken place in recent years, it is surprising that this robust
hymn by Henry Scott Holland (1847–1918), the pioneer Christian
socialist, is not heard more often nowadays. Admittedly the language
of its third verse is rather dated with its references to 'heathen' and
'Empire', but the hymn as a whole breathes a spirit of justice and
social concern. It is a powerful call for God's judgement on our
sinful and divided society, reminiscent in some ways of the Chartist
hymn by Ebenezer Elliott (1781–1849):

> When wilt Thou save the people?
>   O God of mercy, when?
> The people, Lord, the people,
>   Not thrones and crowns, but men!
> Flowers of Thy heart, O God, are they;
> Let them not pass like weeds away,
>   Their heritage a sunless day.
>   God save the people!

Of aristocratic background, Henry Scott Holland was educated at
Eton and Balliol College, Oxford, ordained in 1872, and after a
series of academic and Church appointments became precentor of St
Paul's Cathedral in 1886. From 1910 until his death he was Regius
Professor of Divinity at Oxford.

He had a passionate attachment to social reform. He was one of
the founders of the Christian Social Union, which was set up in 1889
and was an important influence in making the Church of England
more socially and politically conscious. For twenty-two years he
edited the *Commonwealth*, a journal concerned with the social ap-
plication of the Christian faith, and it was in its pages in 1902 that

'Judge Eternal, throned in splendour' first appeared. So far as is known, it was his only hymn. He was, in fact, a great lover of music and notably raised the musical standards at St Paul's during his time there. He was part-editor of the *New Cathedral Psalter* and of the *English Hymnal*, the first edition of which included his hymn.

Those modern hymnals which still include 'Judge Eternal, throned in splendour' have generally altered the third verse to erase its offending references to the heathen and the Empire, so that it reads as follows:

> Crown, O God, thine own endeavour;
>   Cleave our darkness with thy sword;
> Feed the faithless and the hungry
>   With the richness of thy word;
> Cleanse the body of this Nation
>   Through the glory of the Lord.

When this hymn is sung it is invariably to the clean and penetrating Welsh traditional melody Rhuddlan.

Judge Eternal, throned in splendour,
  Lord of lords and King of kings,
With Thy living fire of judgment
  Purge this land of bitter things;
Solace all its wide dominion
  With the healing of Thy wings.

2 Still the weary folk are pining
  For the hour that brings release;
And the city's crowded clangour
  Cries aloud for sin to cease;
And the homesteads and the woodlands
  Plead in silence for their peace.

3 Crown, O God, Thine own endeavour;
  Cleave our darkness with Thy sword;
Feed the faint and hungry heathen
  With the richness of Thy word;
Cleanse the body of this Empire
  Through the glory of the Lord.

72 JUST AS I AM, WITHOUT ONE PLEA

This ever-popular Evangelical hymn, which has both a great simplicity and considerable emotional power, was the work of a remarkable woman who spent fifty years of her life as a confirmed invalid.

Charlotte Elliott (1789–1871) was the grand-daughter of the Revd Henry Venn, one of the members of the famous Clapham Sect which gathered around William Wilberforce. Her father, Henry Venn Elliott, was an Evangelical clergyman who moved from Clapham to Brighton which, like many seaside resorts, was something of a stronghold of 'vital religion' in Victorian times.

At the age of thirty-two Charlotte was stricken by an illness which continued to afflict her for the rest of her life. Although largely confined to bed, she lived to the grand old age of eighty-two and wrote several hundred hymns which appeared in volumes with titles like *The Invalids' Hymn Book* and *Hours of Sorrow Cheered and Comforted*. Among her contemporaries she was probably best known for 'My God and Father, while I stray' and 'Christian, seek ye not repose'.

'Just as I am' was written in 1834 at a time when Charlotte's brother Harry was raising money to build a college in Brighton to educate the daughters of poor clergymen. The whole Elliott household was busily engaged in organizing a bazaar to raise money for the proposed school and Charlotte, sitting in her sickroom, felt particularly useless and helpless. As she sat alone a sense of peace and contentment came over her and in that spirit she wrote the verses which have brought comfort and strength to so many. For the opening phrase of each verse she drew on words which had been addressed to her twelve years earlier by a visiting Swiss evangelist, Dr César Malan. In response to a protestation of her unworthiness to come to Christ, he had told her to come to the Saviour 'just as you are'.

'Just as I am' first appeared in leaflet form in 1835 and was published the following year in *The Invalids' Hymn Book*, headed with the text 'Him that cometh unto Me, I will in no wise cast out' (John 6:37). It ran to six verses, the seventh being added by the author later that year. One of the first to derive spiritual benefit from the hymn was William Wordsworth's daughter Dora, who asked for it to be read to her every morning as she lay dying at her father's house in the Lake District village of Grasmere.

Two other very similar hymns were directly inspired by Charlotte Elliott's verses. In 1850 Russell Sturgis Cook, an American Congregational minister, penned some verses which found their way into *American Hymns Old and New*. The first stanza ran:

> Just as thou art, without one trace
> Of love or joy, or inward grace,
> Or meetness for the heavenly place,
> O wretched sinner, come.

In 1887 Marianne Hearn (1834–1909), a prolific religious lyricist, contributed a six-verse hymn to a Sunday School collection under her pen name of Marianne Farningham. Her hymn, which was designed for healthy young people and achieved considerable popularity, began:

> Just as I am, Thine own to be,
> Friend of the young, who lovest me,
> To consecrate myself to Thee,
> O Jesus Christ, I come.

Of the several tunes which are used as settings for Charlotte Elliott's hymn, the best-known is almost certainly Saffron Walden by Arthur Henry Brown (1830–1926). Strongly influenced by the Oxford Movement, Brown was a pioneer in the restoration of plainchant and did much to revive the use of Gregorian music in Anglican worship.

The Lamb of God

Just as I am, without one plea
But that Thy blood was shed for me,
And that Thou bidd'st me come to Thee,
    O Lamb of God, I come.

2 Just as I am, and waiting not
To rid my soul of one dark blot,
To Thee, whose blood can cleanse each spot,
    O Lamb of God, I come.

3 Just as I am, though tossed about
With many a conflict, many a doubt,
Fightings and fears within, without,
    O Lamb of God, I come.

4 Just as I am, poor, wretched, blind;
Sight, riches, healing of the mind,
Yea, all I need, in Thee to find,
    O Lamb of God, I come.

5 Just as I am, Thou wilt receive,
Wilt welcome, pardon, cleanse, relieve;
Because Thy promise I believe,
    O Lamb of God, I come.

6 Just as I am – Thy love unknown
Has broken every barrier down –
Now to be Thine, yea, Thine alone,
    O Lamb of God, I come.

7 Just as I am, of that free love
The breadth, length, depth, and height to prove,
Here for a season, then above, –
    O Lamb of God, I come.

73 KING OF GLORY, KING OF PEACE

The poems of George Herbert (1593–1633) rightly have a prominent place in nearly all modern hymn-books. Yet although they were written some 350 years ago, it is only in the present century that they have come to be sung in churches.

Herbert was a man who might have risen to high political office but instead chose the life of a country clergyman. Of aristocratic family, and educated at Westminster School and Trinity College, Cambridge, he was a close friend of John Donne and Sir Francis Bacon and attracted the notice of King James I. In 1624 he became Member of Parliament for Montgomery and a glittering public career seemed to beckon. However, the death of his royal patron the following year, coupled with the onset of consumption, led Herbert to reject the career on which he had embarked and to take Holy Orders. He was also strongly influenced by Nicholas Ferrar, the saintly quietist of Little Gidding in Oxfordshire.

After serving as prebendary of Leighton Broomswold in Huntingdonshire, in 1630 he became rector of Bemerton, Wiltshire, where he combined his priestly duties with the writing of some of the finest poetry in the English metaphysical tradition. Greatly loved for his simplicity and saintliness, Herbert only enjoyed three years at Bemerton before he succumbed to consumption.

A few weeks before his death Herbert gave the manuscript of a book of verse to his executor, Edmond Duncon, with the following instructions:

Sir, I pray deliver this little book to my brother Ferrar, and tell him that he shall find in it a picture of the many spiritual conflicts that have passed betwixt God and my soul, before I could subject mine to the will of Jesus my master; in whose service I have now found perfect freedom; desire him to read it, and then, if he can think it may turn to the advantage of any dejected poor soul, let it be made public; if not let him burn it; for I and it are less than the least of God's mercies.

Ferrar edited Herbert's poems and they were published in a book entitled *The Temple* in 1633. It was there that the verses printed overleaf first appeared. They were first turned into a hymn in the *Wellington College Hymn Book* of 1902. Four years later they were chosen, along with several other seventeenth-century devotional poems, for inclusion in the first edition of the *English Hymnal*. To make the hymn, the sixth verse printed here was dropped and the other verses were combined to form three eight-line stanzas.

The last verse of Herbert's poem has striking similarities with the final stanza of the hymn 'When all Thy Mercies, O my God, my rising soul surveys', written by Joseph Addison (1672–1719) and first published as the conclusion of an essay on Gratitude in the *Spectator* of August 1712:

> Through all eternity to thee
> A joyful song I'll raise;
> For O! eternity's too short
> To utter all thy praise.

'King of Glory, King of Peace' is generally sung to the tune *Gwalchmai* by Joseph David Jones (1827–70). Born at Brynerygog in Montgomery, Jones taught singing at Ruthin and published a small collection of psalm tunes.

Praise

King of Glory, King of Peace,
    I will love thee;
And, that love may never cease,
    I will move thee.

2   Thou hast granted my request,
    Thou hast heard me;
Thou didst note my working breast,
    Thou hast spared me.

3   Wherefore with my utmost art
    I will sing thee,
And the cream of all my heart
    I will bring thee.

4   Though my sins against me cried,
    Thou didst clear me,
And alone, when they replied,
    Thou didst hear me.

5   Sev'n whole days, not one in sev'n,
    I will praise thee;
In my heart, though not in heav'n,
    I can raise thee.

6   Thou grew'st soft and moist with tears,
    Thou relentedst:
And when Justice call'd for fears,
    Thou dissentedst.

7   Small it is, in this poor sort
    To enrol thee;
E'en eternity's too short
    To extol thee.

74 LEAD, KINDLY LIGHT, AMID THE ENCIRCLING GLOOM

This is the second great hymn by John Henry Newman (1801–90) which was not originally written to be sung at all. Unlike 'Firmly I believe and truly' (No. 37), 'Lead, kindly Light' was turned into a hymn during the author's lifetime, and although he himself insisted that his verses were 'not a hymn, nor are they suitable for singing', he accepted their inclusion in hymn-books.

Newman wrote this outstanding piece of devotional poetry at a time when he was feeling physically exhausted and intellectually bewildered by the first stirrings of those doubts and convictions that were to take him fifteen years later into the Roman Catholic Church. While travelling in Southern Italy in the spring of 1833, he was struck down by a viral infection of such severity that there were fears for his life. Greatly weakened, he resolved to hasten home and reached the port of Palermo in Sicily at the end of May. However, he had to wait there three weeks for a boat. When at last he got away it was on board an orange boat bound for Marseilles. The vessel was becalmed for a week in the Straits of Bonifacio between Corsica and Sicily and it was during this period, on 16 June, as he sat on the deck in the stifling heat of midsummer waiting for a breeze to spring up and carry him on his way home, that he wrote the verses printed overleaf. There has been much speculation about the exact meaning of the two closing lines, but I do not intend to add to it here and prefer rather to leave them mysterious and elusive – as Newman, I think, meant them to be.

Newman eventually reached his mother's home on 9 July 1833. The following Sunday in his own University Church in Oxford he heard his friend John Keble preach the famous sermon on National Apostasy which began the Oxford Movement.

'Lead, kindly Light' was first published in the *British Magazine* in 1834 and subsequently in *Lyra Apostolica* two years later. It first appeared set to music as a hymn in 1860, but its real popularity dates from its inclusion in the appendix to the original edition of *Hymns Ancient and Modern* in 1868, where it was set to a tune composed for it three years earlier by Dr J. B. Dykes (1823–76), precentor of Durham Cathedral. *Lux Benigna* came to Dykes as he was walking along the Strand past Charing Cross station. Newman typically and modestly attributed the hymn's subsequent great popularity to Dykes's tune rather than to his own words. Other tunes specifically composed for the hymn include Sandon by C. H. Purdy, Bonifacio by David Emlyn Evans, and Alberta, written by Sir W. H. Harris in 1924 while travelling by train through Canada.

Newman's verses rapidly became one of the two or three best-loved Victorian hymns, equally popular with Roman Catholics, Anglicans and Nonconformists. They were a particular favourite of Queen Victoria and were read out to her as she lay dying at Osborne House on the Isle of Wight in January 1901.

A sign of the widespread popularity of Newman's hymn by the early years of this century was the appearance of this rather monotonous and unedifying parody in the First World War:

> We've had no beer,
> We've had no beer today,
> We've had no beer!
> No beer at all today,
> We've had no beer.

Faith – Heavenly Leadings

Lead, kindly Light, amid the encircling gloom,
  Lead thou me on;
The night is dark, and I am far from home,
  Lead thou me on.
Keep thou my feet; I do not ask to see
The distant scene; one step enough for me.

2 I was not ever thus, nor prayed that thou
  Should'st lead me on;
I loved to choose and see my path; but now
  Lead thou me on.
I loved the garish day, and, spite of fears,
Pride ruled my will: remember not past years.

3 So long thy power hath blessed me, sure it still
  Will lead me on,
O'er moor and fen, o'er crag and torrent, till
  The night is gone;
And with the morn those angel faces smile,
Which I have loved long since, and lost awhile.

75 LEAD US, HEAVENLY FATHER, LEAD US

Despite the fact that it refers to Our Lord as 'dreary', this hymn has been a firm favourite with congregations ever since it was first written more than 150 years ago for the inmates of an orphan asylum.

It is the work of James Edmeston (1791–1867), who wrote a grand total of 2,000 hymns for the children of the London Orphan Asylum which he visited regularly. Born and brought up in Stepney in the East End of London and coming from Congregational stock, Edmeston became a successful architect and forsook both the environment and denomination of his childhood, moving to Surrey and espousing Anglicanism. Among his architectural pupils was Sir George Gilbert Scott, the architect responsible for the Albert Memorial, the government buildings in Whitehall, St Pancras station and a host of churches throughout Britain.

It was Edmeston's practice to write a hymn every Sunday and read it at family worship. His first published collection of verses, *The Cottage Minstrel*, was written in response to an advertisement offering £20 for fifty simple hymns suitable for cottage meetings. Subsequent collections included *Infant Breathings* and *Sacred Lyrics*. It was in the latter volume, published in 1821, that 'Lead us, heavenly Father, lead us' first appeared. It was included in *Baptist Hymns and Psalms* in 1858 and from there passed into most hymnals.

This is the only one of Edmeston's hymns still to be sung regularly today. Others found in hymnals current earlier this century include 'Saviour, breathe an evening blessing' and 'God intrusts to all'.

The tune Mannheim normally used for this hymn was adapted from a melody by the German composer Friedrich Filitz (1804–76) in his *Viertimmiges Choralbuch* (1847). Filitz lived in Berlin and

Munich, and brought out a collection of the chorales of the most distinguished masters of the sixteenth and seventeenth centuries. This particular tune was originally set by Filitz to words by Frelinghausen beginning '*Auf, auf, weil der Tag erschienen*'; it was adapted for Edmeston's hymn by Thomas Binney in his *Congregational Church Music* of 1853.

Hymn written for the children of the London Orphan Asylum

Lead us, heavenly Father, lead us
 O'er the world's tempestuous sea;
Guard us, guide us, keep us, feed us,
 For we have no help but thee;
Yet possessing every blessing,
 If our God our Father be.

2   Saviour, breathe forgiveness o'er us:
 All our weakness thou dost know;
Thou didst tread this earth before us,
 Thou didst feel its keenest woe;
Lone and dreary, faint and weary,
 Through the desert thou didst go.

3   Spirit of our God, descending,
 Fill our hearts with heavenly joy,
Love with every passion blending,
 Pleasure that can never cloy;
Thus provided, pardoned, guided,
 Nothing can our peace destroy.

76 LET ALL MORTAL FLESH KEEP SILENCE

This powerful Eucharistic hymn, so full of awe and mystery, is taken from one of the early liturgies of the Greek Orthodox Church. Like 'For the beauty of the earth' (No. 39), it appears in two distinct versions expressing different doctrinal viewpoints. In its original and more common form, printed here, it is a communion hymn. The alternative version tones down its sacramental character and the suggestion of the real physical presence of Christ in the elements of bread and wine in the Eucharist.

The verses are based on a part of the Liturgy of St James which dates from the fourth century and is found in both Greek and Syriac. The whole liturgy was first translated into English by J. M. Neale and R. F. Littledale and published in their *Primitive Liturgies* (1868–9). Shortly after the book's publication, the Revd Gerard Moultrie (1829–85) versified a section entitled 'Prayer of the Cherubic Hymn' to form this hymn. Moultrie was successively chaplain of Shrewsbury School, vicar of South Leigh and warden of St James' College, also in South Leigh. He was responsible for several translations of hymns as well as a number of his own composition.

It is Moultrie's translation which appears overleaf and which is found in most Roman Catholic, Anglican and Presbyterian hymnals. However, there are those for whom the second verse smacks too much of the doctrine of the real presence. To accommodate their views, Dr Percy Dearmer (1867–1936; see notes to hymn No. 63) produced an alternative version for inclusion in *Songs of Praise* in 1931. It appears in several Nonconformist hymnals, including the *Baptist Hymn Book* of 1962. The first two verses of Dearmer's version are as follows:

Let all mortal flesh keep silence,
  And with awe and welcome stand;
Harbour nothing earthly-minded;
  For, with blessing in his hand,
Christ our Lord with us abideth,
  Loving homage to demand.

King is he, yet born a servant,
  Lord of all in human guise,
Truly man, yet God revealing,
  God as love, to mortal eyes;
God with man, he leads and feeds us,
  He the power and he the prize.

The third and fourth verses of Dearmer's hymn differ less radically from Moultrie's original. Both versions are generally sung to the tune Picardy, a French carol melody which probably dates from the seventeenth century.

Let all mortal flesh keep silence,
   And with fear and trembling stand;
Ponder nothing earthly-minded,
   For with blessing in his hand
Christ our God to earth descendeth
   Our full homage to demand.

2   King of kings, yet born of Mary,
   As of old on earth he stood,
Lord of Lords, in human vesture –
   In the Body and the Blood –
He will give to all the faithful
   His own self for heavenly Food.

3   Rank on rank the host of heaven
   Spreads its vanguard on the way,
As the Light of light descendeth
   From the realms of endless day,
That the powers of hell may vanish
   As the darkness clears away.

4   At his feet the six-winged Seraph:
   Cherubim with sleepless eye,
Veil their faces to the Presence,
   As with ceaseless voice they cry,
'Alleluia! Alleluia!
   'Alleluia! Lord most high.'

77 LET ALL THE WORLD IN EVERY CORNER SING

This is another of the poems of George Herbert (1593–1633) which was only turned into a hymn after the author's death. But unlike 'King of Glory, King of peace' (No. 73; see notes to that hymn for biographical details) and 'Teach me, my God and King' (No. 120), this one seems to have been written specifically for singing in church. Not surprisingly, it was the first of Herbert's poems to become a hymn and did not have to wait until the twentieth century to be enjoyed by congregations.

The verses first appeared as set out here in the collection of Herbert's work which was published under the title of *The Temple*, shortly after his death in 1633. They are clearly designed to be sung antiphonally, either by two choirs or by choir and congregation. In 1760 in his *New Book of Psalmody*, John Hill of Lydd set the words to music as Herbert had written them, assigning the first verse to alto and tenor and the second to treble and bass, with a four-part chorus. The rearrangement into a conventional congregational hymn of two verses, with the refrain being repeated at the end of the first as well as the second, seems first to have been made in the volume of *Church Hymns* published by the Society for the Propagation of Christian Knowledge in 1871. It was taken up in the revised edition of *Hymns Ancient and Modern* in 1889 and is the version that now appears in all hymn-books.

Four of the greatest church musicians of the last 150 years have written music for 'Let all the world in every corner sing'. The first was William Henry Monk (1823–89) who composed the melody Herbert for the supplement to *Hymns Ancient and Modern*, of which he was music editor. It was one of the last tunes that he wrote before his death. In his remarkably full life he had been organist of four major London churches, Professor of Vocal Music at King's College, London, and the composer of numerous hymn tunes, including such perennial favourites as Eventide (for 'Abide with me'), Ascension (for 'Hail the day that sees him rise'), and St Ethelwald (for 'Soldiers of Christ, arise').

In the twentieth century Monk's tune has been largely supplanted by Luckington by Basil Harwood (1859–1949), which was first used in the *Oxford Hymnary* of 1908. Born in Gloucestershire and educated at Charterhouse and Trinity College, Oxford, Harwood was successively organist at St Barnabas', Pimlico, Ely Cathedral and Christ Church Cathedral, Oxford. His other hymn tunes include Thornbury (for 'Thy hand, O God, has guided').

In 1915 Martin Shaw (1875–1958) supplied High Road, which was taken up by the *English Hymnal*. A pupil of Sir Charles Stanford, Charles Parry and Walford Davies at the Royal College of Music, he was organist at St Mary's, Primrose Hill, and St Martin-in-the-Fields before becoming director of music for the Anglican diocese of Chelmsford. We have already come across him as the composer of Little Cornard (for 'Hills of the North, rejoice') and as the adapter of the folk melody Royal Oak for 'All things bright and beautiful'.

Most recently, Erik Routley (1917–82) wrote Augustine, which appears in the current edition of the *Church Hymnary*. Any writer on the subject of hymns owes an enormous debt of gratitude to the work of Routley and I am happy to express my own considerable indebtedness to him here. Almost certainly the leading twentieth-century authority on Christian hymnody, he published ten books on the subject and edited the *Bulletin* of the Hymn Society of Great Britain and Ireland, as well as being an active Congregational minister. His last position was as director of Westminster Choir College, Princeton, New Jersey.

Antiphon

Chorus:	Let all the world in ev'ry corner sing, *My God and King!*
Verse:	The heav'ns are not too high, His praise may thither fly; The earth is not too low, His praises there may grow.
Chorus:	Let all the world in ev'ry corner sing, *My God and King!*
Verse:	The Church with psalms must shout, No door can keep them out; But above all, the heart Must bear the longest part.
Chorus:	Let all the world in ev'ry corner sing, *My God and King!*

78 LET US WITH A GLADSOME MIND

This paraphrase of Psalm 136 which forms the basis of an ever-popular hymn was written at the age of fifteen by John Milton (1608–74), the man who is generally regarded as second only to Shakespeare in the roll-call of great English poets. I must admit that I find it coming close to doggerel in parts, but it has an originality and freshness that lifts it high above the level of most adolescent verse and rescues it from the triteness that threatens to creep in.

John Milton was born in Cheapside, London, the son of a scrivener and composer of music. He was educated at St Paul's School and Christ's College, Cambridge, and his father intended that he should pursue a career in the Church. However, his views made it impossible for him to take Anglican Orders and instead he settled into his career of poet, pamphleteer and writer. He came to public attention with powerful tracts against episcopacy, in favour of divorce, and, most notably, with his passionate and elequent defence of freedom of speech and liberty of the press in his *Areopagitica* (1643). During the period of the Commonwealth, Milton was Latin Secretary to the Council of State. It was at this time that he was afflicted with total blindness. At the restoration of the monarchy in 1660 he was arrested and fined, but later released. It was in the years following the Restoration that he completed his greatest work, *Paradise Lost*. He also wrote a treatise on Christian doctrines in which he showed his indifference to all rites and ceremonies and came close to espousing Arianism. He died of gout and was buried next to his father in St Giles, Cripplegate.

Together with a paraphrase of Psalm 114, the verses printed below constitute the earliest example of Milton's work which is still extant. They were written while he was still a pupil at St Paul's and studying French, Italian, Hebrew, Latin and Greek with the aid of a private tutor. The following year he went up to Cambridge. The other youthful paraphrase, which begins 'When the blest seed of Terah's faithfull Son', is strongly reminiscent of the style of Joshua Sylvester (1563–1618), but Milton's approach to Psalm 136 ('O give thanks unto the Lord; for he is good') is much more original and less derivative. Such imagery as that contained in verse 13 ('The floods stood still like Walls of Glass'), for example, seems to be entirely of his own creation.

The paraphrase first appeared in *Poems of Mr John Milton, both English and Latin*, published in 1645. It did not become a hymn until more than 200 years later. The *Congregationalist Hymn Book* of 1855 included the first, second, seventh, eighth, fifteenth, twentieth, twenty-second and twenty-third verses, suitably polished up and made to scan properly. Subsequently the ninth verse was also added. Most modern hymn-books include only six or seven verses in all, including a repeat of the first verse at the end. Only the first verse and the chorus are as Milton originally wrote them. The verses in use today (though not all found together in any one hymn-book) are:

> Let us, with a gladsome mind,
> Praise the Lord, for he is kind:
> *For his mercies aye endure,*
> *Ever faithful, ever sure.*
>
> 2 Let us blaze his name abroad,
> For of gods he is the God:
>
> 7 He with all-commanding might,
> Filled the new-made world with light:
>
> 8 He the golden-tressed sun
> Caused all day his course to run.
>
> 9 Th' horned moon to shine by night,
> Mid her spangled sisters bright:
>
> 15 He his chosen race did bless
> In the wasteful wilderness:
>
> 22 All things living he doth feed;
> His full hand supplies their need:

245

There are a number of other hymns based on Milton's paraphrase. They include 'Praise, O praise our God and King' by Sir Henry Baker (1821–77), 'Praise, O praise our heavenly King' by H. Trend, and 'Come, and let us praises sing' by Thomas Darling (1816–93). In 1873 Arthur Penrhyn Stanley (1815–81), dean of Westminster Abbey, produced a version of Milton's paraphrase suitable for singing on royal and national occasions. It includes the lines:

> Long our island throne has stood,
> Planted on the ocean flood;

'Let us with a gladsome mind' is generally sung to the rather feeble and predictable tune Monkland which is based on the melody of a German song, *'Fahre fort, fahre fort'*, first published in 1704. It first appeared as a hymn tune in Britain in a collection published by the United Brethren in 1790. In 1824 a modified version, similar to that used now, was included in a collection of hymn tunes put together by John Lees, organist at the United Brethren chapel at Leominster, Herefordshire. Some years later J. B. Wilkes (1785–1869), organist at Monkland, a village just a few miles from Leominster, where Sir Henry Baker was vicar, set it to Baker's hymn, mentioned above. It first gained national currency when it was used as a setting for 'O praise our God and King' in *Hymns Ancient and Modern*.

In an effort to produce a livelier tune, the third edition of the *Church Hymnary* offers Harts, a simplified form of a melody by Benjamin Milgrove (1731–1810). I commend its use to those who have had their fill of Monkland.

Psalm 136

Let us with a gladsome mind
Praise the Lord, for he is kind,
For his mercies ay endure,
Ever faithful, ever sure.

2　Let us blaze his Name abroad,
For of gods he is the God;

3　O let us his praises tell,
That doth the wrathfull tyrants quell.

4　That with his miracles doth make
Amazed Heav'n and Earth to shake.

5　That by his wisdom did create
The painted Heav'ns so full of state.

6　That did the solid Earth ordain
To rise above the watry plain.

7　That by his all-commanding might,
Did fill the new-made world with light.

8　And caus'd the Golden-tressed Sun,
All the day long his cours to run.

9　The horned Moon to shine by night,
Amongst her spangled sisters bright.

10　He with his thunder-clasping hand,
Smote the first-born of *Egypt* Land.

11　And in despight of *Pharao* fell,
He brought from thence his *Israel*.

12　The ruddy waves he cleft in twain,
Of the *Erythræan* main.

13　The floods stood still like Walls of Glass,
While the Hebrew Bands did pass.

14 But full soon they did devour
   The Tawny King with all his power.

15 His chosen people he did bless
   In the wastfull Wildernes.

16 In bloody battail he brought down
   Kings of prowess and renown.

17 He foild bold *Seon* and his host,
   That rul'd the *Amorrean* coast.

18 And large lim'd *Og* he did subdue,
   With all his hardy crew.

19 And to his Servant *Israel,*
   He gave their Land therin to dwell.

20 He hath with a piteous eye
   Beheld us in our misery.

21 And freed us from the slavery
   Of the invading enimy.

22 All living creatures he doth feed,
   And with full hand supplies their need.

23 Let us therefore warble forth
   His mighty Majesty and worth.

24 That his mansion hath on high
   Above the reach of mortall eye.

79 'LIFT UP YOUR HEARTS!' WE LIFT THEM, LORD, TO THEE

Worship in the public school chapel may be an imperfect expression of Christianity in many respects (and what earthly and institutional form of worship isn't?), but it has certainly produced an important and distinctive corpus of hymns. 'Lift up your hearts' is perhaps the supreme example of the genre – it is exhilarating, uplifting, uncomplicated and cries out to be sung by a packed congregation anxious to give their vocal chords a good airing. It was written for the boys of Harrow School in 1881 by their headmaster, Henry Montagu Butler (1833–1918), who drew his inspiration from the words of the *Sursum Corda* in the communion service: 'Lift up your hearts', followed by the congregation's response: 'We lift them to the Lord.'

Butler was a leading member of a formidable family which has in the last three generations produced twelve fellows of Oxbridge colleges, three public school headmasters, a leading Tory politician and sundry professors. He himself became headmaster of Harrow at the age of twenty-six and remained there for twenty-six years, until he was appointed Dean of Gloucester. In 1886 he became Master of Trinity College, Cambridge. *The Times* described him as 'the most patriarchal figure in English academic life'.

At Harrow, he was a powerful reforming headmaster in the tradition of Dr Arnold of Rugby. He insisted that his classics masters should have first class degrees and took a strong interest in the development of team games in the school. A keen cricketer, he frequently impressed on pupils the importance throughout life of the maxim, 'Play the game'. In his first year as Master of Trinity College, Cambridge, and at the age of fifty-three, he caused a sensation among the fellows by marrying a young girl who had just come top of the Classical Tripos. 'It is her goodness, not her Greek and Latin, which have stolen my heart,' he assured them. His devotion to his college knew no bounds. He is said to have commented at the end of a sermon on the Day of Judgement, after praising Christ's action in separating the sheep and the goats, 'We would expect no less of him, since he was, after all, in some sense a Trinity man himself.'

The tune Woodlands is also a fine example of public school Christianity at its best – bold, vigorous and eminently singable. It was written for Butler's hymn by Walter Greatorex (1877–1949) when director of music at Gresham's School, Holt, Norfolk. Greatorex was the son of a bank manager and was born in Southwell, Nottinghamshire. Educated at Derby School and St John's College, Cambridge, he was a music master at Uppingham before going to Gresham's in 1906. He remained there for nearly thirty years and was much loved by those boys who got to know him and who shared his love of music and literature. One of the school's most distinguished old boys, the poet W. H. Auden, said that it was to Greatorex that he owed all the knowledge of music that he possessed. The tune was named after the headmaster's boarding house at Gresham's. To generations of boys there, however, it was simply known as 'Gog's Tune', that being Greatorex's nickname. It is also used for 'Tell out, my soul, the greatness of the Lord' (No. 122).

'Lift up your hearts!' We lift them, Lord, to thee;
Here at thy feet none other may we see.
'Lift up your hearts!' E'en so, with one accord,
We lift them up, we lift them to the Lord.

2　Above the level of the former years,
The mire of sin, the slough of guilty fears,
The mist of doubt, the blight of love's decay,
O Lord of Light, lift all our hearts to-day!

3　Above the swamps of subterfuge and shame,
The deeds, the thoughts, that honour may not name,
The halting tongue that dares not tell the whole,
O Lord of Truth, lift every Christian soul!

4　Above the storms that vex this lower state,
Pride, jealousy, and envy, rage, and hate,
And cold mistrust that holds e'en friends apart,
O Lord of Love, lift every brother's heart!

5　Lift every gift that thou thyself hast given;
Low lies the best till lifted up to heaven;
Low lie the bounding heart, the teeming brain,
Till, sent from God, they mount to God again.

6　Then, as the trumpet-call in after years,
'Lift up your hearts!', rings pealing in our ears,
Still shall those hearts respond with full accord,
'We lift them up, we lift them to the Lord!'

80 LO! HE COMES WITH CLOUDS DESCENDING

This is both a theological and a literary oddity. Although most hymn-books put it in the Advent section, it is in reality one of the very few popular hymns which treats of the difficult doctrine of the Second Coming of Christ. It also has a complex literary pedigree, being the work of three different writers. It started life in 1752 when John Cennick (1718–55), an Anglican of Quaker parents who became the first Methodist lay preacher and ended up a Moravian, published a hymn which began:

> Lo! he cometh, endless trumpets
>   Blow before his bloody sign!
> Midst ten thousand saints and angels
>   See the Crucified shine.
>   Alleluia!
> Welcome, welcome, bleeding Lamb!

With such an opening, it is perhaps hardly surprising that in 1758 Cennick's hymn was almost completely re-written by Charles Wesley (1707–88). Two years later Martin Madan (1726–90), founder and chaplain of the Lock Hospital, Hyde Park Corner, and co-author with Wesley and George Whitefield of 'Hark, the herald Angels sing', made a further rearrangement of the hymn, reintroducing some of Cennick's original verses and producing the version which is printed overleaf. The first, second and fifth verses are by Wesley, the third and fourth substantially by Cennick and the sixth an amalgam of the two men's work.

As sung now, the hymn largely follows Madan's version, but several lines have been altered. The fifth verse, which he actually took from another hymn by Wesley, 'Rise, ye dearly purchased sinners', has been universally dropped in favour of the third verse of Wesley's re-writing of Cennick's original:

> Those dear tokens of His Passion
> Still His dazzling Body bears,
> Cause of endless exultation
> To his ransom'd worshippers:
> With what rapture
> Gaze we on those glorious scars.

The hymn is always sung to the magnificent tune Helmsley, which Madan recast from a melody written for Wesley's version by Thomas Olivers (1725–99; see notes to hymn No. 128). There are several stories (all of them probably apocryphal) about its origins. One has it that Olivers heard the tune being whistled in the street, another that it was based on a Scottish melody, and a third that it derived from a popular hornpipe. More likely is the theory that he based it – in part, at least – on a concert-room song, 'Guardian angels, now protect me'. It also bears a passing resemblance to a melody from Thomas Arne's opera, *Thomas and Sally*. A well-known eighteenth-century actress, Miss Catley, danced a hornpipe to the tune in a burlesque; but this was in 1776, eleven years after Olivers had composed Helmsley, and it seems that the hornpipe was based on the hymn tune rather than the other way round. Whatever its origins, it has been extremely popular. It was a particular favourite of Queen Victoria's. When a new organist at her private chapel inadvertently played another tune which had been set to 'Lo! He comes' in *Hymns Ancient and Modern*, a royal request came that in future only Helmsley should be used.

Lo! He comes with clouds descending,
  Once for favour'd sinners slain;
Thousand thousand Saints attending
  Swell the triumph of His train:
    Alleluia!
God appears on earth to reign.

2 Every eye shall now behold Him,
    Robed in dreadful majesty;
  Those who set at nought and sold Him,
    Pierced and nail'd Him to the Tree,
      Deeply wailing,
  Shall the true Messiah see.

3 Every island, sea, and mountain,
    Heav'n and earth, shall flee away;
  All who hate Him must, confounded,
    Hear the trump proclaim the Day:
      Come to judgment!
  Come to judgment! come away!

4 Now redemption, long expected,
    See in solemn pomp appear!
  All His saints, by man rejected,
    Now shall meet Him in the air:
      Alleluia!
  See the Day of God appear!

5 Answer thine own Bride and Spirit,
    Hasten, Lord, the gen'ral Doom!
  The New Heav'n and Earth t'inherit,
    Take thy pining exiles home:
      All creation
  Travails! groans! and bids Thee come!

6 Yea, Amen, let all adore Thee,
    High on Thine eternal throne;
  Saviour, take the power and glory:
    Claim the Kingdom for Thine own:
      O come quickly!
  Alleluia! Come, Lord, come!

81 LORD, ENTHRONED IN HEAVENLY SPLENDOUR

Another public school hymn, this is the work of George Hugh Bourne (1840–1925), headmaster of St Andrew's School, Chardstock, Devon, and later of St Edmund's College, Salisbury. It comes from a series of seven post-communion hymns which he wrote for the use of the latter college and which were privately printed in 1874. It made its first public appearance in the supplement to the revised edition of *Hymns Ancient and Modern* in 1889, when it was printed as the version overleaf. In most modern hymnals the fifth verse is generally omitted.

Bourne was the son of an Anglican clergyman and was educated at Eton and Corpus Christi College, Oxford. He himself was ordained and, in addition to his headmasterly duties, held the positions of chaplain to the Bishop of Bloemfontein, and sub-dean, treasurer and prebendary of Salisbury Cathedral.

The bright and memorable tune St Helen was composed for the 1889 supplement to *Hymns Ancient and Modern* by Sir George Martin (1844–1916). Born at Lambourn in Berkshire, his interest in music was first aroused by hearing Sir Herbert Oakeley play Bach on the organ of the parish church there. He studied under Sir John Stainer whom he succeeded as organist and master of the choristers at St Paul's Cathedral, having earlier served as organist to the Duke of Buccleuch at Dalkeith.

This hymn was very nearly prefaced in this collection with another from the same general stable. Indeed, it was only after considerable heart-searching and with great reluctance that I decided to drop what in many ways is the most distinctive and atmospheric of all public school hymns, 'Lord, dismiss us with thy blessing', which was written for the boys of Rugby by Henry James Buckoll (1803–71). My own memories of singing it in school chapel in the mid 1960s nearly got the better of me, but when I discovered that it is not now to be found even within the covers of *Hymns for Church and School,* as the old *Public School Hymn Book* is now known (let alone in any other modern hymnal), I realized that its inclusion in this book would have been a piece of self-indulgence hard to justify. So out I am afraid it has had to come.

Lord, enthroned in heavenly splendour,
   First-begotten from the dead,
Thou alone, our strong defender,
   Liftest up thy people's head.
     Alleluia!
   Jesu, true and living Bread.

2   Here our humblest homage pay we;
   Here in loving reverence bow;
Here for faith's discernment pray we,
   Lest we fail to know thee now.
     Alleluia!
   Thou art here, we ask not how.

3   Though the lowliest form doth veil thee
   As of old in Bethlehem,
Here as there thine angels hail thee,
   Branch and Flower of Jesse's stem.
     Alleluia!
   We in worship join with them.

4 Paschal Lamb, thine offering, finished
    Once for all when thou wast slain,
In its fulness undiminished
    Shall for evermore remain,
      Alleluia!
    Cleansing souls from every stain.

5 Great High Priest of our profession,
    Through the veil Thou wentest in,
By Thy mighty intercession
    Grace and peace for us to win;
      Alleluia!
    Only sacrifice for sin.

6 Life-imparting heav'nly Manna,
    Stricken Rock with streaming side,
Heaven and earth with loud hosanna
    Worship thee, the Lamb who died,
      Alleluia!
    Risen, ascended, glorified!

82 LORD OF ALL HOPEFULNESS, LORD OF ALL JOY

Three extremely fine twentieth-century hymns are associated with the traditional Irish melody, Slane. One of them we have already come across – 'Be thou my vision' (No. 17). The second, which appears overleaf, is perhaps the best known. It is the work of Mrs Joyce Placzek (1901–53), an English-born *émigré* to the USA who wrote under the pen name of Jan Struther, derived from her maiden name Anstruther.

Born in London, Mrs Placzek pursued a literary career and contributed poetry to a number of periodicals. She was effectively 'discovered' as a hymn-writer by Percy Dearmer (on whom see notes to hymn No. 63) who asked her to contribute to *Songs of Praise* in 1925. He wanted a hymn to fit the tune Slane and she came up with 'Lord of all hopefulness, Lord of all joy' which, in Dearmer's words, was 'a lovely example of the fitting together of thought, words and music'. Other hymns by Mrs Placzek which continue to be sung include 'Round the earth a message runs' and the wedding hymn 'God, whose eternal mind'.

In an effort to keep Slane for 'Be thou my vision', Cyril Taylor (b. 1907) wrote the tune Miniver for this hymn. Taylor, who was educated at Magdalen College School and Christ Church, Oxford, was precentor of Bristol Cathedral and assistant to the head of religious broadcasting at the BBC before becoming warden and chaplain to the Royal School of Church Music. In 1958 he became perpetual curate of Cerne Abbas, Dorset. Miniver first appeared in 1951 in the *BBC Hymn Book*, of which Taylor was editor. He took the title of his tune from the novel *Mrs Miniver*, written by Mrs Placzek and published in 1939, which became a very popular film during the Second World War.

The third modern hymn associated with Slane is 'Lord of creation, to thee be all praise' by Jack Copley Winslow (1882–1974). Educated at Eton and Balliol College, Oxford, Winslow was successively a missionary in India, chaplain to Bryanston School in Dorset and chaplain to Lee Abbey in North Devon. His hymn, which first appeared in 1961 in *A Garland of Verse* and which I quote by permission of his niece, Mrs J. Tyrrell, begins:

> Lord of creation, to thee be all praise!
> Most mighty thy working, most wondrous thy ways!
> Who reignest in glory no tongue can e'er tell,
> Yet deign'st in the heart of the humble to dwell.
>
> Lord of all power, I give thee my will,
> In joyful obedience thy tasks to fulfil.
> Thy bondage is freedom; thy service is song;
> And, held in thy keeping, my weakness is strong.

All Day Hymn

Lord of all hopefulness, Lord of all joy,
Whose trust, ever childlike, no cares
could destroy,
Be there at our waking, and give us,
we pray,
Your bliss in our hearts, Lord,
at the break of day.

2   Lord of all eagerness, Lord of all faith,
Whose strong hands were skilled at the
plane and the lathe,
Be there at our labours, and give us,
we pray,
Your strength in our hearts, Lord,
at the noon of the day.

3   Lord of all kindliness, Lord of all grace,
Your hands swift to welcome, your arms to
embrace.
Be there at our homing, and give us,
we pray,
Your love in our hearts, Lord,
at the eve of the day.

4   Lord of all gentleness, Lord of all calm,
Whose voice is contentment, whose presence
is balm,
Be there at our sleeping, and give us,
we pray,
Your peace in our hearts, Lord,
at the end of the day

From Enlarged Songs of Praise, *by permission of Oxford University Press*

83 LOVE DIVINE, ALL LOVES EXCELLING

This great hymn clearly expresses Charles Wesley's doctrine of perfectionism. It suggests that Christ can transform temporal men into children of God, and that in this life it is possible to be cleansed completely from sin and made totally pure. Many Christians, including the author's own brother, John, have balked at this idea and have toned down the words of the hymn to suggest a slightly less sweeping doctrine of sanctification.

It is said that Charles Wesley (1707–88; see notes to hymn No. 11) had the idea for the hymn from a popular song of the day, 'The Song of Venus', which came from John Dryden's play *King Arthur* and had been set to music by Henry Purcell. It began:

> Fairest isle, all isles excelling,
>   Seat of pleasure and of loves,
> Venus here will choose her dwelling,
>   And forsake the Cyprian groves.

The hymn is printed overleaf as it first appeared in Charles Wesley's *Hymns for those that seek, and those that have Redemption* (1747). In his *Wesleyan Hymn Book* of 1780, John Wesley altered the second line of the fourth verse to 'Pure and spotless let us be', to avoid suggesting that Christians could achieve a sinless perfection in this world. He also omitted the second verse of the hymn, which also clearly expresses the notion of a move towards perfection following conversion to Christianity during which the soul is further cleansed and gradually comes closer to God. The 'second rest' referred to in the fourth line is the relief from the struggle against sin in the life of the true Christian, which comes as a further stage after his initial conversion experience. All subsequent hymn-books have followed John Wesley's changes and some have also altered the second line of the third verse to 'Let us all thy grace receive'. But they have been happy to keep the last verse with its message that individuals will in this life, and before they take their place in heaven, be 'changed from glory into glory' by gradually absorbing and reflecting more and more of the power and influence of Christ.

The first line of this hymn is recalled in another of Wesley's hymns, written a few years later, which begins:

> O Love divine, how sweet thou art!
> When shall I find my willing heart
>   All taken up by thee?
> I thirst, I faint, I die to prove
> The greatest of redeeming love,
>   The love of Christ to me.

The closing line, 'Lost in wonder, love, and praise', was almost certainly lifted from the hymn 'When all thy mercies, O my God' by Joseph Addison (on whom see notes to hymn No. 132), which ended with exactly the same phrase.

There is a rich choice of tunes for this hymn. Purcell's melody, which Wesley had in mind when he wrote it, appeared in the Wesleys' hymn-books of 1761 and 1780 under the name Westminster, but was then dropped and did not reappear until it crept into the *School Hymnal of the Methodist Church* in 1950. Sir John Stainer wrote the tune Love Divine for the 1889 supplement to *Hymns Ancient and Modern*, and Sir Charles Stanford supplied Airedale for the 1904 edition. Nowadays the hymn is generally sung to one of two equally majestic Welsh tunes – Hyfrydol by Rowland Huw Prichard (1811–87), a loom-tender's assistant in the Welsh Flannel Manufacturing Company's mills at Holywell, and Blaenwern by William Penfro Rowlands (1860–1937).

Love divine, all loves excelling,
  Joy of heav'n, to earth come down,
Fix in us thy humble dwelling,
  All thy faithful mercies crown.
Jesu, thou art all compassion,
  Pure unbounded love thou art;
Visit us with thy salvation,
  Enter every trembling heart.

2 Breathe, O breathe thy loving spirit
    Into every troubled breast!
  Let us all in thee inherit,
    Let us find that second rest.
  Take away our bent to sinning,
    Alpha and Omega be;
  End of faith, as its beginning.
    Set our hearts at liberty.

3 Come, almighty to deliver,
    Let us all thy life receive;
  Suddenly return, and never,
    Never more thy temples leave.
  Thee we would be always blessing,
    Serve thee as thy hosts above,
  Pray, and praise thee, without ceasing,
    Glory in thy perfect love.

4 Finish then thy new creation,
    Pure and sinless let us be;
  Let us see thy great salvation,
    Perfectly restored in thee:
  Changed from glory into glory,
    Till in heav'n we take our place,
  Till we cast our crowns before thee,
    Lost in wonder, love, and praise!

84 MAKE ME A CHANNEL OF YOUR PEACE

Most of the modern hymns which have achieved widespread popularity in recent years have come from the Evangelical wing of Protestantism. This simple but highly effective adaptation of the prayer traditionally attributed to St Francis of Assisi comes from the pen of a South African-born Catholic and has been popularized throughout the English-speaking world by the Franciscan Communications Center in Los Angeles, California.

The author, Johann Sebastian von Tempelhoff, who writes under the name Sebastian Temple, was born in Pretoria in 1928. He started writing books at the age of nineteen, and lived in England for seven years before taking up residence in the United States. He now lives in California and has twelve albums of songs and hymns to his credit.

Sebastian Temple wrote the verses overleaf in response to a request for a collection of songs for the Franciscan Third Order's church in downtown Los Angeles. In a letter to me he says:

I wrote so easily and so prolifically that I took for granted that I could write music to the peace prayer of St Francis. The album's other twelve songs fell out of my lips and on to a tape recorder very easily and I wrote them in two days. The third day was left for the peace prayer. Though inspirations for all came easily to me, its strange form drove me crazy. I could not come up with anything that sounded like music to my ears. I tried for a whole morning but nothing came. Finally, I was disgusted, looked at the little statue of St Francis on my shelf and said angrily, 'Well, if you want to write it, YOU do it. I can't.' I got up, went to the kitchen, made a cup of tea and drank it. When I returned to the guitar, I picked it up, had the tape running, and the song fell out of my mouth as it was recorded a few days later.

Modern scholarship tends to cast doubt on the traditional view that the well-known prayer on which the hymn is based was, in fact, written by St Francis (on whom see notes to hymn No. 3). It is rather thought to have been the work of a later Franciscan, Jacopo di Toddi. But whoever the author was, it is a fine prayer. The traditional English version on which Temple based his hymn goes as follows:

Lord, make me an instrument of your peace. Where there is hatred, let me sow love. Where there is injury, pardon. Where there is doubt, faith. Where there is despair, hope. Where there is darkness, light. Where there is sadness, joy.

O Divine Master, grant that I may not so much seek to be consoled, as to console; to be understood as to understand; to be loved, as to love; for it is in giving that we receive, it is in pardoning that we are pardoned and it is in dying that we are born to eternal life.

It is interesting that in the opening line of his hymn Sebastian Temple makes use of an image which was particularly popular with Martin Luther, who often spoke of humans as channels passing on to our neighbours the love that we receive from God. This kind of imagery finds its fullest expression in the writings of the early twentieth-century Swedish Lutheran Anders Nygren, who says in his book *Agape and Eros*:

All that a Christian possesses he has received from God, and all that he possesses he passes on in love to his neighbour. He has nothing of his own to give. He is merely the tube, the channel, through which God's love flows.

Make me a channel of your peace.
Where there is hatred, let me bring you love.
Where there is injury, your pardon, Lord.
And where there's doubt, true faith in you.

2   Make me a channel of your peace.
Where there's despair in life, let me bring hope.
Where there is darkness, only light.
And where there's sadness, ever joy.

3   Oh, Master grant that I may never seek
So much to be consoled as to console,
To be understood as to understand,
To be loved, as to love with all my soul.

4   Make me a channel of your peace.
It is in pardoning that we are pardoned,
In giving to all men that we receive,
And in dying that we're born to eternal life.

85 MINE EYES HAVE SEEN THE GLORY OF THE COMING OF THE LORD

General William Booth of the Salvation Army wasn't the only person determined that the Devil shouldn't have all the best tunes. This hymn was written by an American lady who heard some soldiers singing 'John Brown's body lies a-mouldering in the grave' and felt that such a good tune deserved rather more uplifting words. Written at the height of the American Civil War, it has become a virtually indispensable feature of national parades and presidential inaugurations in the United States.

The author, Julia Ward Howe (1819–1910), came of an upper-class New York family and was a Unitarian lay preacher. Her husband, a Bostonian doctor who worked principally with the mentally handicapped, was an ardent advocate of the abolition of slavery. He helped an abolitionist by the name of John Brown on whom the popular soldiers' song was based, a religious zealot who had planned to set up a stronghold of liberated slaves in the mountains before being hanged for murder and treason at Charlestown, Virginia.

One afternoon in November 1861 the Howes went out to visit the Unionist army of Potomac in action near Washington. They spent the night under canvas with the troops who were singing their song about John Brown. A friend, James Freeman Clarke, who had left the Unitarians to found his own Church of the Disciples in Boston, suggested to Julia that she should write new words for the tune. That evening she thought about it and the following morning she got up early from her camp-bed and lit a candle. 'In the dimness with the old stump of a pen which I remembered to have used the day before, I scrawled the verses almost without looking at the paper.' An early draft of the hymn, still extant, was written out on the writing-paper of the Sanitary Commission in Washington, of which her husband was a member.

In fact, in turning 'John Brown's body' into a hymn Julia Howe was restoring the tune's original purpose, as it seems to have started life in Charleston, South Carolina, in the mid 1850s as the melody of a Methodist hymn, 'Say, brother, will you meet us'. For her own hymn she drew on several powerful biblical images: the trampling of the grapes of wrath comes from Isaiah 63:3; the crushing of the serpent from Genesis 3:15; and the idea of Christ being born in the beauty of the lilies, from the Song of Solomon.

'Mine eyes have seen the glory' was first published in the *Atlantic Monthly* for February 1862, where it was entitled 'The Battle Hymn of the Republic'. For all rights in the piece, Julia Howe was paid just four dollars. Her hymn became one of the major marching songs of the North in the American Civil War. When it is sung nowadays, the third line of the fifth verse is often changed to 'As he died to make men holy, let us live to make men free'.

Although it is almost unthinkable to sing 'Mine eyes have seen the glory' to anything other than the tune of John Brown's Body, two other melodies have been composed specially for it by leading British church musicians. Vision by Sir Walford Davies (1869–1941) and Battle Song by Martin Shaw (1875–1958) both first appeared in 1915.

The Battle Hymn of the Republic

Mine eyes have seen the glory of the coming of the Lord;
He is trampling out the vintage where the grapes of wrath are stored;
He hath loosed the fateful lightning of his terrible swift sword:
His truth is marching on

2 I have seen him in the watchfires of a hundred circling camps;
They have builded him an altar in the evening dews and damps;
I have read his righteous sentence in the dim and flaring lamps;
His day is marching on.

3 I have read a fiery gospel, writ in burnished rows of steel;
As ye deal with my contemners, so with you my grace shall deal:
Let the hero born of woman crush the serpent with his heel;
Our God is marching on.

4 He has sounded forth the trumpet that shall never call retreat;
He is sifting out the hearts of men before his judgment seat;
O be swift, my soul, to answer him, be jubilant, my feet:
Our God is marching on.

5 In the beauty of the lilies Christ was born across the sea
With a glory in his bosom that transfigures you and me;
As he died to make men holy, let us die to make men free:
Our God is marching on.

6 He is coming like the glory of the morning on the wave,
He is wisdom to the mighty, he is succour to the brave;
So the world shall be his footstool, and the soul of time his slave:
Our God is marching on.

86 MORNING HAS BROKEN

Like John Newton's 'Amazing grace' (No. 10), this hymn achieved considerable fame as a pop song in the early 1970s. Recorded by Cat Stevens, it was in the Top Ten in both Britain and the United States for several weeks. Now, thankfully, it has been restored to the use for which it was originally written and is a popular hymn both in church services and school assemblies.

'Morning has broken' was written by Eleanor Farjeon (1881–1965) in the early 1920s at the suggestion of Percy Dearmer (on whom see notes to hymn No. 63), the editor of *Songs of Praise*. Altogether Miss Farjeon wrote four hymns for the new hymnal, the others being 'More lovely than the noonday rest', 'Lord, thou who gav'st me all I have' and the harvest hymn 'Fields of corn, give up your eyes'. She was paid three guineas for each of them.

The verses overleaf were written specifically to fit the Gaelic tune Bunessan which had been noted down in the 1880s from the singing of a wandering Highland singer and first published in *Songs and Hymns of the Gael* in 1888. In 1917 the tune was set to the carol 'Child in the manger' by the Scots poet Mary Macdonald (1789–1872) and named after her birthplace on the Isle of Mull. Her carol can be found set to the tune in the current edition of the *Church Hymnary*. Dearmer wanted to find alternative words for Bunessan and so he approached Miss Farjeon, suggesting to her the theme of thanksgiving for each new day.

Eleanor Farjeon, chiefly remembered today as a children's writer, was in fact an author and poet of wide range and considerable accomplishment. She was born in London; her father was a novelist, playwright and journalist of Jewish descent and her mother came from an American theatrical family. Eleanor led a Bohemian life, and had a strong romantic attachment to the poet Edward Thomas before settling down with George Earle. She had a strong interest in religion throughout her life and flirted with both spiritualism and theories of reincarnation. She finally found her spiritual home in the Roman Catholic Church, into which she was received on her seventieth birthday. She underwent instruction at Farm Street and was much influenced by the thirteenth-century mystical work *The Cloud of Unknowing*, as well as by the writings of St Augustine and the spiritual exercises of St Ignatius Loyola.

In her biography of Eleanor Farjeon, published in 1986, which takes its title from the first line of this hymn, her daughter Annabel writes that 'Catholicism satisfied the ideal longings of this enthusiastic convert, satisfied her innocence and her ripeness with the promise of bliss in a perfect hereafter'. She herself wrote that her coming to Catholicism was less a conversion than 'a progression to a form of faith towards which my own sense of a spiritual life has been moving for the last thirty or forty years. One has to be "converted" from one faith to another – and I've never had another to be converted from. I have had an always increasing sense of the immortal spirit from a source I could only think of as God.'

'Morning has broken' is always sung to the tune Bunessan, for which it was written.

Thanks for a Day

Morning has broken,
Like the first morning.
Blackbird has spoken
Like the first bird.
Praise for the singing!
Praise for the morning!
Praise for them, springing
Fresh from the word!

2   Sweet the rain's new fall
Sunlit from heaven,
Like the first dewfall
On the first grass.
Praise for the sweetness
Of the wet garden,
Sprung in completeness
Where his feet pass.

3   Mine is the sunlight!
Mine is the morning
Born of the one light
Eden saw play!
Praise with elation,
Praise every morning,
God's re-creation
Of the new day!

From The Children's Bells *by Eleanor Farjeon, published by Oxford University Press.*
Reproduced by permission of David Higham Associates Ltd

87 MY GOD! HOW WONDERFUL THOU ART

Until a very late stage in the preparation of this book, this particular 'slot' was occupied by Edward Caswall's hymn, 'My God, I love thee not because I hope for Heaven thereby'. But the more I contemplated its words and overall tone the less I liked them, and I decided to include instead this simple yet profound hymn by Frederick William Faber (1814–63).

It is, indeed, right and proper that Faber should figure in an anthology of the best-loved hymns in the English language. His 'Faith of our fathers! living still', although hardly known in Great Britain, is immensely popular in the United States. For the benefit of British readers, let me quote its first verse:

> Faith of our fathers! living still
> In spite of dungeon, fire and sword;
> Oh how our hearts beat high with joy
> Whene'er we hear that glorious word,
> Faith of our fathers! Holy Faith!
> We will be true to thee till death.

Most modern hymn-books on both sides of the Atlantic include Faber's magnificent 'Souls of men, why will ye scatter', with its well-known third verse which is sometimes taken as the opening of the hymn:

> There's a wideness in God's mercy
> Like the wideness of the sea;
> There's a kindness in his justice
> Which is more than liberty.

Faber was born at Calverley, Yorkshire, where his grandfather was vicar. Educated at Shrewsbury and Harrow Schools and Balliol

College, Oxford, he moved from extreme Evangelicalism to High Anglicanism under the influence of the Oxford Movement. He was ordained into the Church of England in 1837 and became rector of Elton in Huntingdonshire. In 1845 he followed his great friend and mentor, John Henry Newman, into the Roman Catholic Church and set up a small religious community in Birmingham with the name 'Brothers of the Will of God', later shortened to the 'Wilfridians' because Faber took for himself the name Brother Wilfrid. In 1848 he joined Newman's Oratory in Birmingham and the following year he established a branch of the Oratory in London. Faber remained as superior of Brompton Oratory, as it came to be known, for the rest of his life.

Faber's considerable literary output included a 42-volume *Lives of the Saints*, books on meditation and theology, and 150 hymns. He was keen to encourage the practice of hymn-singing in the Catholic Church in Britain and hoped that his work might have the same effect that the *Olney Hymns* had had on Evangelical Anglicanism. Some of his hymns come close to doggerel, but others which no longer appear in hymnals deserve to be brought back into use. Perhaps the best are 'Hark! hark! my soul! angelic songs are swelling', 'O Saviour, bless us as we go' and the Good Friday hymn, 'O come and mourn with me awhile'.

'My God, how wonderful thou art' is almost certainly the most widely sung of Faber's hymns nowadays. It first appeared in his collection *Jesus and Mary*, which was published in 1849. In modern hymnals the first line of the third verse is generally changed to 'How wonderful, how beautiful', and the sixth and eighth verses are omitted.

The hymn is invariably sung to the melody Westminster by James Turle (1802–82), which first appeared in Novello's *The Psalmist* in 1836. Turle was organist and master of the choristers at Westminster Abbey from 1831 to 1875.

Our Heavenly Father

My God! how wonderful thou art,
   Thy Majesty how bright,
How beautiful thy mercy-seat
   In depths of burning light!

2   How dread are thine eternal years,
      O everlasting Lord!
   By prostrate spirits day and night
      Incessantly adored!

3   How beautiful, how beautiful
      The sight of thee must be,
   Thine endless wisdom, boundless power
      And aweful purity!

4   O how I fear thee, living God!
      With deepest, tenderest fears,
   And worship thee with trembling hope
      And penitential tears.

5   Yet I may love thee, living God!
      Almighty as thou art,
   For thou hast stooped to ask of me
      The love of my poor heart.

6   O then this worse than worthless heart
      In pity deign to take
   And make it love thee, for thyself
      And for thy glory's sake.

7   No earthly father loves like thee,
      No mother half so mild
   Bears and forbears, as thou hast done,
      With me, thy sinful child.

8   Only to sit and think of God,
      O, what a joy it is!
   To think the thought, to breathe the Name,
      Earth has no higher bliss!

9   Father of Jesus, love's reward,
      What rapture will it be,
   Prostrate before thy throne to lie,
      And gaze, and gaze on thee!

88 MY SONG IS LOVE UNKNOWN

The rediscovery in the twentieth century of verses by seventeenth-century writers has produced a rich harvest of hymns. We have already come across George Herbert's 'King of Glory, King of Peace' (No. 73) and 'Let all the world in ev'ry corner sing' (No. 77). This fine poem, which is now an extremely popular hymn much in demand at weddings and on other occasions, was written more than 300 years ago but has only been widely sung in church in the last fifty years or so. Its enormous popularity in our own times must be very largely attributable to the haunting tune which John Ireland composed for it shortly after the First World War.

The author of 'My song is love unknown' was Samuel Crossman (1624–83), an Anglican clergyman who spent most of his life attached to Bristol Cathedral. Born in Bradfield Monachorum in Suffolk, he was educated at Cambridge University, and after a long period as prebendary of Bristol Cathedral, he became Dean just a few months before his death. He is buried in the south aisle of the cathedral.

The verses printed below first appeared in a small pamphlet containing nine poems by Crossman that was published in 1664 with the title *The Young Man's Meditation, or some few Sacred Poems upon Select Subjects and Scriptures*. It is possible that they were sung as a hymn in the author's own lifetime, set to a tune composed by Henry Lawes (1596–1662) for Psalm 47, but this is unlikely. 'My song is love unknown' does not appear in any hymn collections published during the eighteenth or the first half of the nineteenth century. It is first found as a hymn in the *Anglican Hymn Book* of 1868, where it was set to Lawes's tune, and then in the *Congregational Hymnal* of 1887. It subsequently appeared in the first edition of the *Public School Hymn Book* in 1903 and has been a firm favourite in school chapels ever since.

It was not, however, until Crossman's words were married with the tune Love Unknown by John Ireland (1879–1962) that the hymn achieved widespread popularity. Geoffrey Shaw, the music editor of *Songs of Praise*, asked Ireland if he could supply a tune for Crossman's verses which Percy Dearmer wished to include in the new hymnal. The story goes that Ireland obliged almost immediately and seemingly without effort, writing out the melody on a scrap of paper in less than a quarter of an hour. His tune first appeared in the 1919 edition of the *Public School Hymn Book* and then in the first edition of *Songs of Praise* (1925).

John Ireland was born at Bowden in Cheshire. His father, Alexander Ireland, was editor of the *Manchester Examiner* and a friend of Thomas Carlyle. John was educated at Leeds Grammar School and at the Royal College of Music where he studied under Sir Charles Stanford. He was successively organist of All Saints', Tufnell Park; St Jude's, Upper Chelsea; Holy Trinity, Sloane Square; and St Luke's, Upper Chelsea, where he remained for twenty-two years. Love Unknown, as it is called, is the only one of his hymn tunes which is regularly used today.

Several of Samuel Crossman's other poems became hymns, but none has survived in modern hymnals. They include 'My life's a shade, my days', 'Sweet place, sweet place, alone' and 'Farewell, poor world, I must be gone'.

This is perhaps an appropriate place to mention some of the other Tudor and Stuart poets whose verses have successfully been turned into hymns in the twentieth century. The *English Hymnal* resurrected verses by two of the best-known writers of that era, Edmund Spenser (1552–99) and John Donne (1573–1631), to make the hymns 'Most glorious Lord of life, that on this day' and 'Wilt thou forgive that sin, by man begun'. The former still appears in the *New English Hymnal*, though the latter has sadly been dropped. *Songs of Praise* was responsible for the rediscovery of 'In this world, the Isle of Dreams' by Robert Herrick (1591–1674), and of that masterpiece by Henry Vaughan (1622–95) which I am delighted to be able to quote in full below as an extra entry in this book. It even comes at the right place alphabetically in the collection!

My soul, there is a country
   Far beyond the stars,
Where stands a winged sentry
   All skilful in the wars.

There, above noise and danger,
   Sweet Peace sits crowned with smiles,
And One born in a manger
   Commands the beauteous files.

He is thy gracious Friend,
   And – O my soul, awake –
Did in pure love descend
   To die here for thy sake.

If thou canst get but thither,
   There grows the flower of peace,
The Rose that cannot wither,
   Thy fortress and thy ease.

Leave then thy foolish ranges,
   Or none can thee secure,
But One, who never changes,
   Thy God, thy Life, thy Cure.

My song is love unknown,
  My Saviour's love to me,
Love to the loveless shown,
  That they might lovely be.
    O, who am I,
      That for my sake
      My Lord should take
    Frail flesh, and die?

2 He came from his blest throne,
    Salvation to bestow:
But men made strange, and none
    The longed-for Christ would know.
      But O, my Friend,
        My Friend indeed,
        Who at my need
      His life did spend!

3 Sometimes they strew his way,
    And his sweet praises sing;
Resounding all the day
    Hosannas to their King.
      Then 'Crucify!'
        Is all their breath,
        And for his death
      They thirst and cry.

4 Why, what hath my Lord done?
    What makes this rage and spite?
He made the lame to run,
    He gave the blind their sight.
      Sweet injuries!
        Yet they at these
        Themselves displease,
    And 'gainst him rise.

5 They rise, and needs will have
   My dear Lord made away;
A murderer they save,
   The Prince of Life they slay.
      Yet cheerful he
         To suffering goes,
         That he his foes
      From thence might free.

6 In life no house, no home,
   My Lord on earth might have;
In death no friendly tomb,
   But what a stranger gave.
      What may I say?
         Heav'n was his home;
         But mine the tomb
      Wherein he lay.

7 Here might I stay and sing,
   No story so divine;
Never was love, dear King,
   Never was grief like thine!
      This is my Friend,
         In whose sweet praise
         I all my days
      Could gladly spend.

89 NEARER, MY GOD, TO THEE

Like 'Mine eyes have seen the glory of the coming of the Lord' (No. 85), this hymn comes from the pen of a Unitarian lady. Mrs Sarah Adams, née Flower (1805–48), was born in Harlow, Essex, the daughter of a Radical journalist who was imprisoned for criticizing the politics of the Bishop of Llandaff. She had a distinguished literary career and was a close friend of Robert Browning.

'Nearer, my God, to Thee' was one of thirteen hymns which Sarah Adams contributed to a Unitarian collection published in 1841 for use in the South Place Religious Society in Finsbury, London. It is based on the story of Jacob's dream at Bethel recounted in Genesis 28:10–22. When the hymn first appeared there were complaints that it did not mention Christ and that it was not suitable for public worship in Trinitarian churches. Several editors composed an additional verse before including it in their hymnals, and William Walsham How, the author of 'For all Thy saints who from their labours rest' (No. 38) re-wrote Mrs Adams's verses with the purpose of 'expressing more definitely Christian faith'. It was, however, in its original form that the hymn achieved widespread popularity in the latter part of the nineteenth century.

Perhaps the best-known tune for the hymn, at least in Britain, is Horbury, which John Bacchus Dykes (1823–76) wrote for the first edition of *Hymns Ancient and Modern* in 1861. He named it after the town in Yorkshire which he had visited two years earlier to make his first confession. In the United States the tune most often used has been Bethany, which was composed in 1856 by Dr Lowell Mason (1792–1872), a bank clerk from Savannah who founded the Boston Academy of Music. Other melodies specially composed for this hymn include *Propior Deo* by Sir Arthur Sullivan (1842–1900), Liverpool by John Roberts (1822–77), and Nenthorn by Thomas Leger-wood Hately (1815–67).

The great question about 'Nearer, my God, to Thee' is, of course, whether it was the hymn that the band struck up on the *Titanic* as that ill-fated liner sank after hitting an iceberg on 14 April 1912. Mrs Eva Hart, one of the few survivors of the disaster still living, is adamant that it was. 'I am as certain about that as I am sitting here,' she is quoted in *The Times* of 13 April 1987 as saying. 'Whether it was the last hymn, I don't know.'

Others, however, are sceptical about the tradition that it was Mrs Adams's hymn that was played as the ship went down. They base their doubts on the fact that contemporary press reports quoted the ship's radio operator, Harold Bride, a trained choirboy who survived the disaster, as saying that what he heard being played from the sinking vessel as he was in the sea waiting to be rescued was the hymn tune Autumn. There are, in fact, three different tunes with this name to be found in early twentieth-century hymn-books, set respectively to Robert Bridges's 'Joy and triumph everlasting', George Horne's 'See the leaves around us falling' and William Wal-sham How's 'The year is swiftly waning'. If it was one of these that the band played, the last is the most likely candidate. The lines which close its first verse would certainly have been appropriate to the melancholy occasion:

> And life, brief life, is speeding;
> The end is nearing fast.

Sir Ronald Johnson, who has made a special study of the whole question of the *Titanic* hymn and with whom I have corresponded at some length on the subject, believes that the tune heard by Bride and wrongly transcribed by reporters was, in fact, Aughton, which ac-companied W. B. Bradbury's hymn, 'He leadeth me! O blessed thought'. Its closing verse would certainly have been apt:

> And when my task on earth is done
> When by Thy grace the victory's won
> E'en death's cold wave I will not flee
> Since God through Jordan leadeth me.

Nearer, my God, to Thee,
  Nearer to Thee!
E'en though it be a cross
  That raiseth me,
Still all my song would be,
'Nearer, my God, to Thee,
  Nearer to Thee!'

2 Though, like the wanderer,
    The sun gone down,
  Darkness be over me,
    My rest a stone,
  Yet in my dreams I'd be
  Nearer, my God, to Thee,
    Nearer to Thee!

3 There let the way appear
    Steps unto heaven,
  All that Thou send'st to me
    In mercy given,
  Angels to beckon me
  Nearer, my God, to Thee,
    Nearer to Thee!

4 Then, with my waking thoughts
    Bright with Thy praise,
  Out of my stony griefs
    Bethel I'll raise,
  So by my woes to be
  Nearer, my God, to Thee,
    Nearer to Thee!

5   Or if on joyful wing
        Cleaving the sky,
    Sun, moon, and stars forgot,
        Upwards I fly,
    Still all my song shall be,
    'Nearer, my God, to Thee,
        Nearer to Thee!'

90 NEW EVERY MORNING IS THE LOVE

This inspiring morning hymn is the work of John Keble (1792–1866; see notes to hymn No. 18). It was written in 1822 while he was a tutor at Oriel College, Oxford, and published five years later in his book, *The Christian Year*.

Like the other Keble hymn in this collection, 'Bless'd are the pure in heart' (No. 18), 'New every morning' is a small section of a much longer poem. It is made up of the sixth, seventh, eighth, ninth, thirteenth, fourteenth and sixteenth verses of a poem entitled 'Morning' which appeared at the beginning of *The Christian Year* with the text: 'His compassions fail not. They are new every morning' (Lamentations 3:22–3). The first five verses of the poem are as follows:

> Hues of the rich unfolding morn,
> That, ere the glorious sun be born,
> By some soft touch invisible
> Around his path are taught to swell;

> Thou rustling breeze so fresh and gay,
> That dancest forth at opening day,
> And brushing by with joyous wing,
> Wakenest each little leaf to sing;

> Ye fragrant clouds of dewy steam,
> By which deep grove and tangled stream
> Pay, for soft rains in season given,
> Their tribute to the genial heaven;

> Why waste your treasures of delight
> Upon our thankless, joyless sight;
> Who day by day to sin awake,
> Seldom of heaven and you partake?

Oh! timely happy, timely wise,
Hearts that with rising morn arise!
Eyes that the beam celestial view,
Which evermore makes all things new!

Several nineteenth- and early twentieth-century hymnals included the above stanzas, or a selection of them, as a separate hymn in addition to 'New every morning'. Others made a hymn by starting with the tenth verse of the original poem in *The Christian Year*:

As for some dear familiar strain
Untir'd we ask, and ask again,
Ever, in its melodious store,
Finding a spell unheard before.

The tune to which 'New every morning' is almost always sung, known variously as Melcombe, Granton and St Philip's, is by Samuel Webbe (1740–1816), a cabinet-maker who became organist at the Sardinian Chapel in London. It first appeared in 1792 in an essay Webbe wrote on church plainchant, where it was written in plain-song notation and set to the words 'O Salutaris Hostia'.

Morning

New every morning is the love
Our wakening and uprising prove;
Through sleep and darkness safely brought,
Restored to life, and power, and thought.

2   New mercies, each returning day,
Hover around us while we pray;
New perils past, new sins forgiven,
New thoughts of God, new hopes of heaven.

3   If on our daily course our mind
Be set to hallow all we find,
New treasures still, of countless price,
God will provide for sacrifice.

4   Old friends, old scenes will lovelier be,
As more of heaven in each we see:
Some softening gleam of love and prayer
Shall dawn on every cross and care.

5   We need not bid, for cloister'd cell,
Our neighbour and our words farewell,
Nor strive to find ourselves too high
For sinful man beneath the sky:

6   The trivial round, the common task,
Will furnish all we ought to ask;
Room to deny ourselves – a road
To bring us, daily, nearer God.

7   Only, O Lord, in thy dear love
Fit us for perfect rest above;
And help us, this and every day,
To live more nearly as we pray.

91 NOW THANK WE ALL OUR GOD

This great hymn of rejoicing, so popular at weddings and other festive occasions, is translated from a German grace which was written around 350 years ago and designed to be sung after meals in devout Lutheran households in the dark days of the Thirty Years War. It is based on Ecclesiasticus 50:22–3, 'Now bless the God of all, who in every way does great things; who exalts our days from birth, and deals with us according to his mercy. May he give us gladness of heart, and grant that peace may be in our days in Israel, as in the days of old.'

The author, Martin Rinkart (1586–1649), was the son of a copper-smith. Educated at the University of Leipzig, he became precentor at the church in Martin Luther's home town of Eisleben. In 1617 he returned to his own native Saxon village of Eilenburg as pastor. For the next thirty years rival armies from across Europe roamed through the parish, pillaging and plundering everything in their way. To make matters worse, the village was struck with plague in 1637. More than 8,000 of the inhabitants perished and Rinkart himself buried 4,000 of his parishioners, some days conducting mass funerals for as many as fifty of the dead.

In the midst of this terrible plague and the severe famine that came in its wake, the Swedish forces that were occupying Eilenburg demanded a tribute of 30,000 thalers from the stricken inhabitants. Rinkart appealed to the Swedes and managed to have the sum reduced to 2,000 thalers. He also appealed to the Almighty, telling his parishioners, 'We can find no mercy with men; let us take refuge with God.'

The story is often told that it was in these grim circumstances that Rinkart wrote his great hymn of thanksgiving and praise. However, the exact date of its composition is uncertain. Some historians suggest that it was written as early as 1630, while others maintain that Rinkart composed it in 1648, having heard of the impending peace settlement at Westphalia that was to end three decades of fighting in Germany. The latter view has now been almost wholly discredited. What is certain is that the hymn was widely sung when the Treaty of Westphalia was signed in 1648. Since then it has been a kind of German Te Deum, sung on occasions of national thanksgiving.

It has had something of the same status in Great Britain over the last 130 years, thanks to the translation that is printed opposite which was made in 1858 by Catherine Winkworth (1829–78). It first appeared in her *Lyra Germanica*, published in 1855. In his *Dictionary of Hymnology*, John Julian lists eleven other translations of Rinkart's 'Nun danket alle Gott', but none approached Miss Winkworth's in quality or came anywhere near it in popularity. Among the other hymns which she translated from the German and which are still widely sung today is *Praise to the Lord! the Almighty, the King of creation* (No. 110 – see notes to this hymn for details of her life).

The tune *Nun Danket* which has always been associated with this hymn is often ascribed to Johann Crüger (1598–1662), cantor of St Nicholas' Church in Berlin and composer of numerous hymn tunes. It was in a book edited by Crüger that the tune and the hymn made their first appearance in 1647. But there is no direct evidence that he composed the tune and some have suggested that the melody came to Rinkart when he was writing the words. This is quite possible as he was himself a noted musician.

Grace

Now thank we all our God,
With heart and hands and voices,
Who wondrous things hath done
In whom his world rejoices;
Who from our mother's arms
Hath blessed us on our way
With countless gifts of love,
And still is ours to-day.

2   O may this bounteous God
Through all our life be near us,
With ever joyful hearts
And blessèd peace to cheer us;
And keep us in his grace,
And guide us when perplexed,
And free us from all ills
In this world and the next.

3   All praise and thanks to God
The Father now be given,
The Son, and him who reigns
With them in highest heaven,
The one eternal God,
Whom earth and heaven adore,
For thus it was, is now,
And shall be evermore.

92 O COME, O COME, EMMANUEL

This Advent hymn is based on the Latin antiphons which were sung in the early Church during the week leading up to Christmas Day. The origin of these short verses is uncertain, although they probably date from the sixth or seventh century and were certainly in use at Rome before the ninth century. There were originally seven antiphons and in monastic institutions they were chanted at the evening service of Vespers by the great officers of the convent, known as obedientiaries, both before and after the Magnificat.

Originally the antiphons were never sung together, but one on each of the seven days leading up to Christmas. However, sometime in the twelfth century five of them were put together to form the verses of a single hymn beginning '*Veni, veni, Emmanuel*', with the refrain '*Gaude, gaude, Emmanuel, nascetur pro te, Israel*' at the end of each verse.

In their original Latin form, as in translation, the verses all began with a long drawn out 'O' to express longing for the Saviour. Each described Christ in a different way – as *Emmanuel* ('God with us'), as in Isaiah, 7:14; *Jesse Virgula* ('the Root of Jesse'), as in Isaiah 11:10; *Oriens* ('the Dayspring'), as in Malachi 4:2; *Clavis Davidica* ('the Key of David'), as in Isaiah 22:22; and *Adonai* ('the Lord of Might'), as in Exodus 3:15.

The first translation of the Latin antiphons into English was made in 1836 by John Henry Newman (1801–90; see notes to hymn No. 37) for his *Tracts for the Times*. In 1851 John Mason Neale (1818–66; see notes to hymn No. 23) translated the five verses which had been made into a hymn. He produced a hymn which began 'Draw nigh, draw nigh, Emmanuel', and which first appeared in his book *Mediaeval Hymns*. The following year he revised his translation to produce the version which is printed overleaf. It was first published in his *Hymnal Noted*. Several other translations have been made of the Latin hymn, but none is as faithful to the original or as fresh as Neale's.

This hymn undoubtedly derives much of its powerful sense of longing from the tune, *Veni Immanuel,* which has accompanied Neale's revised translation since 1854. It seems to have its source in a melody from a French missal in the National Library of Portugal in Lisbon, which itself was an adaptation of a plainsong Kyrie. Some authorities say that Neale himself copied the tune from the missal, others that it was copied by Bishop Jenner during a visit to Lisbon in 1853. The music was arranged by Thomas Helmore (1811–90), an Anglican clergyman who was one of the pioneers in the revival of the use of Gregorian chant in the services of the Church of England.

Veni, veni, Emmanuel

O come, O come, Emmanuel,
And ransom captive Israel,
That mourns in lonely exile here,
Until the Son of God appear:

> *Rejoice! Rejoice! Emmanuel*
> *Shall come to thee, O Israel.*

2   O come, thou Rod of Jesse, free
Thine own from Satan's tyranny;
From depths of hell thy people save,
And give them vict'ry o'er the grave:

3   O come, thou Day-spring, come and cheer
Our spirits by thine advent here;
Disperse the gloomy clouds of night,
And death's dark shadows put to flight:

4   O come, thou Key of David, come,
And open wide our heav'nly home;
Make safe the way that leads on high,
And close the path to misery:

5   O come, O come, thou Lord of Might,
Who to thy tribes, on Sinai's height,
In ancient times didst give the law
In cloud, and majesty, and awe:

93 O FOR A CLOSER WALK WITH GOD

Like 'God moves in a mysterious way', this hymn was written by William Cowper (1731–1800; see notes to hymn No. 45) during one of the comparatively rare periods of sanity that punctuated his almost continuous mental torment.

He wrote it on 9 December 1769 at a time when he was considerably agitated about the illness of his housekeeper, Mrs Unwin, on whom he relied almost totally to keep him going. He was deeply worried at what might happen to him in the event of her death. He attached to the hymn the biblical quotation, 'Enoch walked with God, and he was not, for God took him' (Genesis 5:24).

In a letter to a friend the following day, he wrote of these verses: 'I began to compose them yesterday morning, but fell asleep at the end of the first two lines. When I awakened again the third and fourth were whispered to my heart, in a way which I have often experienced.' The hymn was first published in 1776 in the form printed overleaf and appeared thus in the *Olney Hymns* of 1779. The second and third verses, with their note of deep sadness and sense of loss, are often omitted from modern hymn-books, giving a rather different feel to the hymn from that conveyed in Cowper's original composition.

It was shortly after writing these verses that Cowper composed his hymn 'There is a fountain filled with blood', which is full of rather morbid thoughts on sin and depravity. Its first two verses, which are generally toned down in modern hymnals, originally ran:

> There is a fountain filled with blood
> Drawn from Immanuel's veins;
> And sinners, plunged beneath that flood,
> Lose all their guilty stains.

The dying thief rejoiced to see
That fountain in his day;
And there have I, as vile as he,
Washed all my sins away.

'O for a closer walk with God' is generally sung to one of two Scottish tunes: Caithness, a melody from the 1635 Scottish Psalter, or Stracathro, written in the late 1840s by Charles Hutcheson (1792–1860) to be sung in the church where he worshipped, St George's in Glasgow. This latter tune was named after a village on the banks of the North Esk where a fellow member of the congregation, Sir James Campbell, had just bought a property. Hutcheson gave it the name Stracathro as a tribute to Campbell, a former Lord Provost of Glasgow. The tune fell out of use during the next fifty years but was revived in the twentieth century thanks to the somewhat unlikely combination of the *Public School Hymn Book,* which included in its 1919 edition a version harmonized by Geoffrey Shaw, and the Glasgow Orpheus Choir, whose conductor, Sir Hugh Roberton, arranged a *faux-bourdon* setting (i.e. alternate verses passing to the tenor) of Stracathro for Cowper's hymn.

Walking with God

O for a closer walk with God,
  A calm and heavenly frame,
A light to shine upon the road
  That leads me to the Lamb!

2 Where is the blessedness I knew
    When first I saw the Lord?
  Where is the soul-refreshing view
    Of Jesus and his word?

3 What peaceful hours I once enjoy'd!
    How sweet their mem'ry still!
  But they have left an aching void
    The world can never fill.

4 Return, O holy Dove, return,
    Sweet messenger of rest;
  I hate the sins that made thee mourn
    And drove thee from my breast.

5 The dearest idol I have known,
    Whate'er that idol be,
  Help me to tear it from thy throne,
    And worship only thee.

6 So shall my walk be close with God,
    Calm and serene my frame;
  So purer light shall mark the road
    That leads me to the Lamb.

94 O FOR A THOUSAND TONGUES TO SING

Arguably the greatest and certainly the most popular of the many hymns by Charles Wesley (1707–88; see notes to hymn No. 11), this has had pride of place as the first entry in every edition of the Methodist hymn-book.

It is, in fact, only part of a longer hymn which Wesley wrote in May 1739 to celebrate the first anniversary of his conversion to Evangelical Christianity. As first published in his *Hymns and Sacred Poems* the following year, it ran to eighteen stanzas, beginning:

> Glory to God, and praise and love
> Be ever, ever given;
> By saints below, and saints above,
> The Church in earth and heaven.

> On this glad day the glorious Sun
> Of Righteousness arose,
> On my benighted soul he shone,
> And filled it with repose.

> Sudden expired the legal strife,
> 'Twas then I ceased to grieve,
> My second, real, living life
> I then began to live.

For the *Wesleyan Hymn Book* of 1780 John Wesley selected the ten stanzas printed here, beginning with the seventh verse of his brother's original hymn which is thought to have been inspired by a remark made by Peter Bohler, a Moravian preacher, that: 'Had I a thousand tongues, I would praise Him with them all.' The phrase 'cancelled sin' in the first line of the fourth verse has offended a number of hymnal editors and it has been variously changed to 'death and sin' and 'reigning sin', but most modern hymn-books are happy to stick to the original. Several verses are omitted nowadays, including the ninth with its unfortunate reference to 'wash[ing] the Ethiop white'.

A large number of tunes are associated with this hymn. Probably the most commonly used nowadays is Richmond by Thomas Haweis (1734–1820; see notes to hymn No. 25). Methodists have traditionally favoured Lydia by Thomas Phillips (1735–1805), while Anglicans long preferred a melody by Henry Harington (1727–1816), a physician at Bath and Wells, which is known variously as Landsdowne, Harington, Orlingbury, Bath and Retirement. Other alternatives are Oxford New (from Isaac Smith's collection, *c.* 1770), Selby by A. J. Eyre (1853–1919), and O God of Love (from *The Divine Companion* of 1709).

I myself am particularly fond of the vigorous Lyngham by Thomas Jarman (1782–1862), which divides the second half of each verse contrapuntally between men and women in a very effective way. As far as I know, the only contemporary hymnal which sets 'O for a thousand tongues' to that tune is *Songs and Hymns of Fellowship* (1987), but there may well be others; certainly Lyngham seems to be catching on in a number of different denominations.

Exhorting and beseeching to return to God

O for a thousand tongues to sing
My dear Redeemer's praise!
The glories of my God and King,
The triumphs of his grace.

2   My gracious Master, and my God,
    Assist me to proclaim,
    To spread through all the earth abroad
      The honours of thy name.

3   Jesus, the name that charms our fears,
    That bids our sorrows cease;
    'Tis music in the sinner's ears,
      'Tis life and health and peace!

4   He breaks the power of cancell'd sin;
    He sets the prisoner free;
    His blood can make the foulest clean;
      His blood availed for me.

5   He speaks, and listening to his voice
    New life the dead receive,
    The mournful, broken hearts rejoice,
      The humble poor *believe*.

6   Hear him, ye deaf, his praise, ye dumb,
    Your loosen'd tongues employ,
    Ye blind, behold your Saviour come,
      And leap, ye lame, for joy.

7   Look unto him, ye nations, own
    Your God, ye fallen race!
    Look, and be saved through faith alone,
      Be justified by grace!

8   See all your sins on Jesus laid;
    The Lamb of God was slain,
    His soul was once an offering made
      For every *soul* of man.

9   Awake from guilty nature's sleep.
    And Christ shall give you light,
    Cast all your sins into the deep,
      And wash the *Ethiop* white.

10 With me, your Chief, you then shall know,
    Shall feel your sins forgiven;
    Anticipate your heaven below
      And own, that love is heaven.

95 O GOD OF EARTH AND ALTAR

This is the only hymn ever written by the great Catholic writer G. K. Chesterton (1874–1936), best known today, perhaps, for his Father Brown stories. It first appeared in 1906 in the *Commonwealth,* a Christian socialist magazine edited by Henry Scott Holland, author of 'Judge Eternal, throned in splendour' (No. 71), and was included by Percy Dearmer in the first edition of the *English Hymnal.*

At the time he wrote it, Chesterton was thirty-two and already an accomplished poet, although he knew little about hymns or music. He later told Percy Dearmer that he had written it with the tune Aurelia in mind (see No. 124), since he assumed that its metre was the norm for hymns. In 1906 Chesterton was a lapsed Nonconformist and still sixteen years distant from his conversion to Roman Catholicism, but he had deep religious instincts. He was also firmly committed to social reform and political radicalism, both elements' that come across strongly in these verses which must be counted as one of the greatest expressions of the Christian social gospel in English hymnody.

Erik Routley had a particular admiration for this hymn, which he regarded as 'catholic in every good sense, soaring above sectionalism and yet firmly based on the earth', and it is worth quoting at some length what he wrote about it in his book *Hymns for Today and Tomorrow,* published in 1964:

There are many hymns – good but commonplace – whose argument could be summed up in a sentence. But the condensation of so much into twenty-four lines in this hymn is unparalleled in the history of the form . . . It is the only hymn which exclusively deals with politics in terms of sin and wickedness and confession, not at all in terms of sorrow and healing. It may also be observed how Chesterton uses words in a strictly contemporary sense. He is at heart a militant medievalist – hence his insistence on 'sword': but he is also a modern, for none of any other age could have put quite this sense into the word 'drift'. And none of any other age would have thought of writing 'lies of tongue and pen'. Chesterton was a newspaperman and knew what the pen had lately found itself able to do in the way of corrupting men's minds.'

It is interesting to compare 'O God of earth and altar' with other hymns written around the same time and bearing a similar social and political message. We have already encountered Henry Scott Holland's 'Judge Eternal, throned in splendour' (No. 71), which was written just four years earlier than Chesterton's hymn. 'Son of God, eternal Saviour', written in 1893 by Somerset Corry Lowry (1855–1932), an Anglican clergyman, contains the powerful plea:

> By the patient years of toiling,
> By thy silent hours of pain,
> Quench our fevered thirst of pleasure,
> Shame our selfish greed of gain.

'Father Eternal, Ruler of Creation', a powerful hymn written by Laurence Housman in 1919 which would certainly have been in this collection if there had been more space, makes a similar point equally tellingly:

> Lust of possession worketh desolations;
> There is no meekness in the sons of earth.
> Led by no star, the rulers of the nations
> Still fail to bring us to the blissful birth.

Despite his intentions, Chesterton's hymn is not generally sung to Aurelia, but rather to King's Lynn, a traditional English melody adapted by Ralph Vaughan Williams (1872–1958).

O God of earth and altar,
  Bow down and hear our cry,
Our earthly rulers falter,
  Our people drift and die;
The walls of gold entomb us,
  The swords of scorn divide,
Take not thy thunder from us,
  But take away our pride.

2 From all that terror teaches,
    From lies of tongue and pen,
  From all the easy speeches
    That comfort cruel men,
  From sale and profanation
    Of honour and the sword,
  From sleep and from damnation,
    Deliver us, good Lord!

3 Tie in a living tether
    The prince and priest and thrall,
  Bind all our lives together,
    Smite us and save us all;
  In ire and exultation
    Aflame with faith, and free,
  Lift up a living nation,
    A single sword to thee.

96 O JESUS, I HAVE PROMISED

This hymn was voted eighth in the BBC 'Songs of Praise' poll. It was written in 1866 by the Revd John Ernest Bode (1816–74) for the confirmation of his three children. Although the opening lines are clearly intended to refer to the promises made by candidates at confirmation, there is nothing in the hymn to restrict its use to this particular service and it is sung widely in churches of all denominations in ordinary Sunday worship.

Bode was born in St Pancras, London, his father being head of the Foreign Department of the General Post Office. Educated at Eton, Charterhouse and Christ Church, Oxford, he was ordained in 1841. From 1847 to 1860 he was rector of Westwell, Oxfordshire, and for the remaining fourteen years of his life he held the living of Castle Camps in Cambridgeshire. A considerable poet, he published several volumes of verse and was runner-up in the election for the poetry professorship at Oxford in 1857, coming just one vote behind the victorious Matthew Arnold.

Although he wrote hymns for every Sunday and for each of the festivals in the Christian year, this is the only one of his compositions to have survived in regular use. It was first published as a leaflet by the Society for the Propagation of Christian Knowledge in 1868 with the title 'A Hymn for the newly confirmed'.

Of the many tunes to which this hymn is sung probably the best known and the most fitting is Wolvercote, which was composed around 1910 by the Revd William Harold Ferguson (1874–1950) for use in the chapel of Lancing College where he was then teaching. He went on to become warden of St Edward's School, Oxford, and of St Peter's College, Radley, and finally precentor of Salisbury Cathedral. Of recent years, however, Wolvercote, which first appeared in print in the *Public School Hymn Book* of 1919, has fallen out of favour in certain quarters. In common with other strong unison tunes written around the same period, among them Ferguson's melody Ladywell (used for 'Lift up your voice, ye Christian folk'), it is regarded as being too much a product of the Establishment and the public school chapel, suggesting a superficial camaraderie rather than anything more profound. Donald Webster, who suspects that this feeling lies behind the exclusion of both Ferguson's tunes from the third editon of the *Church Hymnary,* makes some cutting remarks on such 'dismissive dogmatism' in his book *Our Hymn Tunes* (1983). It does certainly seem rather unfair if a fine tune like Wolvercote is being heard less often than it might be because of essentially sociological and political objections.

Still, there are plenty of other tunes to which Bode's hymn has been set. They include Thornbury by Basil Harwood (1859–1949), which is unfortunately open to the same objections as Wolvercote; Day of Rest by J. W. Elliott, originally written for 'O day of rest and gladness' but set to Bode's hymn in the 1875 edition of *Hymns Ancient and Modern;* and *Komm, Seele* by J. W. Franck (b. 1641), which was written for Elmenhorst's poem, '*Komm, Seele, Jesu Leiden soll mein Ergotzung sein'* in 1681.

A Hymn for the Newly Confirmed

O Jesus, I have promised
  To serve thee to the end;
Be thou for ever near me,
  My Master and my Friend;
I shall not fear the battle
  If thou art by my side,
Nor wander from the pathway
  If thou wilt be my Guide.

2 O let me feel thee near me:
    The world is ever near;
  I see the sights that dazzle,
    The tempting sounds I hear;
  My foes are ever near me,
    Around me and within;
  But, Jesus, draw thou nearer,
    And shield my soul from sin.

3 O let me hear thee speaking
    In accents clear and still,
  Above the storms of passion,
    The murmurs of self-will;
  O speak to reassure me,
    To hasten or control;
  O speak, and make me listen,
    Thou Guardian of my soul.

4   O let me see thy features,
      The look that once could make
  So many a true disciple
      Leave all things for thy sake;
  The look that beam'd on Peter
      When he thy name denied;
  The look that draws thy loved ones
      Close to thy piercèd side.

5   O Jesus, thou hast promised
      To all who follow thee,
  That where thou art in glory
      There shall thy servant be;
  And, Jesus, I have promised
      To serve thee to the end;
  O give me grace to follow,
      My Master and my Friend.

6   O let me see thy footmarks,
      And in them plant mine own;
  My hope to follow duly
      Is in thy strength alone;
  O guide me, call me, draw me,
      Uphold me to the end;
  And then in heaven receive me,
      My Saviour and my Friend.

97 O LORD MY GOD, WHEN I IN AWESOME WONDER

This very popular twentieth-century hymn is the result of a double translation from Swedish into English via Russian. Generally known by the words of its chorus as 'How great Thou art', it is the work of the British missionary and evangelist, Stuart K. Hine (b. 1899).

The original Swedish poem on which the hymn is based was written by Carl Boberg (1859–1940), an evangelist, journalist and Member of Parliament. Born at Monsteras on the south-east coast of Sweden, the son of a shipyard worker, Boberg was converted to Evangelical Christianity at the age of nineteen and went to Bible School at Kristinehamn. He returned to his native town as a preacher and it was there in 1886 that he wrote his nine-verse poem beginning 'O store Gud'. He was moved to hymn God's greatness one summer evening as he stood looking across the calm waters of the Monsteras inlet. A rainbow had formed following a storm in the afternoon and the church bell was tolling in the distance. The first verse and refrain of his poem, translated fairly literally into English, reads:

> O Thou great God! When I the world consider
> Which Thou hast made by Thine almighty Word;
> And how the web of life Thy wisdom guideth,
> And all creation feedeth at Thy board:
>
> Then doth my soul burst forth in song of praise:
> O Thou great God! O Thou great God!

Although Boberg's verses were set to music in 1891 and appeared in several Swedish hymn-books around the turn of the century, they seem to have disappeared from view in the 1920s. They were, however, translated into a number of other languages. In 1927 a Russian version appeared in a hymn-book edited by I. S. Prokhanoff. It was this version which Stuart Hine heard being sung in the western Ukraine where he had gone as a missionary in 1923.

The hymn made a considerable impression on Hine. He wrote the first three verses of 'O Lord my God' while engaged in evangelistic work in the Carpathian mountains on the borders of Russia and Romania. The scenery there inspired his second verse, which draws only indirectly on Boberg's original poem while remaining true to its general spirit of wonder at God's creation.

Hine wrote the fourth verse of his hymn when he returned to Britain in 1948. In that year more than 100,000 refugees from Russia and other parts of Eastern Europe streamed into the United Kingdom. The question uppermost in many of their minds was, 'When are we going home?' In an essay on the story of the hymn, Hine writes: 'What better message for the homeless than that of the One who went to prepare a place for the "displaced", of the God who invites into his own home those who will come to him through Christ.'

Stuart Hine published both the Russian and the English versions of the hymn in his Gospel magazine, *Grace and Peace,* in 1949. 'O Lord my God' rapidly caught on in Evangelical circles in both Britain and the United States. One of its prime promoters was Billy Graham, who wrote of it: 'The reason I liked "How great Thou art" was because it glorified God: it turned a Christian's eyes toward God rather than upon himself, as so many songs do.'

The hymn is sung to the Swedish folk melody to which Boberg's verses were set in 1891.

O store Gud

O Lord my God, when I in awesome wonder
    Consider all the works Thy hand hath made,
I see the stars, I hear the mighty thunder,
    Thy power throughout the universe displayed:

Then sings my soul, my Saviour God, to Thee,
    How great Thou art! How great Thou art!
Then sings my soul, my Saviour God, to Thee,
    How great Thou art! How great Thou art!

2   When through the woods and forest glades I wander
    And hear the birds sing sweetly in the trees:
When I look down from lofty mountain grandeur,
    And hear the brook, and feel the gentle breeze;

3   And when I think that God His Son not sparing,
    Sent Him to die – I scarce can take it in:
That on the cross, my burden gladly bearing,
    He bled and died to take away my sin:

4   When Christ shall come with shout of acclamation
    And take me home – what joy shall fill my heart!
Then shall I bow in humble adoration
    And there proclaim, my God, how great Thou art!

Translation, adaption and arrangement © 1953, renewed 1981, by Mann Music, Inc., 25510
Ave. Stanford, Valencia, Ca. 91355. Administered worldwide (excluding USA) by
Thankyou Music. Used by permission

98 O LOVE THAT WILT NOT LET ME GO

I regard this as one of the most moving and profound hymns in the English language. It is one of very few hymns which tackle that most difficult area of human experience for the Christian believer, the reality of suffering, and which does so not in a sentimental or cloying way but in a spirit of Christian hope and with an intense sense of the mystery of life.

The author, George Matheson (1842–1906), was a Church of Scotland minister. Born and educated in Glasgow, he spent eighteen years in the Argyllshire parish of Innellan on the north bank of the Clyde and then moved on to a charge in Edinburgh. As well as being a devoted parish minister, Matheson was a considerable scholar, theologian and scientist. Despite the fact that he was almost totally blind from the age of eighteen, he wrote several books of poems and meditations and a number of serious theological works.

For many years the story was told that he wrote this hymn in a state of abject grief after the girl he had hoped to marry had broken off their engagement on hearing of his blindness. But this is apocryphal. He himself recalled that the hymn was written after his sister Jane, who had been his housekeeper and constant companion, left to be married. In his words:

The hymn was composed in the manse of Innellan on the evening of 6 June 1882. I was at that time alone. Something had happened to me which was known only to myself and which caused me the most severe mental suffering. The hymn was the fruit of that suffering. It was the quickest bit of work I ever did in my life. I am quite sure the whole work was completed in five minutes, and equally sure it never received at my hands any retouching or correction. I had the impression of having it dictated to me by some inward voice.

There are, in fact, two small errors in the above account. It was in

1881, not 1882, that Matheson wrote the hymn and he did make one correction to it. When 'O Love that wilt not let me go' first appeared in print, in the January 1882 issue of the Church of Scotland magazine *Life and Work,* the third line of the third verse was as it is printed opposite – 'I climb the rainbow through the rain'. However, at the request of the editors of the *Scottish Hymnal,* he changed 'climb' to 'trace'. This alteration has been incorporated in all subsequent hymnals.

One of the great strengths of 'O love that wilt not let me go' is that it can be appreciated at so many different levels. It speaks directly and simply to those weighed down with care and grief, and particularly to those approaching death. Yet it also has considerable philosophical depth and some complex mystical allusions. The imagery in the first verse, of the soul returning to the ocean depths, is in some ways closer to Hindu thought or to the ideas of contemporary 'process' theologians than to orthodox Christianity. Matheson himself explained the significance of the puzzling imagery in the two closing lines of the hymn. White blossoms, he said, represented prosperity and red ones self-sacrifice – 'I took red as the symbol of that sacrificial life which blooms by shedding itself.'

The power and intensity of the hymn is greatly enhanced by the tune St Margaret, written specifically for it by Dr Albert Pearce (1844–1912), organist of Glasgow Cathedral. It too was a work of sudden inspiration. Pearce recalled that he read Matheson's hymn while staying at Brodick Manse on the Isle of Arran, and then, 'I wrote the music straight off, and I may say that the ink of the first note was hardly dry when I had finished the tune.'

Self-surrender

O Love that wilt not let me go,
  I rest my weary soul in Thee:
I give Thee back the life I owe,
That in Thine ocean depths its flow
  May richer, fuller be.

2 O Light that followest all my way,
    I yield my flickering torch to Thee:
My heart restores its borrowed ray,
That in Thy sunshine's blaze its day
  May brighter, fairer be.

3 O Joy that seekest me through pain,
    I cannot close my heart to Thee:
I climb the rainbow through the rain,
And feel the promise is not vain,
  That morn shall tearless be.

4 O Cross that liftest up my head,
    I dare not ask to fly from Thee:
I lay in dust life's glory dead,
And from the ground there blossoms red
  Life that shall endless be.

99 O PRAISE YE THE LORD! PRAISE HIM IN THE HEIGHT

The author of this hymn, Sir Henry Williams Baker (1821–77), will always have a prominent place in the history of English hymnody as the driving force behind *Hymns Ancient and Modern*.

The eldest son of a Vice-Admiral, Baker was educated at Trinity College, Cambridge, and ordained in 1844. Seven years later he became vicar of Monkland, near Leominster, on the English–Welsh border. In the same year he succeeded to his father's baronetcy. He remained at Monkland for the rest of his life. The light duties of this small country parish enabled him to devote most of his time to hymnody and particularly to the preparation of *Hymns Ancient and Modern*, which was largely Tractarian in inspiration and did much to promote the practice of hymn-singing throughout the Church of England, and especially in the Anglo-Catholic wing.

Baker was present at the meeting held at the clergy house of St Barnabas, Pimlico, in 1858 which resolved to produce a new hymnal, and was appointed secretary of the committee charged with the book's preparation. He effectively became editor-in-chief of the whole project, which extended over the next seventeen years and involved an enormous amount of work in choosing hymns and commissioning translations, new verses and tunes. Baker was particularly keen to restore to the devotion of the Church of England the treasures of early Latin hymnody, and was instrumental in securing the many fine translations by J. M. Neale which appeared in the first volume of the new work, published in 1861. He also supervised the preparation of an appendix, published in 1868, and a revised edition of the hymnal which came out in 1875 and contained thirty-three of his own hymns and translations, of which this was one.

'O Praise ye the Lord' is based on Psalms 148 and 150. The first verse echoes the first two verses of Psalm 148:

> Praise ye the Lord.
> Praise ye the Lord from the heavens:
> Praise him in the heights.
> Praise him, all his angels:
> Praise him all his hosts.

The third verse echoes verses 3 to 6 of Psalm 150:

> Praise him with the sound of the trumpet:
> Praise him with the psaltery and harp.
> Praise him with the timbrel and dance:
> Praise him with stringed instruments and organs.
> Praise him upon the loud cymbals:
> Let everything that hath breath praise the Lord.

Among Baker's other hymns which are still regularly sung today are 'Lord, thy word abideth' and 'The King of love my Shepherd is' (No. 130).

The tune originally composed for 'O praise ye the Lord' in the 1875 edition of *Hymns Ancient and Modern* was *Laudate Domino* by H. J. Gauntlett (1805–76). In 1894 Sir Charles Hubert Parry (1848–1918) produced a magnificently affirmative and positive melody, which goes under the same name and has become the standard tune for the hymn. It was originally written as the concluding section of an anthem, 'Hear my words, O ye people', for a Salisbury diocesan festival. To avoid confusion, Gauntlett's tune is now known as Gauntlett.

O praise ye the Lord! praise him in the height;
Rejoice in his word, ye angels of light;
Ye heavens, adore him, by whom ye were made,
And worship before him, in brightness arrayed.

2   O praise ye the Lord! praise him upon earth,
In tuneful accord, ye sons of new birth;
Praise him who hath brought you his grace from above,
Praise him who hath taught you to sing of his love.

3   O praise ye the Lord, all things that give sound;
Each jubilant chord re-echo around;
Loud organs, his glory forth tell in deep tone,
And, sweet harp, the story of what he hath done.

4   O praise ye the Lord! thanksgiving and song
To him be outpoured all ages along:
For love in creation, for heaven restored,
For grace of salvation, O praise ye the Lord!

100 O SACRED HEAD, SORE WOUNDED

This powerful Passiontide hymn comes to us from a Latin original via the German, and is now to be found in three quite distinct English translations as well as several hybrid versions.

It is based on a long medieval poem, '*Salve mundi salutare*', which in turn addresses the various parts of Christ's body hanging on the Cross. The last part of the poem, from which the hymn is taken, is an invocation of the Saviour's head and begins '*Salve caput cruentatum*'. The poem is often attributed to St Bernard of Clairvaux (1091–1153), but this seems unlikely as its earliest known appearance is in fourteenth- and fifteenth-century manuscripts.

In the mid seventeenth century the last section of the poem was translated into German by Paul Gerhardt (1607–76) and printed in Frankfurt in 1656 as a hymn beginning '*O Haupt voll Blut und Wunden*'. Gerhardt, who spent much of his life as a Lutheran pastor in Berlin, wrote 123 hymns and is regarded as second only to Luther in his contribution to German hymnody.

The first English translation of Gerhardt's hymn was made in 1752 by John Gambold (1711–71), who was vicar of Stanton Harcourt in Oxfordshire but later resigned his living to join the Moravians. His version began, 'O Head so full of bruises'. In 1830 Dr James Waddell Alexander (1804–59), an American Presbyterian minister who also held the chairs of Rhetoric and Church History at Princeton University, produced a translation which forms the basis of the version of the hymn found in several modern hymn-books. Its first verse runs as follows:

> O sacred head, now wounded,
>   With grief and shame weighed down!
> Now scornfully surrounded,
>   With thorns, thy only crown:
> O sacred Head! what glory,
>   What bliss till now was thine!
> I read the wondrous story!
>   I joy to call thee mine!

A further translation was made by Sir Henry Baker for *Hymns Ancient and Modern* in 1861. The first verse of this version, which can be found in the 'New Standard' edition of *Hymns Ancient and Modern*, is:

> O sacred head, surrounded
>   By crown of piercing thorn!
> O bleeding head, so wounded,
>   So shamed and put to scorn!
> Death's pallid hue comes o'er thee,
>   The glow of life decays;
> Yet angel-hosts adore thee,
>   And tremble as they gaze.

In 1899 Robert Bridges (1844–1930; see notes to hymn No. 6) returned to the original Latin to produce the version that is printed opposite. It appears in the *New English Hymnal* and in several other modern hymn-books.

All these English translations of the hymn are generally sung to the melody Passion Chorale which accompanied Gerhard's German version. It was written around 1600 by Hans Leo Hassler (1564–1612) for a love song, *'Mein Gmuth ist mir verwiret'*. Hassler served as musical director both to the wealthy Fugger family in Augsburg and to the Elector of Saxony. The tune was a favourite of Johann Sebastian Bach and was used five times in his *St Matthew Passion*.

O sacred Head, sore wounded

O sacred Head, sore wounded,
  Defiled and put to scorn;
O kingly Head, surrounded
  With mocking crown of thorn:
What sorrow mars thy grandeur?
  Can death thy bloom deflower?
O countenance whose splendour
  The hosts of heaven adore!

2 Thy beauty, long-desirèd
     Hath vanished from our sight;
   Thy power is all expirèd,
     And quenched the Light of light.
   Ah me! for whom thou diest,
     Hide not so far thy grace:
   Show me, O Love most highest,
     The brightness of thy face.

3 I pray thee, Jesus, own me,
     Me, Shepherd good, for thine;
   Who to thy fold hast won me,
     And fed with truth divine.
   Me, guilty me refuse not,
     Incline thy face to me,
   This comfort that I lose not,
     On earth to comfort thee.

4 In thy most bitter passion
     My heart to thee doth cry,
   With thee for my salvation
     Upon the Cross to die.
   Ah, keep my heart thus movèd
     To stand thy Cross beneath,
   To mourn thee, well-belovèd,
     Yet thank thee for thy death.

5   My days are few, O fail not,
      With thine immortal power,
    To hold me that I quail not
      In death's most fearful hour:
    That I may fight befriended,
      And see in my last strife
    To me thine arms extended
      Upon the Cross of life.

101 O THOU WHO CAMEST FROM ABOVE

One would not expect from a hymn-writer as accomplished as Charles Wesley (1707–88) a phrase that congregations would find it almost impossible to sing. The use of the word 'inextinguishable' in the second line of the second verse of this hymn has been the cause of much tongue-twisting and has prompted several attempts to re-write Wesley's words. It has even led in some instances to this very fine hymn being dropped altogether from hymn-books.

'O Thou who camest from above' first appeared in Wesley's *Short Hymns on Selected Passages of Scripture,* published in 1762. The Scripture passage attached is from Leviticus 6:13, 'The fire shall ever be burning upon the altar; it shall never go out.' It refers to the Jewish practice of burnt offerings, where the fire is kept blazing until the offering is completely consumed. Wesley portrays the faith of the Christian believer in similar terms.

Hymns Ancient and Modern for some time sought to avoid the 'inextinguishable' tongue-twister by substituting the words 'With ever-bright, undying blaze', but it has now reverted to the original. In his *Hymnal Companion* of 1872 Edward Henry Bickersteth, Bishop of Exeter, changed the offending line to 'Unquenched, undimmed in darkest days'. He also sought to give the great Wesley a posthumous lecture on hymn-writing. 'Words of five syllables must be admitted into hymns sparingly,' he wrote, 'but for a whole congregation to be poised on six practically leads for a hymn to be passed by.' The *Church Hymnary* gets round the problem by leaving out verse 2 altogether.

Some hymnals reproduce a revised version of the final verse, which was produced by the compilers of *Hymns Ancient and Modern* because of their concern about Wesley's theology of sacrifice:

Still let me prove thy perfect will,
    My acts of faith and love repeat;
Till death thy endless mercies seal,
    And make the sacrifice complete.

The tune most often associated with this hymn is Hereford by Samuel Sebastian Wesley (1810–76), grandson of Charles. After singing as a boy in the Chapel Royal, he became an organist at the age of sixteen and served in five parish churches and four cathedrals – Hereford, Exeter, Winchester and Gloucester. One of 130 hymn tunes which he composed, Hereford first appeared in his *European Psalmist* (1872), and Charles Wesley's hymn was set to it in the 1909 edition of *Hymns Ancient and Modern*. The *Church Hymnary* offers a rather less satisfying melody by Arthur Hutchings (b. 1906) with the curious title Fudgie.

For Holiness, and for Earnestness in Work

O Thou who camest from above,
    The pure celestial fire to impart,
Kindle a flame of sacred love
    On the mean altar of my heart.

2   There let it for thy glory burn
    With inextinguishable blaze,
And trembling to its source return
    In humble prayer, and fervent praise.

3   Jesus, confirm my heart's desire
    To work, and speak, and think for thee;
Still let me guard the holy fire,
    And still stir up thy gift in me.

4   Ready for all thy perfect will,
    My acts of faith and love repeat,
Till death thy endless mercies seal,
    And make my sacrifice complete.

102 O WORSHIP THE KING, ALL-GLORIOUS ABOVE

This much-loved paraphrase of Psalm 104 ('Bless the Lord, O my soul') is the work of Sir Robert Grant (1785–1838), who in a distinguished public career was successively a barrister, Member of Parliament, Privy Counsellor and colonial governor.

Much of the imagery which Grant employed in his hymn is taken directly from the Psalmist's words. The phrase in the second verse, 'Who maketh the clouds his chariot', becomes 'His chariots of wrath the deep thunder-clouds form'; and the statement in the sixth verse, 'Thou coveredst it with the deep as with a garment: The waters stood above the mountains', becomes 'And round it hath cast, like a mantle, the sea'.

Grant modelled 'O worship the King' on an earlier paraphrase of Psalm 104 made by William Kethe (?–1594), author of 'All people that on earth do dwell' (No. 7). The first two verses of Kethe's hymn are as follows:

> My soul praise the Lord!
> O God, Thou art great:
> In fathomless works
> Thyself Thou dost hide.
> Before Thy dark wisdom
> And power uncreate,
> Man's mind, that dare praise Thee,
> In fear must abide.

This earth where we dwell,
That journeys in space,
With air as a robe
Thou wrappest around:
Her countries she turneth
To greet the sun's face,
Then plungeth to slumber
In darkness profound.

Grant, whose father was Member of Parliament for Inverness, was educated at Magdalen College, Oxford, and called to the Bar. He sat in the House of Commons as a Tory from 1808 to 1834, successively representing the constituencies of Elgin, Inverness, Norwich and Finsbury. Perhaps his most important political action was to carry the Bill which emancipated Jews in Britain. In 1834, shortly after writing this hymn, he was appointed Governor of Bombay.

Grant is the sole representative in this book of a distinguished band of Victorian and Edwardian MPs who were also hymn-writers. Others included Thomas Hughes, the author of *Tom Brown's Schooldays,* who was successively Liberal MP for Lambeth and Frome and who wrote 'O God of Truth, whose living word'; Sir John Bowring, a Radical who represented first Kilmarnock and then Bolton ('Watchman, tell us of the night'); Philip Pusey, Conservative MP for Berkshire from 1835 to 1852 ('Lord of our life, and God of our salvation'); Charles Silvester Horne, a Congregational minister who was Liberal MP for Ipswich from 1910 to 1914 ('For the might of thine arm we bless thee'); and Britain's only hymn-writing Prime Minister, William Ewart Gladstone ('O lead my blindness by the hand').

'O worship the King' was first published in Grant's *Christian Psalmody* (1833). It is normally sung to the tune Hanover, which first appeared in print in 1708 and which used to be attributed to George Frederick Handel. It is now more usually regarded as the work of Dr William Croft (1678–1727), successively organist of St Anne's, Soho, the Chapel Royal and Westminster Abbey.

Psalm civ

O worship the King, all-glorious above;
O gratefully sing his power and his love:
Our Shield and Defender, the Ancient of Days,
Pavilioned in splendour, and girded with praise.

2   O tell of his might, O sing of his grace,
Whose robe is the light, whose canopy space;
His chariots of wrath the deep thunder-clouds form,
And dark is his path on the wings of the storm.

3   The earth with its store of wonders untold,
Almighty, thy power hath founded of old;
Hath stablished it fast by a changeless decree,
And round it hath cast, like a mantle, the sea.

4   Thy bountiful care what tongue can recite?
It breathes in the air, it shines in the light;
It streams from the hills, it descends to the plain,
And sweetly distils in the dew and the rain.

5   Frail children of dust, and feeble as frail,
In thee do we trust, nor find thee to fail;
Thy mercies how tender, how firm to the end,
Our Maker, Defender, Redeemer, and Friend.

6   O measureless Might, ineffable Love,
While angels delight to hymn thee above,
Thy humbler creation, though feeble their lays,
With true adoration shall sing to thy praise.

103 O WORSHIP THE LORD IN THE BEAUTY OF HOLINESS

This Epiphany hymn is the work of John Samuel Bewley Monsell (1811–75), whom we have already come across as the author of 'Fight the good fight with all thy might' (No. 36; see notes to that hymn for details of his life). It was first published in his *Hymns of Love and Praise* (1863).

The hymn rather effectively takes the gifts which the three kings brought with them to present to the baby Jesus and turns them into symbolic offerings which we can all bring to Christ in our lives and worship – the gold of obedience and the incense of lowliness. Although specifically written for and particularly suited for use during the season of Epiphany, 'O worship the Lord' is a general call to worship God and can appropriately be sung at any time in the Christian year.

The opening line of the hymn is taken directly from the ninth verse of Psalm 96 ('O sing unto the Lord a new song'). The 'mornings of joy' and 'evenings of tearfulness' in the fourth verse also have a scriptural derivation, coming from the fifth verse of Psalm 30: 'Weeping may endure for a night, but joy cometh in the morning.'

Altogether, Monsell wrote some 300 hymns. The two included in this collection are probably the most widely sung today. Others which are still in use include 'Sing to the Lord a joyful song', 'Sing to the Lord of harvest' and 'Rest of the weary, Joy of the sad'.

The soaring tune *Was Lebet, was Schwebet* to which 'O worship the Lord' is invariably sung comes from a German manuscript of 1754, *Choral-Buch vor Johann Heinrich Reinhardt*, where it accompanied the song '*Was Lebet, was Schwebet*'.

O worship the Lord in the beauty of holiness,
  Bow down before him, his glory proclaim;
With gold of obedience and incense of lowliness,
  Kneel and adore him: the Lord is his name.

2 Low at his feet lay thy burden of carefulness,
  High on his heart he will bear it for thee,
Comfort thy sorrows, and answer thy prayerfulness,
  Guiding thy steps as may best for thee be.

3 Fear not to enter his courts in the slenderness
  Of the poor wealth thou wouldst reckon as thine;
Truth in its beauty, and love in its tenderness,
  These are the offerings to lay on his shrine.

4 These, though we bring them in trembling and fearfulness,
  He will accept for the name that is dear;
Mornings of joy give for evenings of tearfulness,
  Trust for our trembling, and hope for our fear.

5 O worship the Lord in the beauty of holiness,
  Bow down before him, his glory proclaim;
With gold of obedience and incense of lowliness,
  Kneel and adore him: the Lord is his name.

104 ON JORDAN'S BANK THE BAPTIST'S CRY

This popular Advent hymn, which has been much altered from the original version printed here, was first presented to the British public under somewhat false colours. John Chandler (1806–76), who translated it from the Latin, published it in 1837 in his *Hymns of the Primitive Church*. In fact, the original Latin hymn, *'Jordanis oras praevia'*, is not from the early Church but dates only from the eighteenth century.

'Jordanis oras praevia' was the work of Charles Coffin (1676–1749), and first appeared in the *Paris Breviary* of 1736. Born in Buzancy in the Ardennes, Coffin became principal of the College of Doirmans-Beauvais in the University of Paris. He wrote more than 100 Latin hymns, several of which have been translated and have found their way into English hymn-books. Among other hymns popular today which are based on Coffin's Latin originals are 'O Holy Spirit, Lord of grace', 'Happy are they, they that love God' and 'Great mover of all hearts, whose hand'.

John Chandler, who was educated at Corpus Christi College, Oxford, succeeded his father as vicar of Witley in Surrey. He collected and translated many hymns from the early Church, including 'Blessed city, heavenly Salem' and 'Christ is our corner-stone'.

'On Jordan's bank' has been considerably altered by various hymnal editors, partly to bring the English words more into conformity with the original Latin text than was the case in Chandler's rather free translation. There are various renderings of the last two lines of the first verse. Perhaps the most common is:

> Awake, and hearken, for he brings
> Glad tidings from the King of kings.

Some hymn-books carry the following alternative version of the second verse:

> Then cleansed be every Christian breast,
> And furnished for so great a guest!
> Yea, let us each our hearts prepare
> For Christ to come and enter there.

Nearly all modern hymnals print an amended version of the fourth verse which was first used in *Hymns Ancient and Modern* in an effort by the compilers to follow Coffin's original Latin words more closely:

> To heal the sick stretch out Thine hand,
> And bid the fallen sinner stand;
> Shine forth, and let Thy light restore
> Earth's own true loveliness once more.

The tune Winchester New or Frankfurt first appeared in Hamburg in 1690 as the setting for a German hymn, '*Wer nur den lieben Gott lasst walten*'. John Wesley seems to have been the first to introduce it into England. It appeared in his *Foundery Tune Book* of 1742 where it was described as a 'swift German tune'.

Jordanis oras praevia

On Jordan's bank the Baptist's cry
Announces that the Lord is nigh;
Come then and hearken, for he brings
High tidings of the King of kings.

2 Then cleansed be every breast from sin;
Make straight the way for God within;
Prepare we in our hearts a home,
Where such a mighty Guest may come.

3 For thou art our salvation, Lord,
Our refuge, and our great reward;
Without thy grace we waste away,
Like flowers that wither and decay.

4 Stretch forth thine hand, to heal our sore,
And make us rise and fall no more;
Once more upon thy people shine,
And fill the world with love divine.

5 To him who left the throne of heaven
To save mankind, all praise be given;
Like praise be to the Father done,
And Holy Spirit, Three in One.

105 ONWARD, CHRISTIAN SOLDIERS

Largely misplaced sensibilities about its supposed militaristic message have led this well-known old war-horse to be trotted out of its stable much less often in recent years. Indeed, after generations of raising the roof in school chapels, it is missing altogether from the current edition of *Hymns for Church and School,* as the old *Public School Hymn Book* now discreetly calls itself.

This is a pity. For despite its title, Onward, Christian Soldiers is not a glorification of war; it is a stirring call to Christians to follow the Cross of Christ, and a powerful plea for Christian unity. Admittedly its language is a little naive and its confidence perhaps a shade shallow, but we should remember that it was written for children taking part in an outdoor procession. It may not be a hymn of great depth or subtlety, but set to Sullivan's march tune St Gertrude, it has a tremendous capacity to stir, excite and unite those who are singing it – and that surely can be no bad thing.

'Onward, Christian soldiers' comes from the prolific pen of the Revd Sabine Baring-Gould (1834–1924; see notes to hymn No. 138). He wrote it in 1864 while a curate at Horbury Bridge, near Wakefield in Yorkshire. It was the custom on Whit Monday for children from the village Sunday School to walk in procession to a neighbouring village with their banners held high. Baring-Gould felt the need of a stirring marching song to set the children on their way, and he wrote this hymn during the course of one evening to fit a tune from the slow movement of Haydn's *Symphony in D,* No. 15. It was first published in the *Church Times.*

During his lifetime, Baring-Gould was persuaded by hymn-book compilers to sanction various changes to the words. The *Fellowship Hymn Book* obtained his permission to change the phrase 'one in hope and doctrine' in the penultimate line of the second verse to 'one in hope and purpose'. To please the editors of the 1909 edition of *Hymns Ancient and Modern,* he also changed the fifth line of that verse from 'We are not divided' to 'Though divisions harass'. But although these alterations may more accurately have expressed the sadly divided state of the Church in the world, Baring-Gould's original words have been restored in most modern hymnals.

The melody St Gertrude was specially composed for Baring-Gould's hymn by Sir Arthur Sullivan (1842–1900) in 1871. Still to embark on his collaboration with W. S. Gilbert, he was already a rising star in the British musical firmament, holding a chair at the Royal Academy of Music and having already composed a number of oratorios and orchestral pieces. It is said that he named the tune after a lady in the congregation of one of the fashionable London churches where he was organist. St Gertrude has been inseparable from 'Onward Christian soldiers' and has provided the melody for a number of parodies, of which the best known is the intensely re-petitive 'Lloyd George knew my father'.

A rather more witty parody of Baring-Gould's hymn well ex-presses the frustrations of those who seek to reform the Church:

> Like a mighty tortoise,
>   Moves the Church of God;
> Brothers, we are treading
>   Where we've always trod.

A Hymn for Procession with Cross and Banners

> Onward, Christian soldiers,
>   Marching as to war,
> With the cross of Jesus
>   Going on before.
> Christ, the royal Master,
>   Leads against the foe;
> Forward into battle,
>   See, his banners go!

Onward, Christian soldiers,
Marching as to war,
With the cross of Jesus
Going on before.

2 Like a mighty army,
   Moves the Church of God;
Brothers, we are treading
   Where the saints have trod;
We are not divided,
   All one body we,
One in hope and doctrine,
   One in charity.

3 Crowns and thrones may perish,
   Kingdoms rise and wane,
But the Church of Jesus
   Constant will remain:
Gates of hell can never
   'Gainst that Church prevail;
We have Christ's own promise,
   And that cannot fail.

4 Onward then ye people,
   Join our happy throng;
Blend with ours your voices
   In the triumph-song;
'Glory, laud, and honour
   Unto Christ the King!'
This through countless ages
   Men and angels sing.

106 OUR GOD, OUR HELP IN AGES PAST

This paraphrase of Psalm 90 by Isaac Watts (1674–1748; see notes to hymn No. 29) has been regarded by many as the greatest hymn in the English language. It is said that when Dr Benjamin Jowett, that most eminent Victorian who was master of Balliol College, asked a group of fellow Oxford dons to note down their list of favourite hymns, all of them independently put down just this one, which each felt fulfilled all the conditions of a perfect hymn. In Britain it has almost attained the status of a second National Anthem and is associated particularly with services held on Remembrance Day to commemorate the fallen in the two world wars. Surprisingly, it did not make the 'Songs of Praise' Top Twenty, but it must surely count as one of the nation's favourite hymns.

'Our God, our help in ages past' was written in 1714, shortly before the death of Queen Anne and at a time of acute national anxiety about the succession to the throne. It was first published five years later in Watts's *The Psalms of David imitated in the language of the New Testament*. But it is much more than a mere metrical version of Psalm 90 ('Lord, thou hast been our dwelling-place in all generations'). It is true that some of Watts's phrases are very close to those of the Psalmist, or rather of the psalm as it appears in the Authorized Version. The fifth verse of his hymn, for example, echoes very closely its fourth verse: 'For a thousand ages in thy sight are but as yesterday when it is past, and as a watch in the night.' But more often the hymn amplifies a single line in the psalm and turns it into a piece of inspired poetry with a profound depth and great beauty.

The opening of the fifth verse of the psalm is a good case in point: 'Thou carriest them away as with a flood; they are as a sleep.' Watts takes this simple phrase and turns it, in the fifth and sixth verses of

335

his hymn, into a profound statement about the nature of time and the transience of our earthly lives. These two verses have, in fact, caused much perplexity among Christian commentators, as they seem to conflict with the idea of everlasting life. It has been suggested that the sons of time which 'fly, forgotten as a dream' are to be understood as the minutes, hours and days of our temporal existence. But, given the title which Watts chose for his hymn, should we not take them rather as referring to our own frailty and perishability as human flesh and blood, contrasted with the eternal nature of God?

In 1737 John Wesley changed the first word of Watts's hymn from 'Our' to 'O' when he included it in his *Collection of Psalms and Hymns*. This alteration has been taken up in virtually every subsequent hymn-book, although the Baptists and Congregationalists long retained Watts's original opening. The fourth, sixth and eighth verses of the hymn are nowadays almost always omitted, and the phrase 'Under the shadow' in the second verse is sometimes altered to 'Beneath the shadow' to give a more satisfactory stress.

The tune St Anne which is now almost universally associated with this hymn was not, in fact, attached to it until the publication of *Hymns Ancient and Modern* in 1861. Before that, 'Our God, our help in ages past' was generally sung to Hanover (see notes to hymn No. 102). St Anne first appeared in the 1708 edition of Tate and Brady's book of psalm tunes, where it was set to Psalm 42 ('As pants the hart for cooling streams'). It was probably composed by Dr William Croft (1678–1727), successively organist of St Anne's Church, Soho, the Chapel Royal and Westminster Abbey.

Man frail, and God eternal

Our God, our help in ages past,
Our hope for years to come,
Our shelter from the stormy blast,
And our eternal home.

2   Under the shadow of thy throne
     Thy saints have dwelt secure;
  Sufficient is thine arm alone,
     And our defence is sure.

3   Before the hills in order stood,
     Or earth received her frame,
  From everlasting thou art God,
     To endless years the same.

4   Thy Word commands our flesh to dust,
     Return, ye sons of men;
  All nations rose from Earth at first,
     And turn to earth again.

5   A thousand ages in thy sight
     Are like an evening gone;
  Short as the watch that ends the night
     Before the rising sun.

6   The busy tribes of flesh and blood,
     With all their lives and cares,
  Are carried downwards by the flood
     And lost in following years.

7   Time, like an ever-rolling stream
     Bears all its sons away;
  They fly, forgotten as a dream
     Dies at the opening day.

8   Like flow'ry fields the nations stand
     Pleas'd with the morning light;
  The flowers beneath the Mower's hand
     Lie withering e'er 'tis night.

9   Our God, our help in ages past,
     Our hope for years to come,
  Be thou our guard while troubles last,
     And our eternal home.

107 PRAISE, MY SOUL, THE KING OF HEAVEN

This majestic song of praise is one of Her Majesty the Queen's favourite hymns and she chose it for her wedding in 1947. It is also very popular with her subjects, being voted sixth in the 'Songs of Praise' poll.

It is the work of Henry Francis Lyte (1793–1847), the author of 'Abide with me' (No. 2; see notes to that hymn for details of Lyte's life). He wrote it for his congregation at Lower Brixham in Devon and it was first published in 1834 in a collection called *Spirit of the Psalms*. This book included metrical versions of the Psalms to fit the calendar of the Church of England. Among other hymns in it which are still sung today were 'God of mercy, God of grace', based on Psalm 67, and 'Pleasant are thy Courts above', based on Psalm 84.

'Praise, my soul, the King of heaven' is based on Psalm 103: 'Bless the Lord, O my soul: And all that is within me, bless his holy name.' As Watts did with 'Our God, our help in ages past', Lyte created vivid new images from phrases in the original psalm, although in his case it was achieved more through compression than amplification. Thus the eighth verse of the psalm, 'The Lord is merciful and gracious, slow to anger, and plenteous in mercy. He will not always chide', became 'Slow to chide, and swift to bless' in the hymn. In the same way, the thirteenth and fourteenth verses, 'Like as a father pitieth his children, so the Lord pitieth them that fear him. For he knoweth our frame', became 'Father-like, he tends and spares us; well our feeble frame he knows'.

The fourth verse of the hymn is now often omitted, and in many hymnals the refrain 'Praise him! Praise him!' is replaced by 'Alleluia! Alleluia!'. The editors of *Hymns Ancient and Modern* were unhappy with the notion of angels helping mortals to adore God and even more unhappy with the idea of the sun and moon bowing down before him; for a time the last verse was changed to:

Angels, in the height adore him;
Ye behold him face to face;
Saints triumphant, bow before him,
Gather'd in from every race.
Praise him, praise him,
Praise with us the God of grace.

The tune Praise my Soul was specially written for Lyte's hymn by Sir John Goss (1800–1880) and first appeared in 1869. Born in Fareham, Hampshire, where his father was the parish church organist, Goss was a chorister at the Chapel Royal and later became organist at St Luke's, Chelsea. From 1838 to 1872 he was organist at St Paul's Cathedral.

Psalm ciii

Praise, my soul, the King of heaven;
  To his feet thy tribute bring.
Ransomed, healed, restored, forgiven,
  Who like me his praise should sing?
    Praise him! Praise him!
    Praise the everlasting King!

2 Praise him for his grace and favour
    To our fathers in distress;
  Praise him still the same for ever,
    Slow to chide, and swift to bless.
      Praise him! Praise him!
      Glorious in his faithfulness.

3 Father-like, he tends and spares us;
    Well our feeble frame he knows;
  In his hands he gently bears us,
    Rescues us from all our foes.
      Praise him! Praise him!
      Widely as his mercy flows.

4 Frail as summer's flower we flourish:
    Blows the wind, and it is gone.
  But, while mortals rise and perish,
    God endures unchanging on.
      Praise him! Praise him!
      Praise the high eternal One!

5 Angels, help us to adore him;
    Ye behold him face to face;
  Sun and moon, bow down before him,
    Dwellers all in time and space.
      Praise him! Praise him!
      Praise with us the God of grace!

108 PRAISE THE LORD! YE HEAVENS, ADORE HIM

Virtually everyone knows who composed the tune to which this hymn is almost always sung, but nobody knows who wrote the words.

It first appeared, as printed overleaf, in a leaflet produced around 1800 as a supplement to the collection of psalms, hymns and anthems sung at the London Foundling Hospital. The verses were headed, 'Hymn from Psalm cxlviii, music by Haydn', which makes clear that the hymn was, from the beginning, set to Joseph Haydn's majestic tune Austria. Psalm 148, on which it is based, begins, 'Praise ye the Lord. Praise ye the Lord from the heavens.'

The Foundling Hospital was established by a retired merchant navy captain, Thomas Coram. On his way to a service at St Andrew's, Holborn, one Sunday morning he found an abandoned baby on the steps of the church. He felt moved to found an institution that would care for some of the many illegitimate children in the capital who suffered a similar fate. The hospital was established in High Holborn and had its own chapel with a fine organ which was the gift of George Frederick Handel. This became a fashionable place of worship in the eighteenth century, largely because of the singing by the children. We have already come across another hymn specially written for the inmates of a similar establishment in James Edmeston's 'Lead us, heavenly Father, lead us' (No. 75).

Both John Kempthorne (1775–1838), rector of St Michael's, Gloucester, and Richard Mant (1776–1848), author of 'Bright the vision that delighted' (No. 21) have been credited with the authorship of this hymn, but John Julian produces conclusive proof in his *Dictionary of Hymnody* that neither wrote it. Most hymn-books pair the four verses of the original to form two stanzas, and then add a third which was written in 1836 by Edward Osler (1798–1863):

Worship, honour, glory, blessing,
　Lord, we offer to thy name;
Young and old, their praise expressing,
　Join thy goodness to proclaim.
As the hosts of heaven adore thee,
　We would bow before thy throne;
As thine angels serve before thee,
　So on earth thy will be done.

Interestingly, Joseph Haydn himself attended a service at the chapel of the Foundling Hospital when he was in London in 1792, and wrote afterwards: 'I was more touched by their innocent and reverent music than by anything I had ever heard.' Little can he have thought that a few years later the children would be singing a hymn to a tune which he was to write for a very different purpose. His Austrian Hymn, also known as Haydn, Vienna and Cheadle, was composed at the suggestion of the Austrian Prime Minister and first performed on the Emperor Francis II's birthday, 12 February 1797, when it was set to the words 'Gott erhalte Franz den Kaiser'. It became the Austrian and later the German National Anthem. The tune is said to have been based on a Croatian national song.

Haydn's melody soon passed into use as a hymn tune in England, being found in a volume of Isaac Watts's psalms and hymns in 1805 and set to 'Praise the Lord! Ye heavens, adore him' in the 1809 edition of the Foundling Collection. The tune was a particular favourite of Haydn's in his old age; when the French were bombarding Vienna in May 1809, he asked to be led to his piano so that he might play it. It was the last piece of music that he played.

Psalm cxlviii

Praise the Lord! Ye heavens, adore him;
   Praise him, angels, in the height;
Sun and moon, rejoice before him;
   Praise him, all ye stars and light:

2 Praise the Lord, for he hath spoken;
   Worlds his mighty voice obeyed;
Laws, which never shall be broken,
   For their guidance hath he made.

3 Praise the Lord, for he is glorious!
   Never shall his promise fail;
God hath made his saints victorious;
   Sin and death shall not prevail.

4 Praise the God of our salvation;
   Hosts on high, his power proclaim;
Heaven and earth, and all creation,
   Laud and magnify his name!

109 PRAISE TO THE HOLIEST IN THE HEIGHT

This is the third hymn in the present collection to come from the pen of John Henry Newman (1801–90). Like 'Firmly I believe and truly' (No. 37), it was extracted from the long poem, 'The Dream of Gerontius'. But in this case, as with 'Lead, kindly Light', Newman's meditative verses were turned into a hymn and sung in churches during his own lifetime. It is the most popular of his hymns, at least on the evidence of the 'Songs of Praise' poll, in which it came sixteenth.

'The Dream of Gerontius', which traces the journey of an aged monk through the gate of death into the presence of Christ, was written in 1865 and first appeared in the Catholic publication, *The Month*. There is a story that Newman thought so little of the poem that he threw it into a waste-paper basket from which it was retrieved by a friend.

The lines which make up this hymn come from the last part of a 35-verse 'Hymn to the Angelicals'. There the verse beginning 'Praise to the Holiest in the height' was used at the opening of each of the Hymn's five sections. When in 1868 the editors of *Hymns Ancient and Modern* extracted six stanzas from the poem to make a hymn suitable for congregational singing, they began with this verse and repeated it at the end.

The current third edition of the *Church Hymnary* omits the fourth verse of the hymn on the grounds that there is no higher gift than grace and that its words strongly suggest the doctrine of transubstantiation. This is an unfortunate decision. As Donald Webster points out in his book, *Our Hymn Tunes* (1983), 'In less ecumenical times than our own, Protestants have sung this verse without strain on their consciences and have interpreted the words as referring to Our Lord's earthly ministry.'

The tune Gerontius was written specifically for Newman's hymn by J. B. Dykes (1823–76), precentor of Durham Cathedral, and appeared with it in 1868 in the appendix to the first edition of *Hymns Ancient and Modern*. The 1908 'Historical Edition' carried a new tune specially commissioned by Sir Charles Villiers Stanford (1852–1924) and entitled Alverstone. 'Praise to the Holiest in the height' is also sometimes sung to *Chorus Angelorum* or Somervell by Sir Arthur Somervell (1863–1937). Somervell was a professor at the Royal College of Music and then an inspector of music in schools. His tune, which was written for Newman's hymn, first appeared in *Arundel Hymns* in 1902 and was subsequently used in his oratorio, *The Passion of Christ*. The hymn is also often sung to Richmond by Thomas Haweis (1734–1820; see notes to hymn No. 25) and occasionally to Hebdomadal by Thomas Banks, Bishop of Oxford. The last tune is so called because it was written during a particularly boring session of the University's Hebdomadal Council.

Praise to the Holiest in the height,
And in the depth be praise;
In all his words most wonderful,
Most sure in all his ways.

2 O loving wisdom of our God!
When all was sin and shame,
A second Adam to the fight
And to the rescue came.

3 O wisest love! that flesh and blood,
Which did in Adam fail,
Should strive afresh against the foe,
Should strive and should prevail;

4 And that a higher gift than grace
Should flesh and blood refine,
God's presence and his very self,
And essence all–divine.

5 O generous love! that he, who smote
In Man for man the foe,
The double agony in Man
For man should undergo;

6 And in the garden secretly,
And on the Cross on high,
Should teach his brethren, and inspire
To suffer and to die.

7 Praise to the Holiest in the height,
And in the depth be praise;
In all his words most wonderful,
Most sure in all his ways.

110 PRAISE TO THE LORD! THE ALMIGHTY, THE KING OF CREATION

This is in origin a German hymn and it is traditionally accompanied by a thoroughly German tune. It was a particular favourite of Frederick William III of Prussia, and continues to be extremely popular as an expression of praise and thanksgiving.

The hymn is freely based on the early verses of Psalm 103, 'Bless the Lord, O my soul: And all that is within me, bless his holy name.' The second line of the fourth verse also strongly recalls the last verse of Psalm 150: 'Let every thing that hath breath praise the Lord.'

'Lobe den Herren' was written by Joachim Neander (1650–80), whose brief but full life is covered in the notes to 'All my hope on God is founded' (No. 6). It first appeared in a collection of his hymns entitled *Glaub-und Liebes- übung* (or Alpha and Omega), published in 1680. There it ran to five verses. In 1863 Miss Catherine Winkworth (1829–78) translated the four verses below for her *Chorale Book for England*.

Catherine Winkworth was another of those redoubtable Victorian spinsters who did so much for the Christian cause both through their writings and their active involvement in good works. She spent most of her life in the vicinity of Manchester where her father was a successful businessman, although in later life she moved with the family to Clifton, near Bristol, where she took an active interest in several philanthropic bodies, particularly in the field of women's education.

Miss Winkworth was the foremost translator of German hymns into English in the nineteenth century. Among her translations which are still in common use are 'All my heart this night rejoices', 'How brightly beams the morning star', 'Deck thyself, my soul, with gladness', 'Christ the Lord is risen again', 'Wake, awake! for night is flying' (see hymn No. 142) and 'Now thank we all our God' (No. 91).

The tune, Hast du denn, Jesu (also sometimes found as Hast du denn, Liebster), was taken by Neander from a song book published in Stralsund in 1655, where it had been set to the song *'Hast du denn, Liebster, dein Angesicht ganzlich verborgen'*.

Lobe den Herren

Praise to the Lord! the Almighty, the King of creation!
O my soul, praise him, for he is thy health and salvation!
    All ye who hear,
    Now to his temple draw near,
   Joining in glad adoration.

2 Praise to the Lord, who o'er all things so wondrously reigneth,
Shelters thee under his wings, yea, so gently sustaineth:
    Hast thou not seen?
    All that is needful hath been
   Granted in what he ordaineth.

3 Praise to the Lord, who doth prosper thy work and defend thee;
Surely his goodness and mercy here daily attend thee:
    Ponder anew
    What the Almighty can do,
   If with his love he befriend thee.

4 Praise to the Lord! O let all that is in me adore him!
All that hath life and breath, come now with praises before him!
    Let the Amen
    Sound from his people again:
   Gladly for aye we adore him!

III REJOICE, THE LORD IS KING

This is another of the works of Charles Wesley (1707–88; see notes to hymn No. 11). First published in 1746 in *Hymns for our Lord's Resurrection,* it was clearly intended by the author to be sung at Easter, but it is now more often associated with Ascensiontide services. The refrain is based on St Paul's Epistle to the Philippians 4:4, 'Rejoice in the Lord always; again I say, rejoice.' Most modern hymnals leave out the last two verses.

'Rejoice, the Lord is King' is one of three hymns by Charles Wesley for which George Frederick Handel (1685–1759) wrote tunes. The others are 'Sinners obey the Gospel word' and 'O Love divine, how sweet thou art'. Handel got to know Wesley through a mutual friend, John Rich, the proprietor of the Covent Garden Theatre where the composer's oratorios were performed. Rich's wife was one of the first attenders of West Street Chapel, a favourite preaching place of the Wesleys.

It seems likely that Handel composed his settings for the three Wesley hymns between 1749 and 1752, but the author never heard his words sung to them. The composer seems to have kept the tunes to himself and it was only in 1826, sixty-seven years after his death, that Samuel Wesley, Charles's son, discovered them while he was rummaging through manuscripts in the Fitzwilliam Museum, Cambridge. He immediately arranged for them to be published.

The tune written to accompany 'Rejoice, the Lord is King' was at first called Resurrection and in the *Companion to the Methodist Hymn Book* of 1847 it was set to Arise my soul, arise. The name Gopsal, by which the tune is now generally known, seems first to have been given to it by the Revd W. H. Havergal, father of Frances Ridley Havergal, the author of 'Take my life, and let it be' (No. 119). In

349

1850 Havergal published a botched-up version of Handel's melody in his *Old Church Psalmody* and called it Gopsal after the place near Atherstone in Warwickshire where Charles Jennens, the arranger of the words of Handel's *Messiah,* lived. The tune is also known as Knaresborough, Caernarvon or Handel's 148th.

An alternative tune is Darwall's 148th, composed around 1770 by John Darwall (1731–89), vicar of Walsall, Staffordshire, and more commonly set to 'Ye holy angels bright' (No. 150).

On the Resurrection

Rejoice, the Lord is King!
  Your Lord and King adore;
Mortals, give thanks and sing,
  And triumph evermore:
    Lift up your heart, lift up your voice;
    Rejoice, again I say, rejoice.

2 Jesus, the Saviour, reigns,
    The God of truth and love;
  When he had purged our stains,
    He took his seat above:

3 His kingdom cannot fail,
    He rules o'er earth and heaven;
  The keys of death and hell
    Are to our Jesus given:

4 He sits at God's right hand
    Till all his foes submit,
  And bow to his command,
    And fall beneath his feet:

5 He all his foes shall quell,
   Shall all our sins destroy,
And every bosom swell
   With pure seraphic joy:

6 Rejoice in glorious hope;
   Jesus the Judge shall come,
And take his servants up
   To their eternal home:

     We then shall hear th' Archangel's voice,
     The trump of God shall sound, Rejoice!

112 RIDE ON! RIDE ON IN MAJESTY

This fine hymn for Palm Sunday is by Henry Hart Milman (1791–1868), who was successively vicar of St Mary's, Reading, rector of St Margaret's, Westminster, and Dean of St Paul's Cathedral.

Henry Milman was born in Westminster, the son of Sir Francis Milman, physician to George III. He was educated at Eton and Brasenose College, Oxford, where he won the Newdigate poetry prize. He wrote a number of books on early Church history and a long poem, *The Martyr of Antioch,* which became an oratorio with music by Sir Arthur Sullivan.

'Ride on! ride on in majesty' was written in 1821, while Milman was at St Mary's, Reading, and just before he was elected Professor of Poetry at Oxford University. Reginald Heber (on whose life see notes to hymns Nos. 22 and 41) was at that time preparing a book of hymns to cover all the Sundays and festivals of the Christian year. Milman sent him a copy of 'Ride on! ride on in majesty' and received the enthusiastic reply, 'You have indeed sent me a most powerful reinforcement to my projected hymn-book. A few more such hymns and I shall neither need nor wait for the aid of Scott or Southey.'

Along with twelve other hymns by Milman, 'Ride on! ride on in majesty' was first published in Heber's *Hymns written and adapted to the weekly Church Services of the Year,* which came out in 1827 after its compiler's death. It was there given as the first hymn for Palm Sunday and it has been a regular feature of worship on that day ever since. For some curious reason, the third line of the first verse was long regarded as unacceptable by several hymn-book editors and was generally changed either to 'O saviour meek, pursue thy road' or 'With joyous throngs pursue thy road'.

The hymn is most commonly sung to Winchester New adapted

by W. H. Havergal (1793–1870) from the *Musikalisches Handbuch* published in Hamburg in 1690 (see notes to hymn No. 104). An alternative tune is St Drostane by J. B. Dykes (1823–76), which was written in 1862 and came into *Hymns Ancient and Modern* in 1875.

Palm Sunday

Ride on! ride on in majesty!
Hark, all the tribes hosanna cry;
Thine humble beast pursues his road
With palms and scattered garments strowed.

2   Ride on! ride on in majesty!
In lowly pomp ride on to die:
O Christ, thy triumphs now begin
O'er captive death and conquered sin.

3   Ride on! ride on in majesty!
The wingèd squadrons of the sky
Look down with sad and wondering eyes
To see the approaching sacrifice.

4   Ride on! ride on in majesty!
Thy last and fiercest strife is nigh;
The Father, on his sapphire throne,
Expects his own anointed Son.

5   Ride on! ride on in majesty!
In lowly pomp ride on to die;
Bow thy meek head to mortal pain
Then take, O God, thy power, and reign.

113 ROCK OF AGES, CLEFT FOR ME

In his *Dictionary of Hymnody* Dr Julian wrote of the verses overleaf
that 'no other hymn can be named which has laid so broad and so
firm a grasp upon the English-speaking world'. It certainly came
high on the Victorians' list of favourite hymns. Prince Albert is said
to have repeated it constantly on his deathbed at Windsor Castle,
and it was a particular favourite of W. E. Gladstone who translated
it into Greek, Latin and Italian. After hearing it sung at Gladstone's
funeral, A. C. Benson commented, 'To have written words which
should come home to people in moments of high, deep and passionate emotion; consecrating, consoling, uplifting . . . there can hardly
be anything better worth doing than that.' Oliver Wendell Holmes,
one of the hymn's many American admirers, described it as 'the
Protestant *Dies Irae*'.

Its author, Augustus Montague Toplady (1740–78), was born in
Farnham, Surrey, the son of an army officer, and was educated at
Westminster School and Trinity College, Dublin. He was converted
to Evangelical religion at the age of sixteen by a mission sermon
preached in an Irish barn. Ordained into the Church of England
after a brief flirtation with Methodism, he became curate of Blagdon
in Somerset in 1762. After serving as an assistant curate at Hunger-
ford, Berkshire, he obtained the living of Broadhembury in Devon.
From there he engaged in a vigorous and often acrimonious pamphlet war with his erstwhile friend John Wesley, whose liberal views
and rejection of the doctrine of the Elect he strongly opposed. Toplady was a Calvinist of the narrowest kind, almost totally obsessed
with the subject of sin.

In 1774, suffering from consumption, Toplady obtained permanent leave of absence from his benefice in Devon and moved to

London, where he looked after the French Reformed Church in Orange Street. 'Rock of Ages', one of 133 hymns he composed, first appeared in the form printed here in an article he wrote for the March 1776 issue of the *Gospel Magazine*. In it he made the astonishing calculation that the number of sins committed by the average individual during his lifetime amounted to 2,522,880,000. The article concluded with 'Rock of Ages', which the author described as 'a living and dying prayer for the holiest believer in the world'.

There is a nice but wholly fanciful tale that this hymn was written at the end of an evening during which Toplady and Charles Wesley had met and engaged in long and heated debate. Finally, long after midnight, the two men retired to their rooms, Toplady to write 'Rock of Ages' and Wesley to write 'Jesu, lover of my soul'. In fact Wesley's hymn was published in 1740 – the year of Toplady's birth. Equally apocryphal is the story that Toplady wrote the hymn in 1763 after sheltering during a storm in a rocky gorge in the Mendips known as Burrington Combe. The story goes that lacking a notebook to write down the words that had come to him, he found a playing card lying at his feet and wrote the verses out on the back of it.

However, 'Rock of Ages' was almost certainly written in the autumn of 1774, to be sung after a sermon based on Numbers 20:11 which tells of Moses smiting the rock in the desert to bring forth water for the children of Israel. The second line of the fourth verse is now usually rendered as 'When mine eyelids close in death'.

The tune universally associated with the hymn, Petra or Redhead, was composed by Richard Redhead (1820–1901), organist of St Mary Magdalene, Paddington. It first appeared in his *Church Hymn Tunes* in 1853.

Rock of Ages, cleft for me,
Let me hide myself in Thee;
Let the water and the blood,
From Thy riven side which flowed,
Be of sin the double cure,
Cleanse me from its guilt and power.

2   Not the labours of my hands
Can fulfil Thy law's demands;
Could my zeal no respite know,
Could my tears for ever flow,
All for sin could not atone:
Thou must save, and Thou alone.

3   Nothing in my hand I bring,
Simply to Thy Cross I cling;
Naked, come to Thee for dress;
Helpless, look to Thee for grace;
Foul, I to the fountain fly;
Wash me, Saviour, or I die.

4   While I draw this fleeting breath,
When my eye-strings break in death,
When I soar through tracts unknown,
See Thee on Thy judgment throne,
Rock of Ages, cleft for me,
Let me hide myself in Thee.

114 SHALL WE GATHER AT THE RIVER

I find this Gospel song one of the best and most moving of its kind and its inclusion in this collection is very much a matter of personal preference. It is not to be found in any modern British hymnal that I have seen, although I am glad to say that it does still make an appearance in the *Salvation Army Tune Book* and is requested from time to time on 'Songs of Praise'.

Both the words and music of 'Shall we gather at the river' are by Dr Robert Lowry (1826–99). Born in Philadelphia, he was educated at Lewisburg University, Pennsylvania, where he became Professor of Rhetoric after a few years in the Baptist ministry. He resigned his chair in 1875 to return to pastoral work as minister at Plainfield. He edited several collections of hymns and wrote a number of tunes, including that for the popular Victorian Sunday School hymn by Annie Sherwood Hawks, 'I need thee every hour', for which he also supplied the refrain. Another of Lowry's hymns, 'Low in the grave he lay', was long popular among Methodists at Easter services.

According to Ira Sankey, the words of 'Shall we gather at the river' came to Dr Lowry as he was sitting at his study table in Elliot Place, Brooklyn, on a sultry July afternoon in 1864. An epidemic was raging through the city at the time and he had been pondering the question: 'Why do hymn-writers say so much about the river of death and so little about the pure river of the water of life?' He wrote the words in the space of fifteen minutes and then sat down at his parlour organ to work out the tune. In Lowry's own words, 'It is brass-band music, has a march movement, and for that reason has become popular; though, for myself, I do not think much of it.'

The hymn is based on Revelation 22:1, 'And he showed me a pure river of water of life, proceeding out of the throne of God and of the Lamb.' Some critics have taken Lowry to task for wrongly interpreting this symbolic description of the Holy Spirit proceeding out of God's throne as a literal description of a river flowing by the throne of God. But I myself would not be so harsh on him. The imagery of rivers and flowing water is much used in the Bible to suggest the idea of eternal life and it seems to me to be wholly appropriate to use it in hymns as well.

Lowry's hymn became immensely popular with Sunday Schools both in the United States and in Britain. Its compelling tune also made it a favourite for community singing. Once when he was on a railroad journey between Harrisburg and Lewisburg, Lowry heard it being sung over and over again by a group of half-drunken lumbermen. This experience brought from him the characteristic observation: 'I did not think so much of the music then, as I listened to those singers; but I did think that perhaps the spirit of the hymn, the words so flippantly uttered, might somehow survive and be carried forward into the lives of those careless men, and ultimately lift them upward to the realization of the hope expressed in the hymn.'

At a time when many inferior modern choruses are heard increasingly frequently in churches, it seems a pity that such tried and proven old favourites as this are not also being given an airing. No one would claim it is great poetry or great music, but it has a genuine simplicity and feeling.

Shall we gather at the river

Shall we gather at the river,
  Where bright angel feet have trod,
With its crystal tide for ever
  Flowing by the throne of God?
Yes, we'll gather at the river,
  The beautiful, the beautiful river;
Gather with the saints at the river
  That flows by the throne of God.

2 On the margin of the river
     Dashing up its silver spray,
   We will walk and worship ever
     All the happy, golden day.

3 Ere we reach the shining river,
     Lay we every burden down;
   Grace our spirits will deliver,
     And provide a robe and crown.

4 At the shining of the river,
     Mirror of the Saviour's face,
   Saints whom death will never sever
     Raise their song of saving grace.

5 Soon we'll reach the silver river,
     Soon our pilgrimage will cease;
   Soon our happy hearts will quiver
     With the melody of peace.

115 SOLDIERS OF CHRIST, ARISE

This is yet another of Charles Wesley's hymns and is based on the well-known passage in St Paul's Epistle to the Ephesians which begins with the injunction: 'Put on the whole armour of God, that ye may be able to stand against the wiles of the devil' (Ephesians 6:11–18).

When it first appeared in 1749 in Charles Wesley's *Hymns and Sacred Poems,* this hymn ran to sixteen verses, each eight lines long. It was pruned to a more manageable length by John Wesley and was printed as it is set out below in the *Wesleyan Hymn Book* of 1780. Methodist hymn-books have stuck to this arrangement, but most others have shortened the hymn and split it into six verses, each of four lines, generally omitting the whole of the third verse and the second half of the fourth verse printed below, but adding from Charles Wesley's original version the following verse:

> From strength to strength go on,
> Wrestle, and fight, and pray,
> Tread all the powers of darkness down,
> And win the well-fought day;

Most modern hymn-books also change the order of the verses, putting the four lines that begin 'That having all things done' at the end of the hymn. The last two lines of that verse were for a time changed in *Hymns Ancient and Modern* to:

> Ye may obtain, through Christ alone,
> A crown of joy at last.

Although the original words are now restored in *Hymns Ancient and Modern,* certain other hymn-books alter the last line to 'stand complete at last'.

The most commonly used tunes for this hymn are either St Ethelwald by W. H. Monk (1823–89) which was specially written for the first edition of *Hymns Ancient and Modern* in 1861, or From Strength to Strength by Edward Woodall Naylor (1867–1934) which first appeared in the *Public School Hymn Book* in 1919. Naylor was the son of Dr John Naylor, organist at York Minster, and himself became organist of Emmanuel College, Cambridge, where he was also a lecturer in musical history.

The whole armour of God

Soldiers of Christ, arise,
And put your armour on,
Strong in the strength which God supplies
Though his eternal Son;
Strong in the Lord of Hosts,
And in his mighty power,
Who in the strength of Jesus trusts
Is more than conqueror.

2   Stand then in his great might,
With all his strength endued;
But take, to arm you for the fight,
The panoply of God;
That having all things done,
And all your conflicts passed,
Ye may o'ercome through Christ alone,
And stand entire at last.

3 Stand then against your foes,
  In close and firm array;
Legions of wily fiends oppose
  Throughout the evil day;
  But meet the sons of night,
  But mock their vain design,
Armed in the arms of heavenly light,
  Of righteousness divine.

4 Leave no unguarded place,
  No weakness of the soul;
Take every virtue, every grace,
  And fortify the whole:
  Indissolubly joined,
  To battle all proceed;
But arm yourself with all the mind
  That was in Christ, your Head.

116 STAND UP, AND BLESS THE LORD

This hymn is by James Montgomery (1771–1854), the radical journalist who was also responsible for 'Hail to the Lord's Anointed' (No. 51; see notes to that hymn for details of his life). It was written for the anniversary of the Sheffield Red Hill Wesleyan Sunday School on 15 March 1824.

When Montgomery published the hymn the following year in the *Christian Psalmist* he changed the word 'children' in the second line to 'people', presumably so that it would not be restricted to use in Sunday School, and so it has remained. The fourth verse is now always omitted.

This hymn has strongly Calvinistic overtones, with its clear expression of the doctrine of Election in the second line, but it has won a place in the affections of congregations of many denominations. There is plenty of choice in the tunes to which it is set in contemporary hymn-books, although the favourite seems to be Carlisle by Charles Lockhart (1745–1815). Lockhart, who was blind from childhood, was organist of the Lock Hospital Chapel and his tune was first published in the *Lock Hospital Collection* in 1792. Alternative tunes for 'Stand up, and bless the Lord' are Doncaster, also known as Bethlehem, by Samuel Wesley (1766–1837), and Kerry from Jowett's *Parochial Psalmody* of 1832.

I myself will always associate this hymn with the soaring and vigorous tune Hillside composed by Alan Bunney, the director of music at Tonbridge School from 1940 to 1967. It deserves to be much more widely known and used.

Stand up, and bless the Lord,
Ye children of his choice;
Stand up, and bless the Lord your God
With heart and soul and voice.

2   Though high above all praise,
Above all blessing high,
Who would not fear his holy name,
And laud and magnify?

3   O for the living flame
From his own altar brought,
To touch our lips, our minds inspire,
And wing to heaven our thought!

4   There, with benign regard,
Our hymns He deigns to hear;
Though unrevealed to mortal sense,
Our spirits feel Him near.

5   God is our strength and song,
And his salvation ours;
Then be his love in Christ proclaimed
With all our ransomed powers.

6   Stand up, and bless the Lord,
The Lord your God adore;
Stand up, and bless his glorious name
Henceforth for evermore.

117 STAND UP! – STAND UP FOR JESUS

This rousing hymn by George Duffield (1818–88) came out of a tragedy that might stand as a warning to ministers on the dangers of their garb.

It was inspired by the dying words of a leading nineteenth-century American evangelist, Dudley Atkins Tyng. In the summer of 1858 he carried out a particularly successful summer mission in Philadelphia which drew thousands of young men and secured many conversions. Following a meeting at which he had preached on a text from Exodus 10:11 to a crowd of more than 5000, Tyng was walking alone through the fields of his farm. He stretched out his arm to pat a mule which was working a machine stripping corn from the cob. One of the long sleeves of his preaching gown was caught in a cog and he was drawn into the mill where his arm was torn off. It was some time before he was found by his servants and by then he was bleeding to death. He was carried into his house, and his friends and associates in the mission gathered to witness his agonizing end.

George Duffield, a Presbyterian minister who was a helper in Tyng's mission, was one of those who supported him at the end. Moments before he died, Tyng took Duffield's hand and gave his last instruction for the continuance of the mission. 'Tell them,' he whispered, 'to stand up for Jesus.' Deeply moved, and with the words ringing in his ears, Duffield went home and wrote his hymn. The following Sunday he preached on a text from Ephesians 6:14, 'Stand therefore, having your loins girt about with truth, and having on the breastplate of righteousness.' He concluded the sermon by reading out his hymn. First printed on a single sheet for Sunday School children, it was later published in a Baptist newspaper and soon became immensely popular throughout the

United States, being sung by soldiers on both sides in the Civil War.

The fifth line of the third verse takes up the theme of the text on which Dudley Tyng had preached shortly before his terrible accident: 'Come now, ye that are men, and serve the Lord.' Duffield's original fifth verse is now normally omitted:

> Stand up! – stand up for Jesus!
>   Each soldier to his post;
> Close up the broken column,
>   And shout through all the host.
> Make good the loss so heavy
>   In those that still remain,
> And prove to all around you
>   That death itself is gain.

George Duffield was born at Carlisle, Pennsylvania, and educated at Yale and Union Seminary, New York. He was a minister in New York, New Jersey, Michigan and Illinois. He died in Detroit.

The tune Morning Light, or Stand Up, which gives Duffield's hymn so much of its thrilling punch and urgency, was composed in 1837 by George James Webb (1803–87) for a parlour ballad, 'Tis dawn, the lark is singing'. Born in Britain, near Salisbury, Wiltshire, Webb emigrated to the United States in 1830 and for nearly forty years was organist at the Old South Church in Boston. His tune was used for a number of Methodist and Baptist hymns in the 1840s, and first appeared accompanying Duffield's words in a hymn-book published in 1861.

Stand up! – stand up for Jesus!

> Stand up! – stand up for Jesus!
>   Ye soldiers of the Cross;
> Lift high his royal banner,
>   It must not suffer loss.

From victory unto victory
    His army he shall lead,
Till every foe is vanquished,
    And Christ is Lord indeed,

2 Stand up! – stand up for Jesus!
    The solemn watchword hear,
If while ye sleep he suffers,
    Away with shame and fear,
Where'er ye meet with evil,
    Within you or without,
Charge for the God of battles,
    And put the foe to rout.

3 Stand up! – stand up for Jesus!
    The trumpet call obey,
Forth to the mighty conflict
    In this his glorious day.
Ye that are men now serve him
    Against unnumbered foes;
Let courage rise with danger,
    And strength to strength oppose.

4 Stand up! – stand up for Jesus!
    Stand in his strength alone;
The arm of flesh will fail you,
    Ye dare not trust your own.
Put on the Gospel armour,
    Each piece put on with prayer;
Where duty calls or danger,
    Be never wanting there!

5 Stand up! – stand up for Jesus!
    The strife will not be long;
This day the noise of battle,
    The next the victor's song.
To him that overcometh
    A crown of life shall be;
He with the King of Glory
    Shall reign eternally.

118 STRONG SON OF GOD, IMMORTAL LOVE

This fine hymn by Alfred Tennyson (1809–92) has found its way into this anthology in a rather roundabout way. It was not in my original list of 150 hymns to be included although I intended to include Tennyson's 'Sunset and evening star', which is printed below. However, while I discovered that the latter is not in any modern hymnal that I have seen, I was delighted to find that the former is in the *New English Hymnal* and also features in a list of great hymns produced by the National Council of Churches in the United States.

The verses printed overleaf come from Tennyson's great poem, *In Memoriam*, which was inspired by the death of his close friend Arthur Hallam in 1833 and published anonymously in 1850. The *Congregational Hymnal* of 1887 seems to have been the first to set them to music for congregational singing. Some Christians have found it a shade too liberal for their taste and jibbed at the use of the word 'seemest' in describing Christ's divine and human nature in the third verse. It has none of the confident certainty found in so many Victorian hymns, and in their modern equivalents, but speaks rather with an honesty and sense of perplexity that surely strikes a chord with the mood of our own age.

Alfred Tennyson was the son of the rector of Somersby, Lincoln-shire. He succeeded William Wordsworth as Poet Laureate in 1850. While feeling many doubts about the Christian religion and question-ing some of its doctrines, he retained a strong faith in God. He once observed: 'A good hymn is the most difficult thing in the world to write. In a good hymn you have to be both commonplace and poeti-cal.'

There was a time not so long ago when Tennyson made several appearances in most hymn-books. The *Methodist Hymn Book* of 1933, for example, contains 'Strong Son of God, immortal love', 'Ring out wild bells, across the wild sky' and 'Sunset and evening star'. This last hymn, which Tennyson entitled 'Crossing the Bar', was written in the poet's eighty-first year. He later explained his reference in it to the Pilot as 'that Divine and Unseen who is always guarding us'.

Tennyson is worthy of at least two entries in an anthology of the best hymns in the English language. So here, as a bonus, is 'Crossing the Bar':

> Sunset and evening star
> And one clear call for me!
> And may there be no moaning of the bar,
> When I put out to sea,
> But such a tide as, moving, seems alseep,
> Too full for sound and foam,
> When that which drew from out the boundless deep
> Turns again home.
>
> Twilight and evening bell,
> And after that the dark!
> And may there be no sadness of farewell,
> When I embark;
> For though from out our bourne of time and place
> The flood may bear me far,
> I hope to see my Pilot face to face
> When I have crossed the bar.

369

In Memoriam

Strong Son of God, immortal love,
  Whom we, that have not seen thy face,
  By faith, and faith alone, embrace,
Believing where we cannot prove;

Thou wilt not leave us in the dust:
  Thou madest man, he knows not why;
  He thinks he was not made to die;
And thou has made him; thou art just.

Thou seemest human and divine,
  The highest, holiest manhood, thou;
  Our wills are ours, we know not how;
Our wills are ours, to make them thine.

Our little systems have their day;
  They have their day and cease to be;
  They are but broken lights of thee,
And thou, O Lord, art more than they.

We have but faith: we cannot know;
  For knowledge is of things we see;
  And yet we trust it comes from thee,
A beam in darkness; let it grow.

Let knowledge grow from more to more,
  But more of reverence in us dwell;
  That mind and soul, according well,
May make one music as before,

But vaster. We are fools and slight;
  We mock thee when we do not fear;
  But help thy foolish ones to bear –
Help thy vain worlds to bear thy light.

119 TAKE MY LIFE, AND LET IT BE

This hymn was long to be found in that section of hymn-books entitled 'Consecration and Discipleship'. It is still often sung at confirmation or other services where a commitment, or a re-dedication, is being made to the Christian life.

Its author, Frances Ridley Havergal (1836–79), was born in Astley, Worcestershire, where her father was rector. She showed an early aptitude for both versifying and musical composition, writing her first hymn at the age of seven. A devout Evangelical Christian, she led a classic Victorian spinster's life of good works and pious thoughts. Her health was delicate, and according to a friend, she expressed the hope that 'the angels would have orders to let her alone a bit when she first got to heaven'.

Her output of hymns was considerable and included 'I am trusting thee, Lord Jesus', 'Who is on the Lord's side' (for both of which she also wrote the music), 'Another year is dawning', 'Standing at the portal', 'Thy life was given for me' and 'Lord, speak to me, that I may speak'.

'Take my life, and let it be' was written on 4 February 1874 at the end of a five-day visit by Frances Havergal to friends at Arley House, Worcestershire. She later described the circumstances that led to its composition:

There were ten persons in the house, some unconverted and long prayed for, some converted but not rejoicing Christians. He gave me the prayer, 'Lord, give me all in this house.' And he just did. Before I left the house every one had got a blessing. The last night of my visit after I had retired, a governess asked me to go to the two daughters. They were crying; then and there both of them trusted and rejoiced; it was nearly midnight. I was too happy to sleep, and spent most of the night in praise and renewal of my own consecration. These little couplets formed themselves and chimed in my heart one after another till they finished with 'ever, only, all for thee'.

'Take my life, and let it be' was printed as a consecration hymn in Frances Havergal's *Loyal Responses* (1878). She herself always insisted that it should be sung to her father's tune Patmos, which was written specifically for the hymn and was later known as Consecration. The Revd W. H. Havergal (1793–1870), whom we have already come across in connection with the naming of Handel's tune Gopsal (No. 111), was a noted church musician. A carriage accident, in which he sustained concussion and permanent damage to his eyes, forced him to resign his living soon after Frances's birth. He devoted the rest of his life to improving the quality of church music, which was then at a low ebb in England. His best-known work was the *English Church Psalmody* (1847).

Other tunes used for this hymn are St Bees by J. B. Dykes (1823–76), Vienna by J. H. Knecht (1752–1817), Innocents, a melody of uncertain origin arranged in 1850 by W. H. Monk (1823–89), Lubeck, from Freylinghausen's *Geistreiches Gesangbuch* of 1704, and Nottingham, often thought to be by Mozart, but in fact probably by Jeremiah Clarke (1670–1707).

Self-consecration to Christ

Take my life, and let it be
Consecrated, Lord, to thee;
Take my moments and my days,
Let them flow in ceaseless praise.

2   Take my hands, and let them move
At the impulse of thy love.
Take my feet, and let them be
Swift and beautiful for thee.

3   Take my voice, and let me sing
Always, only, for my King;
Take my lips, and let them be
Filled with messages from thee.

4   Take my silver and my gold;
Not a mite would I withhold.
Take my intellect, and use
Every power as thou shalt choose.

5   Take my will, and make it thine:
It shall be no longer mine.
Take my heart; it is thine own:
It shall be thy royal throne.

6   Take my love; my Lord, I pour
At thy feet its treasure-store.
Take myself, and I will be
Ever, only, all for thee.

120 TEACH ME, MY GOD AND KING

Like 'King of Glory, King of Peace' and 'Let all the world in every corner sing', this hymn started life as a poem by George Herbert (1593–1633; see notes to hymn No. 73) and has only been sung in church in the present century. It is a fine expression of what might rather grandly nowadays be called incarnational theology. Herbert had a strong sense of the metaphysical dimension of ordinary material things and mundane tasks. This hymn positively affirms the goodness and oneness of God's creation and reminds us that the smallest task, if performed in the right spirit and offered to God, can be a noble work. This latter theme is taken up in the sixth verse of John Keble's hymn, 'New every morning is the love' (No. 90).

The verses opposite were extracted in 1906 by the editors of the *English Hymnal* from a poem called 'The Elixir' which was first published in 1633 in Herbert's posthumous work, *The Temple*. The poem plays skilfully on the common seventeenth-century belief in alchemy, the idea that there exists a philosopher's stone which, in the words of verse 5, 'turneth all to gold'. The 'tincture' referred to in verse 3 is the spiritual principle that can be infused into matter. The use of the verb 'touch' in the last verse also continues this metaphor. It was used of the process whereby the fineness of gold was tested by rubbing it with a touchstone, and came to be employed metaphorically, as in Shakespeare's *Timon of Athens*, III.3,6: 'They have all been touched, and found base metal.'

As it originally appeared in *The Temple*, Herbert's poem contained the following additional stanza, which came between the first and second verses:

Not rudely, as a beast,
To run into an action;
But still to make thee prepossest,
And give it his perfection.

A manuscript in Dr Williams' Library, Manchester, contains an earlier draft of the poem, which is there entitled 'Perfection'. It begins:

Lord teach me to refer
All things I do to thee,
That I not only may not err
But also pleasing be.

The same manuscript also includes an additional verse after 'A man that looks on glass' (as with the verse above, I have modernized the spelling):

He that doth aught for thee,
Marketh that deed for thine;
And when the Devil shakes the tree,
Thou saist, this fruit is mine.

It also has a different version of the last verse:

But these are high perfections:
Happy are they that dare
Let in the Light to all their actions
And show them as they are.

The tune to which the hymn is always sung is Sandys, a traditional air which was set to the carol 'This day a child is born' in *Christmas Carols Ancient and Modern* by William Sandys (1833). Vaughan Williams used it as a setting for 'Teach me, my God and King' in the *English Hymnal*.

The Elixir

Teach me, my God and King,
In all things thee to see;
And what I do in any thing,
To do it as for thee.

2   A man that looks on glass,
On it may stay his eye;
Or if he pleaseth, through it pass,
And then the heav'n espy.

3   All may of thee partake:
Nothing can be so mean,
Which with his tincture, 'for thy sake',
Will not grow bright and clean.

4   A servant with this clause
Makes drudgery divine;
Who sweeps a room, as for thy laws,
Makes that and th'action fine.

5   This is the famous stone
That turneth all to gold;
For that which God doth touch and own
Cannot for less be told.

121 TELL ME THE OLD, OLD STORY

This is a good old Gospel song which still finds a place in several hymnals. Like so many others of the same genre, it comes from the pen of a sickly Victorian spinster.

Arabella Catherine Hankey (1834–1911), better known as Kate, was the daughter of Thomas Hankey, a banker and member of the Clapham Sect. While still at school she and her sister began teaching in a Sunday School in Croydon, and at eighteen she started a Bible class in London for girl assistants in the large West End department stores. Some of her pupils kept in touch with her throughout her life and five met at her funeral, fifty years after the class had ceased. She led an uneventful life, except for an exciting trip to South Africa to nurse and bring home an invalid brother; this involved travelling across the veld in bullock waggons and inspired an abiding interest in missions. Her later years were spent in hospital visiting and other good works.

'Tell me the old, old story' was composed on 29 January 1866 when, in the words of the authoress, 'I was weak and weary after an illness, and especially realizing what most of us realize, that simple thoughts in simple words were all that we can bear in sickness.' Her original poem was more than fifty verses long and was published as a leaflet in 1867 entitled *The Story Wanted*. Later it appeared in the form overleaf along with other hymns in a collection. Miss Hankey did not object to it being shortened for the purposes of congregational singing, but she did take exception to the insertion of a refrain between each verse.

The hymn was much sung at Moody and Sankey's revival meetings in both Britain and America, where its power as a conversion agent was helped by the catchy tune written for it by William

Howard Doane (1832–1916). Doane was the principal of a firm of manufacturers of wood-making machinery in Cincinnati, Ohio, and superintendent of the Baptist Sunday School there. He composed numerous hymn tunes, including Refuge, for which, at his request, Fanny Crosby wrote 'Safe in the arms of Jesus' in 1868. He gave the following description of the circumstances in which he wrote the tune for 'Tell me the old, old story':

> In 1867 I was attending the International Convention of the Young Men's Christian Association in Montreal. Among those present was Major-General Russell, then in command of the English forces during the Fenian excitement. He arose in the meeting and recited the words of this song from a sheet of foolscap paper – tears streaming down from his bronzed cheeks as he read. I wrote the music for the song one hot afternoon while on the stage coach between the Glen Falls House and the Crawford House in the White Mountains. That evening we sang it in the parlours of the hotel. We thought it pretty, although we scarcely anticipated the popularity which was subsequently accorded it.

Tell me the old, old story

Tell me the old, old story
  Of unseen things above,
Of Jesus and His glory,
  Of Jesus and His love.

2 Tell me the story simply,
    As to a little child;
For I am weak and weary,
    And helpless, and defiled.

3 Tell me the story slowly,
    That I may take it in, –
That wonderful redemption,
    God's remedy for sin.

4　Tell me the story often,
　　　For I forget so soon;
　　The early dew of morning
　　　Has passed away at noon.

5　Tell me the story softly,
　　　With earnest tones and grave;
　　Remember, I'm the sinner
　　　Whom Jesus came to save.

6　Tell me the story always,
　　　If you would really be,
　　In any time of trouble,
　　　A comforter to me.

7　Tell me the same old story
　　　When you have cause to fear
　　That this world's empty glory
　　　Is costing me too dear.

8　Yes, and, when that world's glory
　　　Shall dawn upon my soul,
　　Tell me the old, old story,
　　　'Christ Jesus makes thee whole.'

122 TELL OUT, MY SOUL, THE GREATNESS OF THE LORD

Among hymns by contemporary British authors, this must come second only to 'I danced in the morning' ('Lord of the Dance') (No. 59) in popularity and frequency of use. In a broadcast in 1976 Sir John Betjeman described it as 'one of very few new hymns really to establish themselves in recent years', while in a poll among readers of the *Church Times* in 1979 it was voted the most popular new hymn.

It is the work of Timothy Dudley-Smith (b. 1926), who was born and brought up in Derbyshire, where his father was a schoolmaster, and educated at Tonbridge School and Pembroke College, Cambridge. He first felt the call to the ordained ministry as a boy of eleven. After serving as a curate in Erith and running the Cambridge University Mission in the East End, he edited *Crusade*, a monthly evangelical magazine established as part of the follow-up to the Billy Graham Crusade of 1955. He then spent thirteen years with the Church Pastoral Aid Society. In 1973 he was appointed Archdeacon of Norwich and since 1981 he has been suffragen Bishop of Thetford in Norfolk.

Timothy Dudley-Smith wrote the verses printed opposite in May 1961. While reading a review copy of the New English Bible New Testament, he was struck by its rendering of the opening phrase of the Magnificat as 'Tell out, my soul, the greatness of the Lord'. He later wrote, 'I saw in it the first line of a poem and speedily wrote the rest.' He had originally intended his verses simply as a poem, but they were included in 1965 in the *Anglican Hymn Book* to which he also contributed 'Lord, who left the highest heaven'. This was the beginning of a prolific career as a hymn-writer. In 1967 he produced a metrical version of the Nunc Dimittis, 'Faithful vigil ended', as a companion to 'Tell out, my soul'.

Although the first line of this hymn follows exactly the New English Bible's translation of Luke 1:46, the rest is a much freer paraphrase of the Magnificat. It is interesting that several other very popular contemporary hymns, particularly of the chorus type, take their words from the Bible with virtually no alterations. Karen Lafferty's 'Seek ye first the kingdom of God' is made up entirely of direct quotations from the Authorized Version of the Gospels, while Stuart Dauermann's highly effective 'You shall go out with joy' uses the words of Isaiah 55:12.

The appeal of 'Tell out, my soul' has undoubtedly been greatly enhanced by its setting to Walter Greatorex's grand and sweeping melody Woodlands, which is also used for 'Lift up your hearts! We lift them, Lord, to thee' (No. 79) and is discussed in the notes to that hymn. It is not, however, the only tune to which Timothy Dudley-Smith's hymn has been set – the *Church Hymnary* provides Mapperley, which was specially composed by Frank Spedding (b. 1929), lecturer and head of department at the Royal Scottish Academy of Music and Drama.

Magnificat

Tell out, my soul, the greatness of the Lord;
  Unnumbered blessings, give my spirit voice;
Tender to me the promise of his word;
  In God my Saviour shall my heart rejoice.

2 Tell out, my soul, the greatness of his name;
    Make known his might, the deeds his arm has done;
  His mercy sure, from age to age the same;
    His holy name, the Lord, the Mighty One.

3 Tell out, my soul, the greatness of his might;
    Powers and dominions lay their glory by,
  Proud hearts and stubborn wills are put to flight,
    The hungry fed, the humble lifted high.

4 Tell out, my soul, the glories of his word;
    Firm is his promise, and his mercy sure,
  Tell out, my soul, the greatness of the Lord
    To children's children and for evermore.

123 TEN THOUSAND TIMES TEN THOUSAND

This stirring hymn, which takes as its subject the Church triumphant, was written by Henry Alford (1810–71), whom we have already encountered as the author of the harvest hymn, 'Come, ye thankful people, come' (No. 31).

Alford was born in Bloomsbury, London. His father, also Henry, was rector of Aston Sandford in Buckinghamshire. He was educated at Ilminster Grammar School and Trinity College, Cambridge, where he subsequently became a fellow. Ordained in 1833, he was curate of Ampton in Suffolk and incumbent of Quebec Chapel, London, before becoming Dean of Canterbury Cathedral in 1857. He remained there until his death. He wrote a number of hymns, including 'Forward! be our watchword' and the baptismal hymn, 'In token that thou shalt not fear'.

Alford wrote 'Ten thousand times ten thousand' in two parts. The first three verses first appeared in 1867 in his *Year of Praise*; the fourth was added in 1870 and was published that year in *The Lord's Prayer illustrated by F. R. Pickersgill, R.A., and Henry Alford, D.D.* The hymn was sung at Alford's funeral on 17 January 1871.

The imagery comes from the Book of Revelation. The opening lines are suggested by the reference in chapter 5, verse 11, to St John the Divine's vision of a mighty throng of angels around the throne of God, 'and the number of them was ten thousand times ten thousand'. The 'rush of hallelujahs' and the 'ringing of a thousand harps' in the second verse are taken from Revelation 19:1–6 and 14:2.

Two tunes have been written for this hymn: Alford by Dr John Bacchus Dykes (1823–76), which first appeared in the 1875 revised

edition of *Hymns Ancient and Modern*, and Gresham by Geoffrey
Shaw (1879–1943), inspector of music for London schools, chairman
of the schools music committee of the BBC and organist at St
Mary's, Primrose Hill.

Processional for Saints' Days

Ten thousand times ten thousand,
In sparkling raiment bright,
The armies of the ransomed saints
Throng up the steeps of light;
'Tis finished, all is finished,
Their fight with death and sin;
Fling open wide the golden gates,
And let the victors in.

2   What rush of hallelujahs
Fills all the earth and sky!
What ringing of a thousand harps
Bespeaks the triumph nigh!
O day for which creation
And all its tribes were made!
O joy, for all its former woes
A thousandfold repaid!

3   O then what raptured greetings
On Canaan's happy shore,
What knitting severed friendships up,
Where partings are no more!
Then eyes with joy shall sparkle
That brimmed with tears of late;
Orphans no longer fatherless,
Nor widows desolate.

4   Bring near Thy great salvation,
        Thou Lamb for sinners slain;
Fill up the roll of Thine elect,
        Then take Thy power and reign;
    Appear, Desire of nations, —
        Thine exiles long for home;
Show in the heaven Thy promised sign;
        Thou Prince and Saviour, come.

124 THE CHURCH'S ONE FOUNDATION

This tremendous hymn was a product of one of those bitter controversies which periodically disturb the generally calm world of the Anglican Church and drive its members into fiercely opposed camps.

In 1863 John Colenso, Bishop of Natal, was deposed by his metropolitan, Bishop Robert Gray of Cape Town, because of his rejection of the doctrine of eternal punishment and his questioning of the traditional authorship of the Pentateuch and the Book of Joshua. Although Gray went on to excommunicate his heterodox junior, Colenso successfully appealed to the Privy Council and remained in his see.

The Colenso affair reopened long-standing divisions between liberals and conservatives within the Church of England. One of those most offended by the Bishop of Natal's heretical views was Samuel John Stone (1839–1900), a young curate at Windsor. In 1866, at the age of twenty-seven, he write this hymn in defence of the orthodox Anglican position. He later said he was moved to write it by admiration for Archbishop Gray's noble stand in defence of the traditional catholic faith. The hymn is based on the ninth article of the Apostles' Creed: 'I believe in the holy Catholic Church; the communion of saints'.

Stone went on to write a number of hymns, including the Lenten hymn 'Weary of earth and laden with my sin'. In 1874 he succeeded his father as vicar of St Paul's, Haggerston, London, and in 1890 he became rector of the City church of All-Hallows-on-the-Wall.

'The Church's one foundation' was first published in the form printed overleaf in Stone's *Lyra Fidelium* in 1866. It was there given the title 'The Holy Catholic Church: The Communion of Saints.

386

"He is the Head of the Body, the Church"'. In 1868 the editors of *Hymns Ancient and Modern* shortened the hymn to five verses by omitting the original third stanza, and the second halves of the sixth and seventh stanzas to give a new composite last verse. It is in that form that the hymn appears in most modern hymn-books. The third verse, not often sung nowadays, is the only one to give a hint of the schisms and heresies which occasioned its writing. Interestingly, another much-loved Anglican hymn, Sir Henry Baker's 'Lord, thy word abideth', was also written to maintain the cause of biblical orthodoxy during the Colenso affair.

In 1885 the following three extra verses were inserted between the original fifth and sixth stanzas to make a processional hymn for use in Salisbury Cathedral:

> So, Lord, she stands before thee,
>   For evermore thine own;
> No merit is her glory,
>   Her boasting this alone;
> That she who did not choose thee
>   Came, chosen at thy call,
> Never to leave or lose thee
>   Or from thy favour fall.
>
> For thy true word remaineth;
>   No creature far or nigh,
> No fiend of ill who reigneth
>   In hell or haunted sky;
> No doubting world's derision
>   That holds her in despite,
> Shall hide her from thy vision
>   Shall lure her from thy light.
>
> Thine, thine! in bliss or sorrow,
>   As well in shade in shine;
> Of old, today, tomorrow,
>   To all the ages, thine!
> Thine in her great commission,
>   Baptized into thy name,
> And in her last fruition
>   Of all her hope and aim.

The tune universally associated with this hymn is the majestic and unforgettable Aurelia by Samuel Sebastian Wesley (1810–76). It was written in 1864 for 'Jerusalem the golden' (No. 62). The circumstances surrounding its composition were recalled by Dr Kendrick Pyne in his book *English Church Music* (1935):

> I was in the drawing room in the Close, Winchester, as a lad of thirteen, with Mrs Wesley, my mother and Mrs Stewart [the mother of the distinguished General Stewart who fell in Egypt]; we were all discussing a dish of strawberries when Dr Wesley came rushing up from below with a scrap of manuscript in his hand, a psalm tune just that instant finished. Placing it on the instrument, he said, 'I think this will be popular.' My mother was the first ever to sing it to the words 'Jerusalem the Golden'. The company liked it, and Mrs Wesley on the spot christened it *Aurelia*.

During the First World War, Allied soldiers kept themselves going with a song to the tune of Aurelia which drew its inspiration from Fred Karno, a comedian famous for his incompetence:

> We are Fred Karno's Army,
> The ragtime infantry;
> We cannot fight, we cannot shoot
> What earthly use are we!
> And when we get to Berlin,
> The Kaiser he will say
> 'Hoch, hoch, Mein Gott,
> What a bloody fine lot
> Are the ragtime infantry.'

The Holy Catholic Church:
The Communion of Saints

The Church's one foundation
  Is Jesus Christ, her Lord;
She is his new creation
  By water and the word:
From heaven he came and sought her
  To be his holy bride,
With his own blood he bought her,
  And for her life he died.

2 Elect from every nation,
  Yet one o'er all the earth,
Her charter of salvation
  One Lord, one faith, one birth;
One holy name she blesses,
  Partakes one holy food,
And to one hope she presses
  With every grace endued.

3 The Church shall never perish!
  Her dear Lord, to defend,
To guide, sustain and cherish,
  Is with her to the end;
Though there be those who hate her,
  And false sons in her pale,
Against or foe or traitor
  She ever shall prevail.

4   Though with a scornful wonder
     Men see her sore oppressed,
  By schisms rent asunder,
     By heresies distressed,
  Yet saints their watch are keeping,
     Their cry goes up, 'How long?'
  And soon the night of weeping
     Shall be the morn of song.

5   'Mid toil and tribulation,
     And tumult of her war,
  She waits the consummation
     Of peace for evermore;
  Till with the vision glorious
     Her longing eyes are blest,
  And the great Church victorious
     Shall be the Church at rest.

6   Yet she on earth hath union
     With God the Three in One,
  And mystic sweet communion
     With those whose rest is won;
  With all her sons and daughters,
     Who by the Master's hand
  Led through the deathly waters,
     Repose in Eden's land.

7   O happy ones and holy!
     Lord, give us grace that we
  Like them, the meek and lowly,
     On high may dwell with thee;
  There past the border mountains
     Where, in sweet vales, the Bride
  With thee, by living fountains,
     For ever shall abide.

125 ('TIS) THE DAY OF RESURRECTION

This joyful Easter hymn comes from the Greek Orthodox tradition where particular stress has always been laid on Christ's Resurrection and Ascension into heaven, gathering up humanity with him.

It formed the first ode in the Golden Canon for Easter Day written by St John of Damascus (*c.* 675–*c.* 749). Often regarded as the last of the Greek fathers, St John served as chief representative of the Christians in the court of the caliph of Damascus. Apparently forced to leave, he entered the monastery of St Sabas between Jerusalem and the Dead Sea and lived in that remote spot for the rest of his life. He was a powerful defender of the use of icons in the church, and wrote *The Fount of Wisdom*, which has long been taken as a textbook on doctrinal matters in the Orthodox Church.

St John's original words are still sung in Greek churches at midnight on Easter eve. As the congregation light candles, everyone joins in the cry, 'Christ is risen! He is risen indeed!' His hymn neatly links the Old Testament idea of the Passover with the New Testament. The reference to 'All hail' in the seventh line of the second verse is to Matthew 28:9, 'Jesus met them, saying, All hail!'

In 1862 Dr J. M. Neale (1818–66) translated all eight odes of St John's Golden Canon for his *Hymns of the Eastern Church*. This first one appeared there as it is printed overleaf, but when it was first published for congregational use the following year in the *Parish Hymn Book*, Neale changed the first line to 'The day of Resurrection', and this form of opening has been found in nearly all subsequent hymnals. The fifth and sixth lines of the last verse are generally changed to:

> Let all things seen and unseen
> Their notes of gladness blend

St John of Damascus also supplies us with the original of another popular Eastern hymn translated by Neale, 'Come ye faithful, raise the strain'. It was the first ode of the canon which he wrote for St Thomas's Sunday, the name given in the Greek calendar to the first Sunday after Easter.

The tune to which 'The day of Resurrection' is most commonly sung, Ellacombe, will be for ever associated in my mind with the film *If*, where it was used for the school hymn, 'Stand up, stand up for college'. The director, Lindsay Anderson, obviously regarded it as epitomizing public school chapel worship with its jaunty confidence and breeziness. In fact, it is an eighteenth-century German melody first found in a song book published in Würtemberg in 1784.

Although Ellacombe is now almost always used for this hymn, there are alternatives, including Lancashire by Henry Smart (1813–1879), Crüger, adapted by Wiliam Henry Monk (1823–89) from a melody in Johann Crüger's *Gesangbuch* of 1640, and even a genuine Greek melody to be found in the fourth volume of *Rassegna Gregoriana*.

'Tis the day of Resurrection,
　Earth, tell it out abroad!
The passover of gladness,
　The passover of God!
From death to life eternal,
　From earth unto the sky,
Our Christ hath brought us over
　With hymns of victory.

2　Our hearts be pure from evil,
　That we may see aright
The Lord in rays eternal
　Of Resurrection-light;
And, listening to his accents,
　May hear, so calm and plain,
His own 'All hail,' and, hearing,
　May raise the victor strain.

3　Now let the heav'ns be joyful,
　Let earth her song begin,
The round world keep high triumph,
　And all that is therein;
Invisible and visible,
　Their notes let all things blend,
For Christ the Lord is risen,
　Our joy that hath no end.

126 THE DAY THOU GAVEST, LORD, IS ENDED

The tendency for churches to drop evening services means that this hymn is heard less and less often, but that did not stop it from being voted No. 1 in the BBC 'Songs of Praise' poll.

It is the work of John Ellerton (1826–93). Educated at King William's College on the Isle of Man, and Trinity College, Cambridge, where he came under the influence of F. D. Maurice and Christian socialism, he was ordained in 1850 and served as a curate first at Midhurst, Sussex, and then at Brighton. In 1860 he became vicar of Crewe Green in Cheshire and it was while living there that he wrote some eighty-six hymns, including two others for evening use, 'Saviour again to thy dear name we raise' and 'Our day of praise is done'. He is said to have composed many of his hymns on his nightly walks to teach classes at the Mechanics Institute patronized by the workers of the London and North Western Railway.

'The day thou gavest' was written in 1870 for a liturgy for missionary meetings. Ellerton got the idea for it from an anonymous hymn with an identical first line. It appeared initially in *Church Hymns*, a collection which he put together with William Walsham How (see hymn No. 38) in 1871. The following year Ellerton moved to Hinstock in Shropshire as rector, and after four years there he went to St Mary's in Barnes, West London. He had a major hand in the preparation, in 1875, of the revised version of *Hymns Ancient and Modern*, a work which contained no less than twenty-six of his own hymns. He was also responsible for a *Children's Hymn Book*, *Hymns for Schools and Bible Classes*, the *Temperance Hymn Book* and the *London Mission Hymn Book*. After an attack of pleurisy in 1884 he was transferred to the less onerous parish of White Roding in Essex; there he lived out his days, saintly, courteous, hard-working and beloved by all who met him. While he lay in a state of semi-consciousness on his deathbed in Torquay, hymns flowed almost unceasingly from his lips.

Perhaps more because of its imperialistic overtones than its suggestion of evening, Queen Victoria chose 'The day thou gavest' for her Diamond Jubilee celebrations in 1897 and it was sung at thousands of churches throughout the land on Sunday, 20 June of that year.

The tune St Clement was composed for Ellerton's hymn in 1874 by the Revd Clement Scholefield (1839–1904), who served curacies at Hove and St Luke's, Chelsea, before becoming chaplain of Eton College and later vicar of St Trinity, Knightsbridge. Although it is now almost universally adored, St Clement was dismissed by many musicians when it first appeared as a feeble waltz tune. Vaughan Williams consigned it to what he called his 'chamber of horrors' in the *English Hymnal* of 1906, and in 1932 the Archbishop of Canterbury, Cosmo Gordon Lang, started a long controversy in the correspondence columns of *The Times* by denouncing it in vehement terms. Sir Charles Stanford produced Joldwynds as an alternative for the 1909 edition of *Hymns Ancient and Modern*, but this never really caught on and it is with St Clement that 'The day thou gavest' is universally associated.

Scholefield's tune may have been the object of attack, but at least it has not been interfered with in the cause of modernity. In their determination to banish the dreaded words 'thou' and 'thy', the editors of *Hymns for Today's Church*, a volume published in 1972 which I shall not be mentioning again in these pages, turned the first two lines of this great hymn into this trite piece of doggerel:

> The day you gave us, Lord is ended,
> The sun is sinking in the west.

The day thou gavest, Lord, is ended,
  The darkness falls at thy behest;
To thee our morning hymns ascended,
  Thy praise shall sanctify our rest.

2 We thank thee that thy Church unsleeping,
  While earth rolls onward into light,
Through all the world her watch is keeping,
  And rests not now by day or night.

3 As o'er each continent and island
  The dawn leads on another day,
The voice of prayer is never silent,
  Nor dies the strain of praise away.

4 The sun that bids us rest is waking
  Our brethren 'neath the western sky,
And hour by hour fresh lips are making
  Thy wondrous doings heard on high.

5 So be it, Lord; thy throne shall never,
  Like earth's proud empires, pass away;
Thy kingdom stands, and grows for ever,
  Till all thy creatures own thy sway.

127 THE EARTH BELONGS UNTO THE LORD

We will shortly be encountering the jewel of Scottish metrical psalmody, 'The Lord's my Shepherd' (No. 131). This hymn, which comes from the same quarry, the Revised Psalter of 1650, is equally precious in the eyes of many Scots. Its last two verses are regularly sung during the bringing up of the elements in communion services in the Church of Scotland.

The first Scottish Psalter was produced in 1564 by John Knox and other Protestants who had returned from exile in Geneva to lead the Scottish Reformation. It was revised in 1650 by a committee of the Westminster Assembly of divines, the body which also drew up the Westminster Confession which remains the doctrinal authority for the Church of Scotland and other reformed Churches. It is from that revision that this paraphrase of Psalm 24 comes. The original psalm begins: 'The earth is the Lord's, and the fulness thereof'.

This metrical psalm clearly asserts God's sovereignty over the earth, and has a powerful message in these days of concern about ecology and the destruction being wreaked by man on the natural environment. The concluding lines of the first verse accurately reflect the ancient Israelite view of the cosmos as contained in the Book of Genesis, where the earth is seen as floating on the sea out of which it was created when God first moved over the face of the waters.

The ubiquity of Macbrayne's steamers around the west coast of Scotland in the early years of this century inspired the following parody, which is sadly no longer apt in these days of greatly diminished ferry services:

397

> The earth belongs unto the Lord,
> And all that it contains
> Excepting the West Highland piers
> And they are all MacBrayne's.

The last two verses of the hymn, which are so effectively used in Scottish communion services, are closely based on the latter part of the 24th Psalm. This contains an ancient Hebrew liturgy, possibly dating back to the time of King Solomon, which was used by the Israelites when re-enacting the procession bearing the Ark of the Covenant into the Temple at Jerusalem where Yahweh was acclaimed as king. As the procession reached the entrance to the Holy City, the cry went up, 'Lift up your heads, O ye gates'. This powerful command also provided the inspiration for a fine hymn by James Montgomery (on whom see notes to hymn No. 51), 'Lift up your heads, ye gates of brass'.

The first three verses of this hymn are generally sung to the tune St Matthew, which was probably by Dr William Croft (1678–1727), organist of Westminster Abbey. It first appeared in 1708 in a supplement to Tate and Brady's new version of the Psalms, where it was set to Psalm 33. The fourth and fifth verses are sung as a communion hymn to the thrilling tune St George's Edinburgh, written by Andrew Mitchell Thomson (1778–1831) and first published in 1820. Thomson was educated at Edinburgh University and after a period as a schoolteacher in Markinch, Fife, was ordained into the Church of Scotland. After serving as a minister in Kelso and then in Perth he moved to Edinburgh, where he was incumbent first at New Greyfriars and then at St George's. He did much to improve psalmody and congregational singing.

Psalm xxiv

The earth belongs unto the Lord,
  And all that it contains;
The world that is inhabited,
  And all that there remains.
For the foundations thereof
  He on the seas did lay,
And he hath it established
  Upon the floods to stay.

2 Who is the man that shall ascend
    Into the hill of God?
  Or who within his holy place
    Shall have a firm abode?
  Whose hands are clean, whose heart is pure,
    And into vanity
  Who hath not lifted up his soul,
    Nor sworn deceitfully.

3 He from th' Eternal shall receive
    The blessing him upon,
  And righteousness, ev'n from the God
    Of his salvation.
  This is the generation
    That after him enquire,
  O Jacob, who do seek thy face
    With their whole heart's desire.

4 Ye gates, lift up your heads on high;
    Ye doors, that last for aye,
  Be lifted up, that so the King
    Of glory enter may.
  But who of glory is the King?
    The mighty Lord is this;
  Ev'n that same Lord, that great in might
    And strong in battle is.

5   Ye gates, lift up your heads; ye doors,
     Doors that do last for aye,
Be lifted up, that so the King
     Of glory enter may.
But who is he that is the King
     Of glory? Who is this?
The Lord of hosts, and none but he,
     The King of glory is.

128 THE GOD OF ABRAHAM PRAISE

Many Christian hymns have been inspired by and closely based on those first songs of praise to God which were sung by the Hebrew people, and which we know today as the the Psalms. This particular hymn is interesting in that it derives both its inspiration and its tune from modern Jewish synagogue worship.

Its author, Thomas Olivers (1725–99), was born in Tregynon in Montgomeryshire. His parents died when he was four years old and he grew up with little supervision or education. After a somewhat profligate youth he became a cobbler, and was converted to Evangelical Christianity by the preaching of George Whitefield, the great itinerant preacher of the early eighteenth century, who is often regarded as the father of the Evangelical Revival. Apparently it was hearing Whitefield preach on the text, 'Is not this a brand plucked out of the fire?' (Zechariah 3:2) that changed Olivers' life. He went on to become one of John Wesley's most active itinerant preachers, working first in Cornwall and then throughout England and Wales.

While staying in London in 1770, Olivers visited the Jewish synagogue at Duke's Place in Westminster. There he heard the Yigdal, a paraphrase in metrical form of the thirteen articles of the Jewish faith, sung antiphonally by the congregation and a chorister. He was much affected by the music and resolved to write a Christian text to fit it.

The Yigdal is read at the opening of morning service in all synagogues and is sung to traditional tunes on the eve of the Sabbath and on the evenings of the major Jewish festivals. It is believed to have been composed by Daniel ben Judah early in the fifteenth century. The thirteen articles on which it is based were drawn up by Moses Maimonides (1130–1205), who first formulated the Dogmas of Judaism. The following is a literal translation of the Hebrew original:

Extolled and praised be the living God, who exists unbounded by time.
He is one of unparalleled unity, invisible and eternal.
Without form or figure – incorporeal, holy beyond conception.
Prior to all created things, the first, without date or beginning.
Lo! He is Lord of all the world and all creation, which evince His greatness and dominion.
The flow of His prophetic spirit has He imparted to men selected for His glory.
No one has appeared in Israel like unto Moses; a prophet, beholding His glorious semblance.
God has given the true law to His people, by the hands of His trusty prophet.
This law, God will never alter, nor change for any other.
He perceives and is acquainted with our secrets, sees the end of all things at their very beginning.
He rewards man with kindness according to his work; dispenses punishment to the wicked, according to his misdeeds.
At the end of days by Him appointed, will He send our Messiah, to redeem those who hope for final salvation,
God, in His great mercy, will recall the dead to life. Praise be His glorious name for evermore.

As can be seen, Olivers' hymn is only loosely based on the words of the Yigdal. He himself is reported to have told a friend during a conference in Wesley's City Road Chapel: 'Look at this; I have rendered it from the Hebrew, giving it, as far as I could, a Christian character.' His hymn, which was first published in the form printed below in a pamphlet around 1770, is made up almost entirely of either direct quotations or close paraphrases of passages from the Hebrew Bible, the Christian Old Testament. Olivers thoughtfully produced references for virtually every line of his text.

John Wesley included the hymn in his *Pocket Hymn Book for the Use of Christians of All Denominations* in 1785 and it became extremely popular in Methodist circles. James Montgomery, the author of 'Hail to the Lord's Anointed' and 'Stand up, and bless the Lord' (Nos. 51 and 116 in this collection), wrote of Olivers' hymn:

That noble ode, 'The God of Abrah'm praise', though the essay of an unlettered man, claims especial honour. There is not in our language a lyric of more majestic style, more elevated thought, or more glorious imagery; its structure, indeed, is unattractive; and, on account of the short lines, occasionally uncouth; but, like a stately pile of architecture, severe and simple in design, it strikes less on the first view than after deliberate examination, when its proportions become more graceful, its dimensions expand, and the mind itself grows greater in contemplating it.

The striking tune in the minor key to which 'The God of Abrah'm praise' is always sung is a traditional Jewish melody, the origins of which are uncertain. This was the music to which Olivers heard the Yigdal being sung at the Great Synagogue in Duke's Place. He named it Leoni after the chorister who was singing the solo part there – Meyer Lyon, whose liturgical name was 'Leoni'. Meyer Lyon, who also sang publicly at Drury Lane and Covent Garden, went on to become the first qualified *chazan* of the English and German Synagogue in Jamaica.

A Hymn to the God of Abraham

The God of Abrah'm praise	(Ex. 3:6)
Who reigns enthron'd above;	
Ancient of everlasting days,	(Dan. 7:22)
And God of Love;	(2 Cor. 13:11)
Jehovah, Great I am	(Ex. 6:3; 3:14)
By earth and heav'n confest;	(Rev. 4:8–11)
I bow and bless the sacred Name	
For ever bless'd.	(Rom. 1:25)
2 The God of Abrah'm praise,	
At whose supreme command	(Gen. 12:1)
From earth I rise – and seek the joys	
At his right hand:	
I all on earth forsake,	Gen. 12:4
Its wisdom, fame and power;	
And him my only portion make,	(Gen. 15:1)
My Shield and Tower.	(Ps. 18:2)

403

3   The God of Abrah'm praise,
       Whose all-sufficient grace   (Gen. 17:1)
   Shall guide me all my happy days   (Gen. 28:15)
        In all my ways:
✗   He calls a worm his friend!   (James 2:23)
       He calls himself my God!   (Ex. 3:6)
   And he shall save me to the end   (1 Pet. 1:5)
        Thro' Jesu's blood.

4   He by himself hath sworn,   (Gen. 22:16–17)
       I on his oath depend,   (Rom. 4:20–21)
   I shall on eagle's wings up-borne   (Ex. 19:4)
        To heaven ascend;
       I shall behold his face,   (John 17:24)
       I shall his power adore,   (Ex.15:2)
   And sing the wonders of his grace   (Ps. 145:1; 146:2)
        For evermore.

5   Tho' nature's strength decay   (Gen. 15:4, 6; Rom. 4:19)
       And earth and hell withstand,   (Ex. 5:2)
   To Canaan's bounds I urge my way,   (Ex. 14:15)
        At his command:
       The wat'ry deep I pass,   (Ex. 14:22)
       With Jesus in my view;   (Ex. 13:21)
   And through the howling wilderness   (Ex. 13:18)
        My way pursue.

6   The goodly land I see,   (Ex. 3:8)
       With peace and plenty bless'd;   (Deut. 8:7–9)
   A land of sacred liberty,   (Lev. 25:42)
        And endless rest.   (Ex. 33:14)
       There milk and honey flow,   (Ex. 3:8)
       And oil and wine abound   (Deut. 32:13–14)
   And trees of life for ever grow,   (Is. 61:3)
        With mercy crown'd.

7 There dwells the Lord our King,   (Gen. 14:18; Heb. 7:1–2)
   The Lord our Righteousness   (Jer. 33:16)
  (Triumphant o'er the world and sin)   (Eph. 4:8; Phil. 2:9–11)
    The Prince of Peace: (Is. 9:6)
   On Sion's sacred height,   (Ps. 50:2)
   His kingdom still maintains;
  And glorious with his saints in light   (Is. 24:23)
   For ever reigns.

8 He keeps his own secure,   (Ps. 12:7)
   He guards them by his side,
  Arrays in garments, white and pure   (Rev. 4:4; 19:7–8)
   His spotless bride;   (Eph. 5:27)
   With streams of sacred bliss   (Rev. 7:17; 22:1)
   With groves of living joys –
  With all the fruits of Paradise   (Rev. 2:7; 22:2)
   He still supplies.

9 Before the great Three-One   (Rev. 7:9–10)
   They all exulting stand;
  And tell the wonders he hath done
   Thro' all their land:
   The list'ning spheres attend,   (Rev. 7:11–12)
   And swell the growing fame;
  And sing, in songs which never end
   The wondrous Name.

10 The God who reigns on high,   (Rev. 4:8)
   The great arch-angels sing,
  And 'Holy, Holy, Holy,' cry,
   'Almighty King!
   Who was and is, the same;
   And evermore shall be;
  Jehovah – Father – great I am!
   we worship thee.'

11 Before the Saviour's face   (Rev. 5:8–10; 15:24)
    The ransom'd nations bow;
    O'erwhelmed at his almighty grace,
        For ever new:
    He shews his prints of love –   (Jn. 20:27)
    They kindle – to a flame!
    And sound thro' all the worlds above
        the slaughter'd Lamb

12 The whole triumphant host,   (Rev. 5:13; 19:1–7)
    Give thanks to God on high;
    'Hail, Father, Son and Holy Ghost,'
        They ever cry;
    Hail, Abraham's God – and *mine*   (Ps. 89:26; Jn. 20:17, 28)
    (I join the heavenly lays)   (Ps. 103:1–5)
    All might and majesty are thine   (Rev. 4:11; 5:12; 7:10, 12)
    And endless praise.

129 THE HEAD THAT ONCE WAS CROWNED WITH THORNS

This Ascensiontide hymn picks up the theme of Christ's two crowns, the crown of thorns placed mockingly on his head by the Roman soldiers (Mark 15:17–19) and the vision of St John the Divine in Revelation 19:12, 'On his head were many crowns'.

The author, Thomas Kelly (1769–1855), was the son of an Irish judge and was educated at Trinity College, Dublin, with the intention that he should read for the Bar. He experienced a conversion to Evangelical religion and was ordained into the episcopal Church of Ireland in 1792. However, he fell foul of the Archbishop of Dublin on account of his 'Methodistical' leanings and seceded from the episcopal Church to found his own sect. He was by all accounts a magnetic preacher, and also a genuine friend to the poor and oppressed. He was a prolific hymn-writer. His collection, *Hymns on Various Subjects*, first published in 1804, had by its 1853 edition reached 765 entries, all of them from his own pen. He also produced music to go with them. Among his other hymns which are still sung today are 'The Lord is risen indeed!' and 'We sing the praise of him who died'.

'The head that once was crowned with thorns' first appeared in the fifth edition of his hymn-book, issued in 1820. Kelly attached to it the following text from Hebrews 2:10, 'For it became him, for whom are all things, and by whom are all things, in bringing many sons unto glory, to make the Captain of their salvation perfect through sufferings.'

The opening line of this hymn is identical to that of a verse in a poem on the subject of heaven by John Bunyan (1628–88), the author of *Pilgrim's Progress* and of the hymn 'Who would true valour see' (No. 147). It seems highly likely that Kelly drew the inspiration for his hymn from this poem, which was first published in 1688 in Bunyan's *One thing is needful, or serious meditations upon the four last things*. The thirty-ninth verse of the poem ran as follows:

> The head that once was crowned with thorns,
>   Shall now with glory shine;
> That heart that broken was with scorns,
>   Shall flow with life divine.

Kelly's hymn is almost always sung to the tune St Magnus (also known as Nottingham, Birmingham or Greenock), which is possibly by Jeremiah Clarke (1670–1707). It is found in the third edition of Playford's *Divine Companion* of 1709 which contains many tunes attributed to Clarke, but this particular one is anonymous. Clarke was organist first at Winchester Cathedral and then at St Paul's, and joint organist with Dr Croft at the Chapel Royal. He met an unhappy end. In a state of deep depression over an unsuccessful love affair, he resolved either to shoot or drown himself. He tossed a coin beside a pond to determine which it should be but the coin fell on its edge, embedded in the mud; he returned to his house by St Paul's and shot himself. In recent times he has been accorded the posthumous honour of being official composer to the short-lived Social Democratic Party, his 'Trumpet Tune' having been adopted as the party's theme tune.

Christat perfect through sufferings

The head that once was crowned with thorns
  Is crowned with glory now;
A royal diadem adorns
  The mighty Victor's brow.

2 The highest place that heav'n affords
    Is his, is his by right,
  The King of Kings and Lord of Lords
    And heav'n's eternal Light;

3 The joy of all who dwell above,
    The joy of all below,
  To whom he manifests his love,
    And grants his name to know.

4 To them the Cross with all its shame,
    With all its grace, is given;
  Their name an everlasting name,
    Their joy the joy of heav'n.

5 They suffer with their Lord below,
    They reign with him above,
  Their profit and their joy to know
    The mystery of his love.

6 The Cross he bore is life and health,
    Though shame and death to him;
  His people's hope, his people's wealth,
    Their everlasting theme.

130 THE KING OF LOVE MY SHEPHERD IS

I think I am on safe ground in asserting that more hymns have been based on the 23rd Psalm than on any other. There is space for only two of them in this collection – this fine paraphrase by Sir Henry Baker and the version from the 1650 Scottish Psalter that forms the next entry. Also worthy of mention are Joseph Addison's 'The Lord my pasture shall prepare', Joseph Gelineau's 'The Lord is my Shepherd' and George Herbert's beautiful 'The God of love my shepherd is'.

Biographical notes about Sir Henry Williams Baker (1821–77) can be found in the notes to hymn No. 99, 'O praise ye the Lord! praise him in the height'. He was chairman of the editorial committee of *Hymns Ancient and Modern* and it was in the appendix to the first edition of that book that this hymn first appeared in 1869. In his *Notes on English Church Hymns*, published four years after Baker's untimely death at the age of fifty-six, John Ellerton wrote: 'It may interest many to know that the third verse of this lovely hymn, perhaps the most beautiful of all the countless versions of Psalm xxiii, was the last audible sentence upon the dying lip of the lamented author.'

The melody universally associated with the hymn is *Dominus Regit Me* which was written especially for it in 1869 by the Revd John Bacchus Dykes (1823–76). The son of a banker and grandson of a well-known Evangelical clergyman, he was educated at Wakefield and at St Catherine's College, Cambridge. At the time he wrote this tune Dykes was vicar of St Oswald's, Durham, where his high-churchmanship got him into serious difficulties. He needed two curates to assist him in the work of the large and demanding parish, but the bishop refused to license them unless a pledge was given that they would not be required to wear coloured stoles, have anything to do with incense, or turn their backs on the congregation during the celebration of Holy Communion. Dykes refused to give such a pledge and lost an appeal to the Court of Queen's Bench against the bishop's refusal to issue a licence for the curates. Without any extra help in the church his health gave way and he died at the age of fifty-three.

Dominus Regit Me has rightly won much praise in high places. Ralph Vaughan Williams singled it out for special praise in his preface to the *English Hymnal*, while in his book *The Musical Wesleys* (1968), Erik Routley noted:

> To speak of a 'Victorian hymn tune' is to set off in any remotely musical mind the strains of John Bacchus Dykes' tune to 'The King of Love'. There is nothing more centrally Victorian in all English religion than those words set to that tune. Probably, without the least consciousness that he was doing anything of the kind, that folk-genius Dykes gathered up there everything that this kind of Victorian music has to say . . . The tune does exactly what the words do with Psalm 23. Sir Henry Baker writes, not a pastoral paraphrase like George Herbert's or an eighteenth-century country house paraphrase like Addison's but an English parish church paraphrase . . . This is the purest Anglican Herefordshire, and the tune comes flying across the country from Anglican Durham to meet it.

Psalm xxiii

The King of love my Shepherd is,
  Whose goodness faileth never;
I nothing lack if I am his
  And he is mine for ever.

2 Where streams of living water flow
    My ransomed soul he leadeth,
And where the verdant pastures grow
    With food celestial feedeth.

3 Perverse and foolish oft I strayed,
    But yet in love he sought me,
And on his shoulder gently laid,
    And home rejoicing brought me.

4 In death's dark vale I fear no ill
    With thee, dear Lord, beside me;
Thy rod and staff my comfort still,
    Thy Cross before to guide me.

5 Thou spread'st a table in my sight;
    Thy unction grace bestoweth;
And O what transport of delight
    From thy pure chalice floweth!

6 And so through all the length of days
    Thy goodness faileth never:
Good Shepherd, may I sing thy praise
    Within thy house for ever.

131 THE LORD'S MY SHEPHERD

Voted No. 2 in the BBC 'Songs of Praise' poll and almost certainly the most frequently requested hymn for weddings and funerals, this metrical version of the 23rd Psalm was, rather surprisingly, the work of a committee. Long loved in Scotland, it has only really been popular in England since it was chosen by the Queen for her marriage service in 1947.

'The Lord's my Shepherd' first appeared in the form printed overleaf in the Scottish Psalter of 1650, which was drawn up by the Westminster Assembly. This assembly of divines also drew up the Westminster Confession, which still represents the official doctrinal statement of the Church of Scotland and other reformed churches. An earlier paraphrase of the 23rd Psalm, which began 'The Lord is only my support', had appeared in the earlier Scottish Psalter produced in 1564 by John Knox and others, but it is completely different from the one sung now.

For their version, the divines meeting at Westminster put together lines taken from several different sources. The first line comes from the pen of Zachary Boyd (1585–1654). Born in Kilmarnock and a graduate of St Andrews University, he spent sixteen years in France and was subsequently minister of the Barony Church in Glasgow and vice-chancellor of Glasgow University. In 1646 he wrote a metrical version of the 23rd Psalm which began:

> The Lord's my shepheard, I'le not want.
> He makes me by good will
> Ly in green pastures, he me leads
> Beside the waters still.

The second line comes from a psalter produced in 1643 by Francis

Rous (1579–1658), a Cornishman who was a close adherent of Oliver Cromwell and became Member of Parliament for Truro, Speaker in the Barebones Parliament and provost of Eton College. His version began:

> My shepheard is the living Lord,
>   and he that doth me feed:
> How can I then lack any thing
>   whereof I stand in need?
> In pastures green and flourishing
>   he makes me down to lye:
> And after drives me to the streames
>   which run most pleasantly.

Most of the other lines come either from a metrical version of the psalm produced in 1639 by Sir William Mure of Rowallan (1594–?), an Ayrshire soldier who served in Cromwell's forces, or from a revised version of the old 1564 Psalter which was compiled by the Westminster Assembly of divines in 1646. Only the phrases 'He leadeth me the quiet waters by' and the word 'furnished' were original to the compilers of the 1650 edition.

For nearly 300 years this version of the 23rd Psalm was not much sung outside the Church of Scotland, although it entered the *Methodist Hymnal* in 1876 and the *Congregational Hymnal* in 1916. It did not appear in an Anglican hymn-book until 1965, eighteen years after its use at the wedding of Princess Elizabeth and Prince Philip, when it had been set to the tune Crimond. It is with this tune that it has been associated ever since. Crimond is often attributed to Jessie Irvine (1836–87), whose father was minister of the village of Crimond in Aberdeenshire. It first appeared in 1872 in the *Northern Psalter*, where it was set to the hymn 'I am the Way, the Truth, the Life', and attributed to David Grant, an Aberdeen tobacconist. Modern scholarship tends to support the accuracy of this attribution. The tune's association with 'The Lord's my Shepherd' undoubtedly owes much to the influence of the Glasgow Orpheus Choir under Sir Hugh Robertson, who frequently broadcast and recorded it in the early part of this century.

Psalm xxiii

The Lord's my Shepherd, I'll not want.
　　He makes me down to lie
In pastures green; he leadeth me
　　The quiet waters by.

2　My soul he doth restore again,
　　And me to walk doth make
Within the paths of righteousness,
　　E'en for his own name's sake.

3　Yea, though I walk in death's dark vale,
　　Yet will I fear none ill;
For thou art with me, and thy rod
　　And staff me comfort still.

4　My table thou hast furnishèd
　　In presence of my foes;
My head thou dost with oil anoint,
　　And my cup overflows.

5　Goodness and mercy all my life
　　Shall surely follow me;
And in God's house for evermore
　　My dwelling-place shall be.

132 THE SPACIOUS FIRMAMENT ON HIGH

This fine piece of poetic writing is the work of Joseph Addison (1672–1719), essayist, versifier, dramatist and co-founder, with Richard Steele, of the *Spectator*. It has rightly won high praise from a number of quarters. Lord Selbourne, Lord Chancellor in Gladstone's first two governments and a distinguished amateur hymnologist, described it as a 'very perfect and finished composition, taking rank among the best hymns in the English language ... If it be not poetry, I do not know what is; and to prove that it is song, and soul-stirring song too, it is only necessary to hear it, as I often have, heartily sung to an appropriate tune.' The fastidious Scots included it as one of only five hymns authorized to be printed at the end of the Scottish Paraphrases in 1781. Two of the other hymns allowed in were also by Addison.

Addison was born in Milston, Wiltshire, where his father, who later went on to become Dean of Lichfield, was rector. He was educated at Charterhouse, and Queen's College and Magdalen College, Oxford, and was himself originally destined for the Church. However, literature and politics caught his imagination and he served as a minister in several governments before retiring from public life in 1710 to devote himself to writing essays.

'The spacious firmament on high' first appeared at the end of an essay in the *Spectator* of 23 August 1712. It is based on the first four verses of Psalm 19, which begins: 'The heavens declare the glory of God; and the firmament sheweth his handywork.' In his essay Addison observed that the psalm 'furnishes very noble matter for an ode'. His hymn also makes much use of the Platonic idea of the music of the spheres, a theme which was to be taken up again by another hymn-writer 150 years later, when the American Unitarian

John White Chadwick wrote his 'Eternal ruler of the ceaseless round of circling planets singing on their way'.

Another of Addison's hymns, 'When all thy mercies, O my God, my rising soul surveys', also originally appeared in a *Spectator* essay and is still found in most modern hymnals. Both hymns gained wide circulation when they were added by the printers to the 1818 edition of Tate and Brady's version of the Psalms.

The best tune by far for this hymn is one specially composed for it by Sir Henry Walford Davies (1869–1941). Born in Oswestry, Shropshire, Davies was successively a teacher at the Royal College of Music, conductor of the London Bach Choir, organist of the Temple Church, Professor of Music at the University College of Wales, Aberystwyth, organist of St George's, Windsor, and Master of the King's Music. His tune for 'The spacious firmament on high' was first published in the *Fellowship Hymn Book Supplement* of 1920 with the name *Laudare Domino*, and is now known as Firmament.

Ode

The spacious firmament on high,
With all the blue, ethereal sky,
And spangled heav'ns, a shining frame,
Their great Original proclaim.
Th'unwearied sun, from day to day,
Does his Creator's power display,
And publishes to every land
The work of an Almighty Hand.

2   Soon as the evening shades prevail,
The moon takes up the wondrous tale,
And nightly to the listening earth
Repeats the story of her birth;
Whilst all the stars that round her burn,
And all the planets in their turn,
Confirm the tidings as they roll,
And spread the truth from pole to pole.

3   What though, in solemn silence, all
Move round the dark terrestrial ball?
What though nor reäl voice nor sound
Amid their radiant orbs be found?
In reason's ear they all rejoice,
And utter forth a glorious voice,
For ever singing, as they shine,
'The Hand that made us is Divine'.

133 THE STRIFE IS O'ER, THE BATTLE DONE

This dignified and measured Easter hymn is a translation by Francis Pott (1832–1909) of a Latin original, '*Finita iam sunt praelia*'. Dr J. F. Neale, who included it in his *Hymni Ecclesiae* of 1851, reckoned that the original Latin verses dated from the twelfth century, but the earliest source in which they have been found is a book published in Cologne in 1695 with the title *Symphonia Sirenum* and it may be that they date only from the seventeenth century.

Francis Pott was educated at Brasenose College, Oxford, and ordained in 1856. He held curacies at Bishopsworth in Somerset, and Ardingly and Ticehurst, both in Sussex, before becoming rector of Northill, Bedfordshire, in 1866. In 1891 deafness forced him to retire and he spent the last years of his life in Speldhurst, Kent. He was a keen student of hymnology and was on the original committee which produed *Hymns Ancient and Modern*. 'The Strife is o'er' first appeared in his *Hymns fitted to the Order of Common Prayer* in 1861. Among his other hymns which are still widely sung today are 'Angel voices, ever singing' and 'Forty days and forty nights'.

This Easter hymn portrays Christ's death as the victorious end to a battle with the principalities and powers of darkness. The imagery is of battle and the Word of God is seen as having come down from heaven in the person of Christ to do battle with the Devil and slay him. This way of looking at Christ's saving work as essentially doing battle with the Devil (rather than paying a ransom for the sins of men or showing a depth of love which begets love on the part of man) was first developed by Iranaeus and was common in the early Middle Ages. To some extent it was taken up again by Luther at the Reformation.

Two tunes are commonly used for this hymn: Victory, adapted by W. H. Monk from the *Gloria Patri* of a Magnificat by G. P. da Palestrina (d.1594) and *Gelobt sei Gott*, harmonized by F. Layriz in

1844 from a tune by Melchior Vulpius (1560–1616), cantor at Weimar, in his 1609 *Gesangbuch*. When this latter tune (which is often known as Vulpius) is used, the word 'Alleluia!' is repeated three times at the end of each verse. In the original Latin version, three Alleluias were sung at the beginning of the hymn. In the medieval Church the word Alleluia, which is a Greek rendering of the Hebrew phrase for 'Praise Yahweh', was banished from worship during Lent, but taken up on Easter Sunday when it was used with great frequency in hymns and psalms of praise.

Finita iam sunt praelia

The strife is o'er, the battle done;
Now is the Victor's triumph won;
O let the song of praise be sung:
Alleluia!

2   Death's mightiest powers have done their worst,
And Jesus hath his foes dispersed;
Let shouts of praise and joy outburst:
Alleluia!

3   On the third morn he rose again,
Glorious in majesty to reign;
O let us swell the joyful strain:
Alleluia!

4   He brake the age-bound chains of hell;
The bars from heav'n's high portals fell;
Let hymns of praise his triumph tell:
Alleluia!

5   Lord, by the stripes which wounded thee,
From death's dread sting thy servants free,
That we may live, and sing to thee:
Alleluiah!

134 THERE IS A GREEN HILL FAR AWAY

Opinions vary about this children's hymn which is perhaps not so popular now as it once was. Some consider it to be a commendably clear, if simple, explanation of why the Crucifixion had to happen, while others regard it as a wholly inadequate, and even misleading, statement of the doctrine of the Atonement.

It comes from the prolific pen of Mrs Cecil Frances Alexander (1818–95), whom we have already encountered as the author of 'All things bright and beautiful' (No. 8), 'I bind unto myself to-day (No. 58) and 'Jesus calls us: o'er the tumult' (No. 66). The story goes that this particular hymn was written while Frances Humphreys, as she then was, sat by the bedside of a sick child. It was published in 1848, two years before her marriage to William Alexander, later to become Bishop of Derry and Archbishop of Armagh, in her *Hymns for Little Children*. This volume provided hymns to illustrate the Catechism and Creed. 'There is a green hill far away' was intended to explain and amplify the credal statement, 'He suffered under Pontius Pilate, was crucified, dead and buried'. In the same book, 'All things bright and beautiful' appeared to illustrate the phrase 'Maker of heaven and earth', and 'Once in royal David's city' to explain 'Born of the Virgin Mary.'

At the time she wrote this hymn, Frances Humphreys was living in the Northern Irish city of Londonderry, and it has been suggested that the high city walls with their vista of green hills beyond suggested to her the opening line. She later altered the word 'without' in the second line to 'outside', but the original has been retained in most hymnals. Some modern hymn-books have now incorporated her amendment, ending confusion for generations of children puzzled at how hills could lack walls.

Several learned New Testament scholars have admired the theology of this hymn. Professor A. M. Hunter, Professor of New Testament Exegesis at Aberdeen University from 1945 to 1971, has commented: 'It was given to an Irish woman in a hymn she wrote for children, to express better than many a learned tome the purpose, the necessity and the challenge of that sacrifice which has in principle redeemed our prodigal human race.' However, other theologians have questioned the picture of the Atonement given in the fourth verse of this hymn, pointing out that there is no such thing as a price of sin, only a penalty for sin and a price of redemption which Christ paid. This verse is, indeed, often omitted nowadays.

The French composer Charles Gounod was so moved by the hymn when he read it that he composed a tune for it which he sent to Mrs Alexander; but it is to another tune, Horsley, written by William Horsley (1774–1858), organist of the Female Orphan Asylum and later of Charterhouse, and first published in 1844, that 'There is a green hill far away' is invariably sung.

There is a green hill far away,
  Without a city wall,
Where the dear Lord was crucified,
  Who died to save us all.

2 We may not know, we cannot tell,
    What pains he had to bear,
  But we believe it was for us
    He hung and suffered there.

3 He died that we might be forgiven,
    He died to make us good;
  That we might go at last to heaven,
    Saved by his precious blood.

4 There was no other good enough
    To pay the price of sin;
  He only could unlock the gate
    Of heaven, and let us in.

5 O dearly, dearly has he loved,
    And we must love him too,
  And trust in his redeeming blood,
    And try his works to do.

135 THINE BE THE GLORY

Because of its magnificent eighteenth-century tune, based on a chorus by Handel, this hymn always seems much older than it actually is. It also seems quintessentially British. It comes as something of a surprise to discover that it comes from a Swiss original and that the author died only a little over fifty years ago.

In 1904 the *YMCA Hymn Book*, published in Lausanne, Switzerland, contained a hymn which began:

> *À toi la gloire, O Réssuscite,*
> *À toi la victoire pour l'éternité.*
> *Brillant de lumière, l'ange est descendu,*
> *Il roule la pierre de tombeau vaincu.*

The author of the hymn was Edmond L. Budry (1854–1932). Educated at Lausanne, he became a minister in the Église Évangélique Libre du Canton de Vaud, an Evangelical breakaway from the Swiss National Reformed Church. After serving in Cully and Sainte Croix he spent thirty-five years as the pastor of Vevey, near Montreux on Lake Geneva. He wrote '*À toi la gloire*' in 1896 following the death of his first wife, Marie de Hayenborg. It was translated into English by Richard Birch Hoyle (1875–1937), a Baptist minister whose last pastorate was at Kingston-upon-Thames and who translated hymns from twelve different languages, all of which he read fluently. The hymn is found in many other languages – I have sung it in Norwegian on Easter Sunday in a small church at the end of a fjord.

The tune which Budry's hymn was written to fit, and to which 'Thine be the glory' is always sung, was written in 1746 by George Frederick Handel (1685–1759) for the chorus 'See the conquering hero comes' in his oratorio *Judas Maccabeus*. Born in Halle, Germany, the son of the surgeon to the Duke of Saxony, Handel was originally marked out by his father for a legal career. However, he early showed his considerable musical talents and after studying at Halle, Hamburg and in Italy he became chapelmaster to the Elector of Hanover, later King George I of England. Handel first visited Great Britain in 1710 and liked the country so much that he made it his permanent home from 1713. He became chapelmaster to the Duke of Chandos, a position which gave him the security from which to write more than forty operas, seven oratorios and numerous psalms and Te Deums, as well as many orchestral and instrumental pieces.

À toi la gloire

Thine be the glory, risen conquering Son,
Endless is the victory Thou o'er death hast won;
Angels in bright raiment rolled the stone away.
Kept the folded grave-clothes, where Thy body lay.
  Thine be the glory, risen conquering Son,
  Endless is the victory Thou o'er death hast won.

2 Lo! Jesus meets us, risen from the tomb;
Lovingly He greets us, scatters fear and gloom;
Let the Church with gladness, hymns of triumph sing,
For her Lord now liveth, death hath lost its sting.

3 No more we doubt Thee, glorious Prince of life;
Life is nought without Thee: aid us in our strife;
Make us more than conquerors, through Thy deathless love;
Bring us safe through Jordan to Thy home above.

136 THOU, WHOSE ETERNAL WORD

This hymn was written to be sung to the tune of the National Anthem. Its author, John Marriott (1780–1825), was too modest to publish it during his lifetime and it was not sung in any church until after his death.

John Marriott was educated at Rugby and Christ Church, Oxford. Ordained in 1804, he spent four years at Dalkeith Palace near Edinburgh as domestic chaplain to the fourth Duke of Buccleuch and private tutor to his eldest son, Lord George Scott. When his young charge died suddenly at the age of ten, Marriott was presented by the Duke to the living of Church Lawford in Warwickshire. However, ill-health made it impossible for him to live there and instead he served a series of curacies in Devon. In 1824 he was attacked by ossification of the brain. By all accounts he was a saintly individual and was highly thought of by Sir Walter Scott, who got to know him when he was at Dalkeith. Marriott contributed three ballads to Scott's *Minstrelsy of the Scottish Border* and wrote several hymns.

Too modest to publish his hymns during his own lifetime, Marriott would not even allow the words of 'Thou, whose eternal Word', which he wrote around 1813, to be copied by friends. Six weeks after his death, the verses of the hymn were read out to a meeting of the London Missionary Society by the Revd Thomas Mortimer. It was much acclaimed by those who heard it there and was printed later that year (1825) in both the *Evangelical Magazine* and the *Friendly Visitor*.

The hymn is based on Genesis 1:3, 'And God said, Let there by light: and there was light.' It is printed opposite as it was written by Marriott. The version which is familiar to us today, with 'almighty' substituted for 'eternal' in the first line, is that which appeared in the first edition of *Hymns Ancient and Modern* in 1861. The editors of that work made two further changes to Marriott's original, reversing the order of 'Blessed and holy' in the first line of verse 4 and changing 'world' to 'earth' in the penultimate line. Most modern hymnals have reverted to Marriott's original version of the fourth verse, but all retain the alteration made to his first line. Perhaps it is time to return to the original here too.

The tune, known variously as Moscow, England, Trinity or Giardini, was written by Felice Giardini (1716–96) and first printed in the *Lock Hospital Collection of Psalm and Hymn Tunes* in 1769. Giardini was a chorister at Milan Cathedral, led the Italian Opera orchestra in London and was himself a composer of operas. He lived for most of his life in London, but after losing favour with the English public he went to Russia and died in Moscow.

Missionary Hymn

Thou, whose eternal Word
Chaos and darkness heard,
 And took their flight,
Hear us, we humbly pray,
And, where the Gospel-day
Sheds not its glorious ray,
 Let there be light!

2 Thou, who didst come to bring
On thy redeeming wing
 Healing and sight,
Health to the sick in mind,
Sight to the inly blind,
O now, to all mankind,
 Let there be light!

3 Spirit of truth and love,
Life-giving, holy Dove,
 Speed forth thy flight;
Move o'er the waters' face,
Bearing the lamp of grace,
And, in earth's darkest place,
 Let there be light!

4 Blessed and holy Three,
Glorious Trinity,
 Wisdom, Love, Might;
Boundless as ocean's tide
Rolling in fullest pride,
Through the world, far and wide,
 Let there be light!

137 THROUGH ALL THE CHANGING SCENES OF LIFE

Like 'As pants the hart for cooling streams' (No. 13), this fine paraphrase of Psalm 34 ('I will bless the Lord at all times; his praise shall continually be in my mouth') comes from the New Version of the Psalter produced in 1696 by Nahum Tate and Nicholas Brady.

This particular paraphrase has generally been credited to Nahum Tate (1652–1715), who must stand as one of the most colourful figures in the history of English hymnody. He was born in Dublin, where his father, Faithful Teate, was a divine. Young Nahum seems to have changed his name to Tate when he came to London. He aspired to be a poet, but to make a living meanwhile he translated French and Latin texts for publishers, including a cautionary treatise on *Syphilis, or a Poetical History of the French Disease*. As well as poems, he wrote plays and altered the works of established dramatists, including Shakespeare. He gave *King Lear* a happy ending by allowing Cordelia to escape death and marry Edgar, and omitted the character of the Fool completely. Probably his best-known work besides the version of the Psalms on which he collaborated with his fellow Irishman, Nicholas Brady, is his libretto for Purcell's opera, *Dido and Aeneas*. In 1692 he became Poet Laureate and was later appointed Historiographer Royal. However, he turned to drink and died ignominiously in a debtors' refuge housed within the precincts of the Royal Mint.

The text printed overleaf forms the first ten verses of the paraphrase as it appeared in 1696 in Tate and Brady's *New Version of the Psalms of David fitted to the tunes used in the churches*. The spelling has been updated. The original version ran to eighteen verses, but no hymn-book has ever printed the paraphrase in its entirety – most take verses 1 to 4 and 7 to 9, plus the following doxology:

429

To Father, Son and Holy Ghost,
    The God whom we adore,
Be glory, as it was, is now,
    And shall be evermore.

The fine tune, Wiltshire, was written by Sir George Smart (1776–1867) when he was only nineteen and organist at St James's Chapel, London. When it was first published it was as a setting for Psalm 18. Scots, who long knew the tune as New St Ann, are used to singing other metrical psalms to it including 'The Lord's my Shepherd'. Smart went on to become organist at the Chapel Royal.

Psalm xxxiv

Through all the changing scenes of life,
    In trouble and in joy,
The praises of my God shall still
    My heart and tongue employ.

2 Of his deliverance I will boast,
    Till all that are distress'd
From my example courage take
    And soothe their griefs to rest.

3 O magnify the Lord with me,
    With me exalt his name;
4 When in distress to him I called,
    He to my rescue came.

5 Their drooping hearts were soon refreshed,
    Who looked to him for aid;
Desired success in every face,
    A cheerful air displayed.

6 'Behold,' say they, 'Behold the man
   Whom providence relieved;
The man so dangerously beset,
   So wondrously retrieved!'

7 The hosts of God encamp around
   The dwellings of the just;
Deliverance he affords to all
   Who on his succour trust.

8 O make but trial of his love;
   Experience will decide
How blest they are, and only they,
   Who in his truth confide.

9 Fear him, ye saints, and you will then
   Have nothing else to fear;
Make you his service your delight,
   Your wants shall be his care.

10 While hungry lions lack their prey,
   The Lord will food provide
For such as put their trust in him,
   And see their needs supplied.

138 THROUGH THE NIGHT OF DOUBT AND SORROW

As far as I know, this is the only Danish hymn to find its way into English-language hymn-books. Its author, Bernhard Severin Ingemann (1789–1862), was a legendary figure in his country, whose influence on children was second only to that of the great Hans Christian Andersen.

Born on the island of Falster, Ingemann, a devout Lutheran, became Professor of Danish Language and Literature at the Academy of Sorö in Zealand. He wrote historical romances which were much influenced by the work of Sir Walter Scott, but it was his stories for children which won him his greatest fame. On his seventieth birthday he was presented with a golden horn ornamented with figures from his poems and stories, and paid for by halfpenny donations from every child in the land.

Ingemann wrote his hymn, 'Igjennem Nat og Traengsel', based on the Israelites' journey to the Promised Land, in 1825 and it was published in a Copenhagen *Psalmebog* in 1859. Sabine Baring-Gould (1834–1924) came across a copy of the hymn and translated it. His translation was first published in the *People's Hymnal* in 1867 and later, in an altered state, in *Hymns Ancient and Modern* in 1875. It is the earlier version which appears here and is to be found in most modern hymnals.

Baring-Gould, who is best known as the author of 'Onward Christian soldiers' (No. 105), was the son of an Indian cavalry officer who tried to settle in Devon but found the milieu there too conservative and spent the latter part of his life on a perpetual grand tour of the spas and cities of Europe. Young Sabine was not sent to school but succeeded in obtaining a place at Clare College, Cambridge. He was ordained into the Church of England and married a

432

Yorkshire mill-girl half his age who bore him five sons and nine daughters. In 1872 his uncle, who was rector of Lew Trenchard in Devon, died and he presented himself to the living. He spent the rest of his life as parson and squire of the village.

A strong Anglo-Catholic and a considerable scholar, Baring-Gould published a sixteen-volume *Lives of the Saints*. He also wrote novels and collected the folk songs of Devon and Cornwall, including the immortal 'Widdecombe Fair'. Other hymns by him which are still sung today include 'Daily, daily sing the praises' and 'Now the day is over'.

'Through the night of doubt and sorrow' has recently been in trouble on account of its sexist language. In a piece in the *Daily Telegraph* on 29 July 1987, Fritz Spiegel revealed that during a rehearsal for BBC Radio 4's morning service a female preacher objected to the line 'Brother clasps the hand of brother'. He went on: 'According to a friend who was singing in the choir she tried (fortunately in vain) to get it changed to "Person clasps the hand of person". In the end a compromise was reached and the offending verse omitted.'

The hymn has been set to a number of tunes, but by far the best – which is now almost universally used – is Marching, which was specially written for it by Martin Shaw (1875–1958). Shaw wrote it in 1915 for use at St Mary's, Primrose Hill, where he was organist.

Igjennem Nat og Traengsel

Through the night of doubt and sorrow
  Onward goes the pilgrim band,
Singing songs of expectation,
  Marching to the Promised Land.

2 Clear before us through the darkness
    Gleams and burns the guiding light;
Brother clasps the hand of brother,
    Stepping fearless through the night.

3 One the light of God's own presence
    O'er his ransomed people shed,
Chasing far the gloom and terror,
    Brightening all the path we tread;

4 One the object of our journey,
    One the faith which never tires,
One the earnest looking forward,
    One the hope our God inspires:

5 One the strain that lips of thousands
    Lift as from the heart of one;
One the conflict, one the peril,
    One the march in God begun;

6 One the gladness of rejoicing
    On the far eternal shore,
Where the one almighty Father
    Reigns in love for evermore.

7 Onward, therefore, pilgrim brothers,
    Onward with the Cross our aid;
Bear its shame, and fight its battle,
    Till we rest beneath its shade.

8 Soon shall come the great awakening,
    Soon the rending of the tomb;
Then the scatt'ring of all shadows,
    And the end of toil and gloom.

139 THY HAND, O GOD, HAS GUIDED

This hymn was the work of Edward Hayes Plumptre (1821–91) and first appeared in the 1889 supplement to *Hymns Ancient and Modern*. Its title, 'Church Defence', might suggest that it was written in circumstances similar to those which prompted Samuel Stone to pen 'The Church's one foundation' (No. 124). However, 'Thy hand, O God, has guided' does not seem to have been born out of any particular controversy; it was rather an expression of confidence in the Church in general, and the Church of England in particular, at a time when there was much scepticism and religious uncertainty in the land.

According to W. K. Lowther Clarke in his book *A Hundred Years of Hymns Ancient and Modern* (1960), Plumptre's hymn originally contained a verse which began:

> God bless our merry England,
> > God bless our Church and Queen,
> God bless our great Archbishop,
> > The best there's ever been.

This the editors of the 1889 supplement quite understandably refused to print. I find it slightly hard to believe that Plumptre should have seriously proposed such a verse as the one quoted above, but I suppose it is possible.

E. H. Plumptre (1821–91) was a notable figure in the Victorian Church of England. Educated at King's College, London, and University College, Oxford, he became a fellow of Brasenose and was ordained in 1846. He was successively chaplain of King's College, London, assistant preacher at Lincoln's Inn, Dean of Queen's College, Oxford, prebendary of St Paul's Cathedral and Professor of New Testament at King's College, London. He held the livings of Pluckley and Bickley in Kent before in 1881 becoming Dean of Wells. A

435

considerable scholar, he translated Aeschylus, Dante and Sophocles. His other hymns include 'O Light, whose beams illumine all', 'Rejoice, ye pure in heart' and 'Thine arm, O Lord, in days of yore'. This last hymn would certainly have found a place in this anthology if there had been more room. Let me at least print its first verse:

> Thine arm, O Lord, in days of old
>   Was strong to heal and save;
> It triumphed o'er disease and death,
>   O'er darkness and the grave:
> To thee they went, the blind, the dumb,
>   The palsied and the lame,
> The leper with his tainted life,
>   The sick with fevered frame.

The tune Thornbury was specially composed for 'Thy hand, O God, has guided' by Basil Harwood (1859–1949), organist at Ely Cathedral and Christ Church Cathedral, Oxford. It was first used at an annual festival of the London Church Choir Association in 1898 but did not come into *Hymns Ancient and Modern* until 1916.

Church Defence

> Thy hand, O God, has guided
>   Thy flock, from age to age;
> The wondrous tale is written,
>   Full clear, on every page;
> Our fathers owned thy goodness,
>   And we their deeds record;
> And both of this bear witness:
>   One Church, one Faith, one Lord.

> 2 Thy heralds brought glad tidings
>   To greatest, as to least;
> They bade men rise, and hasten
>   To share the great King's feast;

436

And this was all their teaching,
 In every deed and word,
To all alike proclaiming
 One Church, one Faith, one Lord.

3 When shadows thick were falling,
 And all seemed sunk in night,
Thou, Lord, didst send thy servants,
 Thy chosen sons of light.
On them and on thy people
 Thy plenteous grace was poured,
And this was still their message:
 One Church, one Faith, one Lord.

4 Through many a day of darkness,
 Through many a scene of strife,
The faithful few fought bravely,
 To guard the nation's life.
Their Gospel of redemption,
 Sin pardoned, man restored,
Was all in this enfolded:
 One Church, one Faith, one Lord.

5 And we, shall we be faithless?
 Shall hearts fail, hands hang down?
Shall we evade the conflict,
 And cast away our crown?
Not so: in God's deep counsels
 Some better thing is stored;
We will maintain, unflinching:
 One Church, one Faith, one Lord.

6 Thy mercy will not fail us,
 Nor leave thy work undone;
With thy right hand to help us,
 The vict'ry shall be won;
And then, by men and angels,
 Thy name shall be adored,
And this shall be their anthem:
 One Church, one Faith, one Lord.

140 TO GOD BE THE GLORY

This is another rousing Evangelical hymn by Frances Crosby (1820–1915), whom we have already come across as the author of 'Blessèd assurance, Jesus is mine' (No. 19).

'To God be the glory' was written in the early 1870s and was popular with Ira Sankey, who used it in his British crusade with fellow American evangelist, Dwight Moody, in 1873. Sankey also included the hymn in his *Sacred Songs and Solos*, which was published in Britain in 1873, but for some reason he did not include it in his *Gospel Hymns*, which appeared in the United States after his return there in 1875. It seems to have lapsed into relative obscurity for the next three-quarters of a century until it was rediscovered by members of the Billy Graham evangelistic organization in the 1950s.

Cliff Barrows, one of the Billy Graham team, included 'To God be the glory' in the song book for the 1954 London crusade 'because of its strong text of praise and its attractive melody'. It was immediately popular with the audiences in the Harringay Arena and became the theme hymn of the crusade, being repeated every night.

Returning to America in the summer of 1954, the Billy Graham team used Fanny Crosby's hymn in their crusade in Nashville, Tennessee. It was quickly taken up and found its way into several American hymnals, notably the *Baptist Hymnal*, and the *Trinity Hymnal* of the Presbyterian Church. It now finds a place in many modern British and American hymnals.

This is a hymn which is definitely much better heard sung than read on a page. Some of the language in which it expresses its message of salvation by faith alone is less than inspiring, although it does have a certain originality – where else in English hymnody does one find the word 'transport' used to describe what happens to us when we see Jesus?

Much of the hymn's popularity is undoubtedly attributable to the tune by W. H. Doane (1832–1916), which seems to cry out for tambourines and foot-tapping. For details of Doane's life, see notes to 'Tell me the old, old story' (No. 121).

To God be the glory

To God be the glory! great things He hath done:
So loved He the world that He gave us His Son;
Who yielded His life an atonement for sin,
And opened the Life gate that all may go in.

Praise the Lord! Praise the Lord!
Let the earth hear his voice!
Praise the Lord! Praise the Lord!
Let the people rejoice!
Oh, come to the Father through Jesus the Son;
And give Him the glory! great things He hath done!

2 O perfect redemption, the purchase of blood,
To every believer – the promise of God;
The vilest offender who truly believes,
That moment from Jesus a pardon receives.

3 Great things He hath taught us, great things He hath done,
And great our rejoicing through Jesus the Son;
But purer, and higher, and greater will be
Our wonder, our transport, when Jesus we see.

141 TURN BACK, O MAN, FORSWEAR THY FOOLISH WAYS

Considering the amount of great poetry that came out of the First World War, it is perhaps surprising how few hymns we have from that period when so many sensitive hearts and minds were made painfully aware of the sinfulness of humanity. These powerful verses by Clifford Bax (1886–1962) are very much a product of that war to end all wars and have the same mixture of despair tinged with optimism that is found in the work of Rupert Brooke and Wilfred Owen.

Bax was educated privately and studied art at the Slade School. After living on the Continent for some years, he returned to England and pursued a successful career as a writer of poems, plays, comedies and short stories. He wrote 'Turn back, O man', in 1916 at the behest of the composer Gustav Holst (on whom see notes to hymn No. 60). The hymn first appeared in the League of Arts *Motherland Song Book* of 1919. It was often sung at Assemblies of the League of Nations.

Erik Routley has described this hymn as 'very largely humanistic'. Bax himself later became a Buddhist and it is certainly a hymn which adherents to virtually all the world's great religions could equally happily sing. But if there is nothing very specifically Christian in its message, its strong condemnation of man's foolish and wanton destruction of God's world is surely a theme which strikes a deep chord with all religious people in the late twentieth century. It seems to me also to be a shining example of the Christian doctrine of hope, with the establishment of Christ's kingdom on earth held out as the goal for which we must all strive and which will one day come to pass.

Surprisingly, this hymn is missing from most moden English hymnals, although it does find a place in the third edition of the *Church Hymnary*. That volume also contains another superb hymn which came out of the First World War, and which has the same streak of idealism arising from despair. It is 'Peace' written in 1918 by Laurence Housman (1865–1959), the brother of the poet A. E. Housman, at the request of Dr H. R. L. Shepherd, rector of St Martin-in-the-Fields, London. It was used in the Life and Liberty movement and first published in *Songs of Praise* in 1925 set to the fine tune Langham, specially written for it by Geoffrey Shaw. The first verse, which I quote by permission of Oxford University Press who own the copyright, runs as follows:

> Father Eternal, Ruler of Creation,
> Spirit of Life, which moved ere form was made,
> Through the thick darkness covering every nation,
> Light to man's blindness, O be thou our aid!
> Thy Kingdom come, O Lord, thy will be done.

These two hymns deserve a much wider currency and it would be good to see them in all modern hymn-books. Interestingly, they are both now usually sung to the Old 124th from the Geneva Psalter of 1551. It was, in fact, for an arrangement that he had made of the Old 124th that Gustav Holst asked Bax to write a hymn in 1916.

Turn back, O man, forswear thy foolish ways.
Old now is earth, and none may count her days,
Yet thou, her child, whose head is crowned with flame,
Still wilt not hear thine inner God proclaim –
'Turn back, O man, forswear thy foolish ways.'

2 Earth might be fair and all men glad and wise.
Age after age their tragic empires rise,
Built while they dream, and in that dreaming weep:
Would man but wake from out his haunted sleep,
Earth might be fair and all men glad and wise.

3 Earth shall be fair, and all her people one:
Nor till that hour shall God's whole will be done.
Now, even now, once more from earth to sky,
Peals forth in joy man's old undaunted cry –
'Earth shall be fair, and all her folk be one!'

Reproduced by permission of A. D. Peters & Co. Ltd

142 WAKE, O WAKE! WITH TIDINGS THRILLING

This powerful Advent hymn is German in origin. It was written at the very end of the sixteenth century by Philipp Nicolai (1556–1608) in circumstances very similar to those that may have inspired another Lutheran pastor, Martin Rinkart, to compose 'Now thank we all our God' a generation or so later (see notes to hymn No. 91).

Nicolai, who was educated at the Universities of Erfurt and Wittenberg, was ordained into the Lutheran Church at the age of twenty. At the time of writing this hymn, he was pastor at Unna in Westphalia. In 1597 there was a terrible plague in the town; in just six months over 1,300 people died and Nicolai was regularly burying up to thirty of his parishioners a day. In his despair he re-read St Augustine's *City of God* and then wrote a book of meditations which he called *A Mirror of Joy*. He wrote of it:

> There seemed to me nothing more sweet, delightful and agreeable than the contemplation of the noble, sublime doctrine of eternal life . . . I gave to my manuscript the name and title of Mirror of Joy and took this thus composed, to leave behind me (if God should call me from the world) as the token of my peaceful, joyful Christian departure, or (if God should spare me in health) to comfort other sufferers whom He should also visit with the pestilence.

'*Wachet auf, ruft uns die Stimme*', to give this hymn its original German title, is one of two hymns in *A Mirror of Joy* which became very popular, The other, '*Wie schon leuchtet uns der Morgenstern*', which became a favourite marriage hymn in Germany, is also found in a number of English hymnals in a translation which begins 'How brightly beams the morning star'.

'*Wachet auf*' makes much of the image of Christ as the bridegroom which is found in the parable of the wise and foolish virgins in St

Matthew 25:1–13. The hymn was originally entitled 'Of the voice at midnight and the wise Virgins who meet their heavenly Bridegroom'. The reference to the watchmen in the first and second verses is taken from Isaiah 52:8, 'Thy watchmen shall lift up the voice; with the voice together they shall sing: for they shall see eye to eye, when the Lord shall bring again Zion.' The gates of pearl mentioned in the last verse are found in Revelation 21:21.

In his book *Hymns for Today and Tomorrow* (page 37), Erik Routley described this as 'one of the perfect hymns of all time. It conveys a single overall impression of pageantry, energy, light, colour and expectancy. This is entirely faithful to the biblical teaching about the relation between the temporal world and the eternal world.'

The translation printed below was made for the *English Hymnal* by Francis Crawford Burkitt (1864–1935), a distinguished biblical and patristic scholar who was Norrisian Professor of Divinity at Cambridge from 1905 to 1935. It appears in the *New English Hymnal*. There are a number of other translations in current use. The New Standard edition of *Hymns Ancient and Modern* uses one by Frances E. Cox (1812–97) which begins: 'Sleepers, wake! the watch-cry pealeth', while the *Church Hymnary* favours a version by Catherine Winkworth (1829–78) which begins: 'Wake, awake! for night is flying'.

Common to all these translations is the majestic tune *Wachet auf*, which Nicolai himself composed for the hymn. It was later adapted and harmonized by J. S. Bach in one of his best-known cantatas. Felix Mendelssohn also made use of the tune.

Wachet auf, ruft uns die Stimme

Wake, O wake! with tidings thrilling
The watchmen all the air are filling,
  Arise, Jerusalem, arise!
Midnight strikes! no more delaying,
'The hour has come!' we hear them saying.

Where are ye all, ye virgins wise?
　The Bridegroom comes in sight,
　Raise high your torches bright!
　　Alleluia!
The wedding song
Swells loud and strong:
Go forth and join the festal throng.

2　Zion hears the watchmen shouting,
Her heart leaps up with joy undoubting,
　　She stands and waits with eager eyes;
See her Friend from heaven descending,
Adorned with truth and grace unending!
　　　Her light burns clear, her star doth rise.
　　　Now come, thou precious Crown,
　　　Lord Jesu, God's own Son!
　　　　Alleluia!
　　Let us prepare
　　To follow there,
　　Where in thy supper we may share.

3　Every soul in thee rejoices;
From men and from angelic voices
　　Be glory giv'n to thee alone!
Now the gates of pearl receive us,
Thy presence never more shall leave us,
　　　We stand with Angels round thy thone.
　　　Earth cannot give below
　　　The bliss thou dost bestow.
　　　　Alleluia!
　　Grant us to raise,
　　To length of days,
　　The triumph-chorus of thy praise.

445

143 WE PLOUGH THE FIELDS, AND SCATTER

This much-loved harvest hymn which seems to come from the very depths of the English countryside is, in fact, another translation from a German original. *'Wir pflugen und wir streuen/Den Samen auf das Land'* was written by Matthias Claudius (1740–1815).

Born in Reinfeld near Lübeck, Claudius was the son of a Lutheran pastor and was originally destined for the same profession. However, an affliction of the chest coupled with the rationalist influence of the University of Jena, where he studied, combined to change his course and he became a journalist instead. He edited several newspapers, wrote poetry and was a close friend of the poet Goethe. After a period of atheism, he renewed his Christian faith. At the time he wrote this hymn, he was editor of the local paper in Hesse Darmstadt, where he also served as a Commissioner of Agriculture.

Claudius's harvest hymn first appeared in a play which he wrote in 1783 about a harvest thanksgiving in a North German village. It was closely based on a peasants' song which he heard sung at the home of one of the farmers. In its original version it ran to seventeen four-line verses with a refrain to each, but when the hymn was published in a collection of melodies for schools in 1800 it was shortened to six verses with a chorus.

It was this shorter version of the hymn which was translated into English in 1861 by Jane Montgomery Campbell (1817–78). The daughter of the vicar of St James's, Paddington, she translated many German hymns and assisted in the compilation of two hymn-books for children. She lived in Bovey Tracey, Devon, and met an unfortunate death in a carriage accident while driving across Dartmoor.

The tune Wir Pflugen, or Dresden, is by J. A. P. Schultz (1747–1800) and first appeared set to Claudius's hymn in 1800. Schultz, who is famous for his *Christmas Cantata*, was *Kapellmeister* to Prince Henry of Prussia and then occupied the same office at the Court of Copenhagen.

Miss Campbell's translation has been altered slightly in most modern hymnals so that the last four lines of the third verse now run:

> Accept the gifts we offer
> For all thy love imparts,
> And, what thou most desirest,
> Our humble, thankful hearts.

It is now quite common for an updated version of the hymn to be sung at harvest festivals. This begins:

> We plough the fields with tractors,
> With drills we sow the land;
> But growth is still the wondrous gift
> Of God's almighty hand.
> We add our fertilizers
> To help the growing grain,
> But for its full fruition
> It needs God's sun and rain.

I have to say that I find this modern version, whose origins I have been unable to trace, all too reminiscent of John Betjeman's splendid parody which begins:

> We spray the fields and scatter
> The poison on the ground.

Those who want a modern-day harvest hymn would, I think, do much better to turn to John Arlott's 'God, whose farm is all creation'.

Wir pflugen und wir streuen

We plough the fields, and scatter
 The good seed on the land,
But it is fed and watered
 By God's almighty hand;
He sends the snow in winter,
 The warmth to swell the grain,
The breezes and the sunshine,
 And soft refreshing rain.
  All good gifts around us
   Are sent from heav'n above;
  Then thank the Lord, O thank the Lord,
  For all his love.

2 He only is the Maker
 Of all things near and far,
He paints the wayside flower,
 He lights the evening star.
The winds and waves obey him,
 By him the birds are fed;
Much more to us, his children,
 He gives our daily bread:

3 We thank thee then, O Father,
 For all things bright and good;
The seed-time and the harvest,
 Our life, our health, our food.
No gifts have we to offer
 For all thy love imparts,
But that which thou desirest,
 Our humble, thankful hearts:

144 WHAT A FRIEND WE HAVE IN JESUS

This hymn has fallen out of favour in recent years. It is not found in the current editions of the *Church Hymnary*, the *New English Hymnal* or *Hymns Ancient and Modern*. But there is no doubt that it is still held in very great affection by many people – and rightly so, for though it may not be great poetry, it conveys in a simple but sincere and effective way the love that God has for his creatures and the consolation which he can offer them in times of distress.

It was certainly born out of bitter personal experience. Its author, Joseph Medicott Scriven (1820–86), had more than his fair share of misfortune. Born in Dublin, his early hopes for a military career were dashed by ill-health which continued to dog him throughout his life. He emigrated to Canada at the age of twenty-five, after his intended bride had been drowned the evening before their wedding. He settled first at Rice Lake and then at Port Hope, Ontario, where he gained a living as a tutor, while spending most of his time working tirelessly among the poor and destitute. He became engaged again, only to see his second fiancée die after a brief illness. In October 1886 he was found drowned in a water-run near Rice Lake. A monument to his memory was erected near the lake by local people.

Scriven did not publish 'What a Friend we have in Jesus' during his lifetime. A friend who was with him shortly before he died came across the manuscript and was much impressed by it. Scriven told him that he had written the verses for his mother back home in Ireland at a time of particular sorrow. When asked whether he had written it unaided, he replied, 'The Lord and I did it between us.'

The tune Converse is the work of Charles Converse (1832–1918). Having studied music in Germany, where he was friendly with Franz Liszt and Louis Spohr, he went on to become a successful lawyer in his native USA. He was equally at home composing symphonies, oratorios and Gospel songs. There is some doubt as to whether he wrote the tune specifically for this hymn or whether it was originally written for another sacred song and put to Scriven's words by Ira Sankey for the first edition of his *Gospel Hymns*.

This hymn was much parodied by soldiers in the First World War. The text below is one of the more salubrious versions, which was used with particular effect in the film *Oh What a Lovely War*; it was sung contrapuntally, against the words of Scriven's original, in an open-air service:

> When this lousy war is over,
> Oh, how happy I will be!
> When I get my civvy clothes on,
> No more soldiering for me.
> No more church parades on Sundays,
> No more asking out for leave,
> I shall kiss the Sergeant-Major,
> How he'll miss me, how I'll grieve.

Pray without ceasing

What a Friend we have in Jesus,
  All our sins and griefs to bear!
What a privilege to carry
  Everything to God in prayer!
O what peace we often forfeit,
  O what needless pain we bear,
All because we do not carry
  Everything to God in prayer!

2 Have we trials and temptations?
     Is there trouble anywhere?
   We should never be discouraged:
     Take it to the Lord in prayer.
   Can we find a friend so faithful,
     Who will all our sorrows share?
   Jesus knows our every weakness:
     Take it to the Lord in prayer.

3 Are we weak and heavy-laden,
     Cumbered with a load of care?
   Jesus only is our refuge:
     Take it to the Lord in prayer.
   Do thy friends despise, forsake thee?
     Take it to the Lord in prayer;
   In His arms He'll take and shield thee;
     Thou wilt find a solace there.

145 WHEN I SURVEY THE WONDROUS CROSS

These much loved and much sung verses by Isaac Watts (1674–1748; see notes to hymn No. 29) have an important place in the history of English hymnody. They introduced a new note of subjective religious experience into a genre which had previously been studiously objective. This is the first known hymn in the English language to include the personal pronoun 'I' and to express the experience of Christian faith rather than simply limiting itself to matters of doctrine.

It has long been acknowledged as one of the finest hymns ever written. It was certainly so regarded by the great Victorian essayist and poet Matthew Arnold, who heard it sung in Sefton Park Presbyterian Church, Liverpool, on the last Sunday of his life, and who was overheard repeating the third verse shortly before his sudden death a few days later. In his *Dictionary of Hymnology*, first published in 1892, John Julian described the hymn as 'one of the four which stand at the head of all hymns in the English language', the others being 'Awake, my soul, and with the sun', 'Hark! the herald angels sing' and 'Rock of Ages, cleft for me'. It was voted fourth in the BBC 'Songs of Praise' poll.

Watts wrote 'When I survey the wondrous Cross' as a communion hymn and it first appeared in 1707 in his *Hymns and Spiritual Songs*. He there appended the text on which it is based, from Paul's Epistle to the Galatians 6:14, 'God forbid that I should glory, save in the cross of our Lord Jesus Christ, by whom the world is crucified to me, and I to the world.'

In 1709 Watts changed the second line to 'On which the Prince of Glory died'. It is not clear why he made this alteration. The fourth verse was dropped from many eighteenth- and nineteenth-century hymnals, being considered rather too gory, and it continues to be generally omitted today. In the second line of the fifth verse the word 'present' is sometimes changed to 'offering'.

The tune Rockingham (also known as Caton and Communion), to which the hymn is almost invariably sung in Britain, is first found in *The Psalms of David for the Use of Parish Churches*, published in 1790 with music selected and composed by Edward Miller. Dr Miller was organist at Doncaster Parish Church from 1756 to 1807. He took the name Rockingham from his patron and friend the Marquis of Rockingham, the Whig statesman who was three times Prime Minister. In his book the tune accompanied nine different psalms. It seems to have been adapted from an earlier tune called Tunbridge, which is found in a *Supplement to Psalmody in Miniature* by Aaron Williams (1778). Rockingham was not used for 'When I survey the wondrous Cross' until 1854. Before that, Watts's words were sung to a debased version of Tallis's Canon, known as Suffolk. In the United States the hymn is often sung to Hamburg, arranged by Lowell Mason (1792–1872).

Crucifixion to the world by the Cross of Christ

When I survey the wondrous Cross,
   Where the young Prince of Glory died,
My richest gain I count but loss,
   And pour contempt on all my pride.

2 Forbid it, Lord, that I should boast
   Save in the death of Christ my God;
All the vain things that charm me most,
   I sacrifice them to his blood.

3 See from his head, his hands, his feet,
   Sorrow and love flow mingled down;
Did e'er such love and sorrow meet,
   Or thorns compose so rich a crown?

4 His dying crimson, like a robe,
   Spreads o'er his body on the Tree;
Then am I dead to all the globe,
   And all the globe is dead to me.

6 Were the whole realm of nature mine,
   That were a present far too small;
Love so amazing, so divine,
   Demands my soul, my life, my all.

146 WHEN MORNING GILDS THE SKIES

This is not, as its title might suggest, a morning hymn but rather a general hymn of praise to Christ which is suitable for use at any time or season. The German original on which it is based is of unknown authorship. Beginning *'Beim fruhen Morgenlicht'*, and running to fourteen verses, it first appeared anonymously in the *Katholisches Gesangbuch* published in Würzburg in 1828.

The translation printed here was made by Edward Caswall (1814–78). Educated at Marlborough and Brasenose College, Oxford, he was ordained into the Church of England but in 1847 he became a Roman Catholic. Following the death of his wife, he joined John Henry Newman's Oratory in Birmingham. He wrote a large number of hymns, many of them translations, including the Advent hymn, 'Hark! a thrilling voice is sounding', 'My God, I love thee; not because', and the Good Friday hymn, 'At the Cross her station keeping'.

Caswall's translation was first published in *Catholic Hymns*, a collection edited by the Revd Henry Formby and published in 1854. In 1873 he published a longer translation, covering all fourteen verses of the German original. At the same time he made some alterations to his earlier translation. He changed the first two lines of the second verse to:

> The sacred minster bell,
> It peals o'er hill and dell,

and altered the last line of verse 6 to 'Through all the ages on'. These alterations appear in the version of the hymn contained in the *New English Hymnal*, which also includes the following additional verses from the later translation:

When sleep her balm denies,
My silent spirit sighs,
　　May Jesus Christ be praised;
When evil thoughts molest,
With this I shield my breast,
　　May Jesus Christ be praised.

In heaven's eternal bliss,
The loveliest strain is this,
　　May Jesus Christ be praised;
Let air, and sea, and sky
From depth to height reply,
　　May Jesus Christ be praised.

The 'New Standard' edition of *Hymns Ancient and Modern* contains Caswall's original six-verse translation, as printed below. The third edition of the *Church Hymnary* and *Hymns for Church and School* print another six-verse translation of the hymn, which has the same first three lines as Caswall's but differs considerably thereafter. It is the work of Robet Bridges (1844–1930).

The tunes normally used for this hymn are either *Laudes Domini* by Joseph Barnby (1838–96) or *O Seigneur*, a tune by Louis Bourgeois (1510–61) set to Marot's version of Psalm 3 in the French Psalter of 1551. 'When morning gilds the skies' also goes particularly well to the tune of Count Danilo's song, 'I'm off to Chez Maxim's' from *The Merry Widow* by Franz Lehar.

Beim frühen Morgenlicht

When morning gilds the skies,
My heart awaking cries,
　　May Jesus Christ be praised:
Alike at work and prayer
To Jesus I repair;
　　May Jesus Christ be praised.

2 Whene'er the sweet church bell
Peals over hill and dell,
  May Jesus Christ be praised:
O hark to what it sings,
As joyously it rings,
  May Jesus Christ be praised.

3 My tongue shall never tire
Of chanting with the choir,
  May Jesus Christ be praised:
This song of sacred joy,
It never seems to cloy,
  May Jesus Christ be praised.

4 Does sadness fill my mind?
A solace here I find,
  May Jesus Christ be praised:
Or fades my earthly bliss?
My comfort still is this,
  May Jesus Christ be praised.

5 The night becomes as day,
When from the heart we say,
  May Jesus Christ be praised:
The powers of darkness fear,
When this sweet chant they hear,
  May Jesus Christ be praised.

6 Be this, while life is mine,
My canticle divine,
  May Jesus Christ be praised:
Be this the eternal song
Through ages all along,
  May Jesus Christ be praised.

147 WHO WOULD TRUE VALOUR SEE

This hymn is sung today in two very different versions. It comes from John Bunyan's great spiritual classic, *Pilgrim's Progress*. The verses printed overleaf originally appeared in the book at the point where Mr Greatheart and Mr Valiant-for-truth, near the end of their long pilgrimage, have reached the enchanted ground. It is introduced into the narrative with these words by Mr Valiant-for-truth: 'I believed, and therefore came out, got into the way, fought all that set themselves against me, and, by believing, am come to this place.'

John Bunyan (1628–88) is one of the great figures of English Protestantism. Born in the village of Elstow, Bedfordshire, the son of a tinker, he served in Cromwell's army during the Civil War and then returned to his native village as a brazier and itinerant Independent preacher. Following the imposition of anti-Nonconformist laws at the restoration of the monarchy in 1660, Bunyan was imprisoned in Bedford gaol for twelve years. It was during a second much briefer period of imprisonment that he began writing *Pilgrim's Progress*, the first part of which was published in 1678, and the second part, in which these verses appear, in 1684.

As with many other fine examples of seventeenth-century religious verse, it is only in the present century that Bunyan's poem has been sung as a hymn. It owes its popularity to Dr Percy Dearmer (1867–1936), who included a heavily edited version in the *English Hymnal* in 1906. Dearmer's version, which can be found in the *New English Hymnal*, has the following changes from Bunyan's original:

Verse 1, lines 1–4:   He who would valiant be
                      'Gainst all disaster,
                    Let him in constancy
                    Follow the Master.

Verse 2, lines 5–8:

No foes shall stay his might,
Though he with giants fight:
He will make good his right
    To be a pilgrim.

Verse 3:

Since, Lord, thou dost defend
    Us with thy Spirit,
We know we at the end
    Shall life inherit.
Then fancies flee away!
I'll fear not what men say,
I'll labour night and day
    To be a pilgrim.

In a lengthy passage in his book *Songs of Praise Discussed*, Dr Dearmer defended his substantial re-writing of Bunyan's words on the grounds that the original was never meant for congregational singing. In recent years, however, more and more hymnals have reverted to Bunyan's original, hobgoblins and foul fiends not-withstanding, and this is surely right; it has a power and directness which is lost in the more modern version.

The tune Monks Gate was one of the thirty-five traditional folk songs which Ralph Vaughan Williams adapted for use in the *English Hymnal*. It is based on a song called 'Our Captain Calls', and was collected by Vaughan Williams from Mrs Verral in the village of Monks Gate, near Horsham in West Sussex.

Who would true valour see,
   Let him come hither;
One here will constant be,
   Come wind, come weather;
There's no discouragement
Shall make him once relent
His first avowed intent
   To be a pilgrim.

2   Who so beset him round
     With dismal stories
Do but themselves confound;
     His strength the more is.
No lion can him fright;
He'll with a giant fight;
But he will have a right
     To be a pilgrim.

3   Hobgoblin nor foul fiend
     Can daunt his spirit;
He knows he at the end
     Shall life inherit.
Then fancies fly away,
He'll fear not what men say;
He'll labour night and day
     To be a pilgrim.

148 WILL YOUR ANCHOR HOLD

This rousing hymn by Priscilla Jane Owens (1829–99) is the official hymn of the Boys' Brigade.

Priscilla Owens was born in Baltimore, but came of Scottish and Welsh descent. For more than fifty years she was active in Sunday School work in her home town, and most of her hymns and songs were written for Sunday school children. She is also remembered for another spirited hymn which begins:

> We have heard the joyful sound –
>   'Jesus saves, Jesus saves!'
> Spread the gladness all around:
>   'Jesus saves, Jesus saves!'
> Bear the news to every land,
>   Climb the steeps and cross the waves;
> Onward! – 'tis our Lord's command,
>   Jesus saves! Jesus saves!

Miss Owens was not the first to compare Christian faith to an anchor. St Paul's Epistle to the Hebrews 6:19 talks of the 'hope we have as anchor of the soul, both sure and steadfast'. It was almost certainly that biblical reference which inspired this particular hymn. Several other popular Gospel songs of the nineteenth century also use nautical imagery to powerful effect. The catchy Salvation Army chorus 'Count your blessings' begins: 'When upon life's billows you are tempest tossed'. Philip Bliss (1838–76), author of 'Ho, my comrades', produced at least two songs with a maritime flavour. We have already had cause to quote from one of them, 'Brightly beams our Father's mercy' (see note to hymn No. 54). The other has the following first verse and chorus:

Light in the darkness, sailor, day is at hand!
See o'er the foaming billows fair Heaven's land.
Drear was the voyage, sailor, now almost o'er;
Safe within the lifeboat, sailor, pull for the shore!
Pull for the shore, sailor; pull for the shore!
Heed not the rolling waves, but bend to the oar;
Safe in the lifeboat, sailor, cling to self no more;
Leave the poor old stranded wreck, and pull for the shore.

The tune to which the hymn is sung, Will Your Anchor Hold?, was written by William J. Kirkpatrick (1838–1921). A carpenter from Philadelphia, Pennsylvania, he became much involved in church work and composed many Gospel songs. Altogether he compiled eighty-seven books of such songs, the sales of which ran into millions. He is best remembered for his tune 'Cradle Song', which is universally used for the Christmas carol 'Away in a manger'.

Will your anchor hold in the storms of life,
When the clouds unfold their wings of strife?
When the strong tides lift, and the cables strain
Will your anchor drift, or firm remain?
We have an anchor that keeps the soul
Steadfast and sure while the billows roll;
Fastened to the Rock which cannot move,
Grounded firm and deep in the Saviour's love!

2 Will your anchor hold in the straits of fear?
When the breakers roar and the reef is near;
While the surges rave, and the wild winds blow,
Shall the angry waves then your bark o'erflow?

3 Will your anchor hold in the floods of death,
When the waters cold chill your latest breath?
On the rising tide you can never fail,
While your anchor holds within the veil.

4 Will your eyes behold through the morning light
The city of gold and the harbour bright?
Will you anchor safe by the heavenly shore,
When life's storms are past for evermore?

149 YE CHOIRS OF NEW JERUSALEM

This Easter hymn derives from a medieval original, '*Chorus novae Ierusalem*', which was the work of St Fulbert of Chartres (d. 1028). Little is known about the author, who was consecrated Bishop of Chartres in 1007, but his hymn was widely taken up in England during his lifetime and became one of the office hymns in the Sarum, York and Hereford breviaries for the Sundays after Easter.

The hymn was translated in the late 1840s by Robert Campbell (1814–68) and first appeared in his *Hymns and Anthems* (1850). Born at Troehraig, Ayrshire, Campbell became an advocate. He translated a large number of Latin hymns, including 'At the Lamb's high feast we sing' and 'Thy work on earth, O Christ, is done'. In 1852 he moved from Episcopalianism to Roman Catholicism.

The opening words of the second verse are a curious amalgam of the description of Christ as the lion of 'the tribe of Judah' in Revelation 5:5 and God's promise to the serpent in Genesis 3:15 that He will bruise its head because of its beguiling of Eve.

Hymns Ancient and Modern prints Campbell's original first verse but goes on to use its own different version of verses two to five. There have been several other translations of St Fulbert's hymn. Their first lines include 'Thou New Jerusalem on high', 'Wake, choir of our Jerusalem' and 'Jerusalem, thy song be new'. The compilers of *Hymns Ancient and Modern* also made a translation which preserves the metre of the original. It begins:

> Up, new Jerusalem and sing
> The sweet new song of Christ thy King;
> In sober joy thy children call
> To keep the Paschal festival.

The tune normally used for Campbell's hymn is St Fulbert by H. J. Gauntlett (1805–76). It was actually written for the hymn 'Now Christ our Passover is slain', and first appeared in the *Church Hymn and Tune Book* in 1852.

Chorus novae Jerusalem

Ye choirs of new Jerusalem,
  Your sweetest notes employ,
The Paschal victory to hymn
  In strains of holy joy.

2 How Judah's Lion burst his chains,
  And crushed the serpent's head;
And brought with him, from death's domains,
  The long-imprisoned dead.

3 From hell's devouring jaws the prey
  Alone our Leader bore;
His ransomed hosts pursue their way
  Where he hath gone before.

4 Triumphant in his glory now
  His sceptre ruleth all,
Earth, heaven, and hell before him bow,
  And at his footstool fall.

5 While joyful thus his praise we sing,
  His mercy we implore,
Into his palace bright to bring
  And keep us evermore.

6 All glory to the Father be,
  All glory to the Son,
All glory, Holy Ghost, to thee,
  While endless ages run. Alleluya!

150 YE HOLY ANGELS BRIGHT

This is yet another hymn which is derived from the rich storehouse of seventeenth-century devotional verse. It is based on a poem by John Bunyan's near contemporary and fellow Puritan, Richard Baxter (1615–91).

Baxter was born at Rowton in Shropshire and educated at Wroxeter School. He was ordained into the Church of England and served at Bridgnorth and Kidderminster. He developed a strong distrust of episcopacy and during the English Civil War served as one of Oliver Cromwell's chaplains. In 1660 he became chaplain to Charles II who nominated him for the vacant bishopric of Hereford. However, he refused to accept it and, following the passage of the Act of Uniformity in 1662, he left the Established Church. In 1673 he became a Nonconformist minister, and in 1685 he was tried before the notorious Judge Jeffreys for sedition and imprisoned for eighteen months. His most famous literary composition is *The Saints' Everlasting Rest*, but he was also a pioneer hymn-writer, believing that singing in church should not be limited to metrical psalms but should also embrace 'hymns more suitable to gospel times'.

In 1672 Baxter published 'a psalm of praise to the tune of Psalm cxlviii'. It ran to sixteen stanzas, the first two of which were:

> Ye holy angels bright,
> Which stand before God's throne,
> And dwell in glorious light,
> Praise ye the Lord, each one!
> You were so nigh,
> Fitter than we
> Dark sinners be,
> For things so high.

You blessed souls at rest,
　Who see your Saviour's face,
Whose glory, ev'n the least,
　Is far above our grace,
　　God's promise sound
　　As in his sight
　　With sweet delight
　You do abound.

In 1838 John Hampden Gurney (1802–62) took Baxter's verses as the basis of a new hymn which was published in his *Collection of Hymns for Public Worship*. It is Gurney's work which appears overleaf and which has become a favourite congregational hymn. Educated at Trinity College, Cambridge, Gurney entered the Church after studying for a legal career. He was for twenty-three years curate at Lutterworth in Leicestershire, and in 1847 he became rector of St Mary's, Bryanston Square, London. In 1857 he was made a prebendary of St Paul's Cathedral. His other hymns include 'Fair waved the golden corn' and 'Lord, as to thy dear cross we flee'.

In many modern hymnals the word 'light' is erroneously given instead of 'sight' in the sixth line of verse 2.

The best tune for this hymn is surely Darwall's 148th by John Darwall (1731–89), which is first found in Williams's *New Universal Psalmodist* (1770), set to Psalm 148. Darwall, successively curate and vicar of Walsall, Staffordshire, was an enthusiastic musician and composed tunes for all the 150 metrical psalms.

Ye holy angels bright,
  Who wait at God's right hand,
Or through the realms of light
  Fly at your Lord's command,
    Assist our song,
      Or else the theme
      Too high doth seem
    For mortal tongue.

2   Ye blessèd souls at rest,
  Who ran this earthly race,
And now, from sin released,
  Behold the Saviour's face,
    His praises sound,
      As in his sight
      With sweet delight
    Ye do abound.

3   Ye saints, who toil below,
  Adore your heavenly King,
And onward as ye go
  Some joyful anthem sing;
    Take what he gives,
      And praise him still
      Through good and ill,
    Who ever lives.

4   My soul, bear thou thy part,
  Triumph in God above,
And with a well-tuned heart
  Sing thou the songs of love.
    Let all thy days
      Till life shall end,
      Whate'er he send,
    Be filled with praise.

FURTHER READING

Among the books which I have found most useful in preparing the notes to this volume are:

A Companion to the Baptist Church Hymnal (Psalms and Hymns Trust, 1953).
A Dictionary of Hymnology, edited by John Julian (John Murray, 1907).
John Barkley, *Handbook to the Church Hymnary* (Oxford University Press, 1979).
Frank Colquhoun, *A Hymn Companion* (Hodder & Stoughton, 1985).
Frank Colquhoun, *Preaching on Favourite Hymns* (Mowbray, 1986).
A. P. Davis, *Isaac Watts* (Independent Press, 1948).
F. J. Gilman, *The Evolution of the English Hymn* (Allen & Unwin, 1927).
C. P. Hancock, *A Hymn Lovers Companion* (Orphans Press, Leominster, 1984).
Handbook to the Church Hymnary (Oxford University Press, various editions).
Historical Companion to 'Hymns Ancient and Modern', edited by Maurice Frost (Proprietors of *Hymns Ancient and Modern*, 1962).
M. A. Hodges and A. M. Allchin, *A Rapture of Praise* (Hodder & Stoughton, 1966).
H. A. L. Jefferson, *Hymns in Christian Worship* (Rockliff, 1950).
James Lightwood, *Hymn Tunes and Their Story* (Charles Kelly, 1905).
R. M. Moorsom, *A Historical Companion to 'Hymns Ancient and Modern'* (1889).
Millar Patrick, *Four Centuries of Scottish Psalmody* (Oxford University Press, 1949).
Erik Routley, *Hymns and Human Life* (John Murray, 1952).
Erik Routley, *Hymns Today and Tomorrow* (Darton, Longman & Todd, 1964).
Erik Routley, *The Musical Wesleys* (Herbert Jenkins, 1968).
Erik Routley, *Church Music and the Christian Faith* (Collins, 1978).
Erik Routley, *A Panorama of Christian Hymnody* (The Liturgical Press, Collegeville, Minnesota, 1979).
Erik Routley, *Christian Hymns Observed* (Mowbray, 1983).
Ira Sankey, *My Life and Sacred Songs* (Hodder & Stoughton, 1906).
Cyril Taylor, *Hymns for Today Discussed* (Canterbury Press, Norwich, 1984).
Donald Webster, *Our Hymn Tunes, Their Choice and Performance* (St Andrew Press, Edinburgh, 1983).
Tyler Whittle, *Solid Joys and Lasting Treasures* (Ross Anderson Publications, 1985).
Your Favourite Songs of Praise (Oxford University Press and BBC Books, 1987).

There is also much useful information to be gained from the quarterly bulletins of the Hymn Society of Great Britain and Ireland.

INDEX OF FIRST LINES

Hymn
number

1 A safe stronghold our God is still
2 Abide with me: fast falls the eventide
3 All creatures of our God and King
4 All glory, laud, and honour
5 All hail the power of Jesus' name
6 All my hope on God is founded
7 All people that on earth do dwell
8 All things bright and beautiful
9 Alleluia! sing to Jesus
10 Amazing grace
11 And can it be, that I should gain
12 And did those feet in ancient time
13 As pants the hart for cooling streams
14 At the name of Jesus
15 Awake, my soul, and with the sun

16 Be still, my soul: the Lord is on thy side
17 Be thou my vision, O Lord of my heart
18 Bless'd are the pure in heart
19 Blessèd assurance, Jesus is mine
20 Breathe on me, Breath of God
21 Bright the vision that delighted
22 Brightest and best of the sons of the morning

23 Christ is made the sure Foundation
24 Christ, whose glory fills the skies
25 City of God, how broad and far
26 Come, come, ye Saints
27 Come down, O Love divine
28 Come, Holy Ghost, our souls inspire
29 Come, let us join our cheerful songs
30 Come, ye faithful, raise the anthem
31 Come, ye thankful people, come
32 Crown Him with many crowns

33 Dear Lord and Father of mankind

34   Eternal Father, strong to save

35   Father, hear the prayer we offer
36   Fight the good fight with all thy might
37   Firmly I believe and truly
38   For all Thy saints who from their labours rest
39   For the beauty of the earth
40   Forth in thy name, O Lord, I go
41   From Greenland's icy mountains

42   Glorious things of thee are spoken
43   God be with you till we meet again
44   God is working his purpose out as year succeeds to year
45   God moves in a mysterious way
46   God save our gracious Queen
47   God, whose city's sure foundation
48   Guide me, O thou great Jehovah

49   Hail the day that sees him rise
50   Hail thee, Festival Day! blest day that art hallowed for ever
51   Hail to the Lord's Anointed
52   Hark the glad sound! the Saviour comes
53   Hills of the North, rejoice
54   Ho, my comrades! see the signal
55   Holy, Holy, Holy! Lord God Almighty
56   How lovely on the mountains are the feet of Him
57   How sweet the name of Jesus sounds

58   I bind unto myself to-day
59   I danced in the morning
60   I vow to thee, my country – all earthly things above
61   Immortal, invisible, God only wise

62   Jerusalem the golden
63   Jesu, good above all other
64   Jesu, lover of my soul
65   Jesus bids us shine
66   Jesus calls us: o'er the tumult
67   Jesus Christ is risen today, Halle-Halle-lujah
68   Jesus lives! no longer now
69   Jesus loves me! this I know
70   Jesus shall reign where'er the sun
71   Judge Eternal, throned in splendour

INDEX OF FIRST LINES

72   Just as I am, without one plea

73   King of Glory, King of Peace

74   Lead, kindly Light, amid the encircling gloom
75   Lead us, heavenly Father, lead us
76   Let all mortal flesh keep silence
77   Let all the world in ev'ry corner sing
78   Let us with a gladsome mind
79   'Lift up your hearts!' We lift them, Lord, to thee
80   Lo! He comes with clouds descending
81   Lord, enthroned in heavenly splendour
82   Lord of all hopefulness, Lord of all joy
83   Love divine, all loves excelling

84   Make me a channel of your peace
85   Mine eyes have seen the glory of the coming of the Lord
86   Morning has broken
87   My God! how wonderful thou art
88   My song is love unknown

89   Nearer, my God, to Thee
90   New every morning is the love
91   Now thank we all our God

92   O come, O come, Emmanuel
93   O for a closer walk with God
94   O for a thousand tongues to sing
95   O God of earth and altar
96   O Jesus, I have promised
97   O Lord my God, when I in awesome wonder
98   O Love that wilt not let me go
99   O praise ye the Lord! praise him in the height
100   O sacred Head, sore wounded
101   O Thou who camest from above
102   O worship the King, all-glorious above
103   O worship the Lord in the beauty of holiness
104   On Jordan's bank the Baptist's cry
105   Onward, Christian soldiers
106   Our God, our help in ages past

107   Praise, my soul, the King of heaven
118   Praise the Lord! Ye heavens, adore him
109   Praise to the Holiest in the height
110   Praise to the Lord! the Almighty. the King of creation

111   Rejoice, the Lord is King
112   Ride on! ride on in majesty
113   Rock of Ages, cleft for me

114   Shall we gather at the river
115   Soldiers of Christ, arise
116   Stand up, and bless the Lord
117   Stand up! – stand up for Jesus
118   Strong Son of God, immortal love

119   Take my life, and let it be
120   Teach me, my God and King
121   Tell me the old, old story
122   Tell out, my soul, the greatness of the Lord
123   Ten thousand times ten thousand
124   The Church's one foundation
125   ('Tis) the day of Resurrection
126   The day thou gavest, Lord, is ended
127   The earth belongs unto the Lord
128   The God of Abrah'm praise
129   The head that once was crowned with thorns
130   The King of love my Shepherd is
131   The Lord's my Shepherd, I'll not want
132   The spacious firmament on high
133   The strike is o'er, the battle done
134   There is a green hill far away
135   Thine be the glory, risen, conquering Son
136   Thou, whose eternal Word
137   Through all the changing scenes of life
138   Through the night of doubt and sorrow
139   Thy hand, O God, has guided
140   To God be the glory! great things he hath done
141   Turn back, O man, forswear thy foolish ways

142   Wake, O wake! with tidings thrilling
143   We plough the fields, and scatter
144   What a Friend we have in Jesus
145   When I survey the wondrous Cross
146   When morning gilds the skies
147   Who would true valour see
148   Will your anchor hold in the storms of life

149   Ye choirs of new Jerusalem
150   Ye holy angels bright

INDEX OF AUTHORS,
TRANSLATORS AND
COMPOSERS

(This index refers to the hymn numbers printed beside each title in the text)

Adams, Sarah, 89
Addison, Joseph, 73, 132
Ainger, A. C., 44
Akeroyd, Samuel, 11
Alington, C. A., 47
Alexander, Mrs C. F., 8, 58, 66, 134
Alford, Henry, 31, 123
Armes, Philip, 70

Baker, H. W., 99, 130
Banks, Thomas, 109
Baring-Gould, Sabine, 105, 138
Barnby, Joseph, 38, 146
Barthelemon, F. H., 15
Bax, Clifford, 141
Baxter, Richard, 150
Bernard of Clairvaux, St, 100
Bernard of Murles, St, 62
Blake, William, 12
Bliss, Philip, 54
Boberg, Carl, 97
Bode, J. E., 96
Borthwick, Jane, 16
Bourgeois, Louis, 7, 146
Bourne, G. H., 81
Boyce, William, 37
Boyd, William, 36
Bradbury, W. B., 69
Brady, Nicholas, 13, 137

Bridges, Matthew, 32
Bridges, Robert, 6, 100
Brierley, J. M., 14
Brown, A. H., 72
Budry, E. L., 135
Bull, John, 46
Bunney, Alan, 116
Bunyan, John, 147
Burkitt, F. C., 142
Butler, H. M., 79
Byrne, Mary, 17

Campbell, Jane, 143
Campbell, R., 149
Campbell, Thomas, 11
Carlyle, Thomas, 1
Carter, Sydney, 59
Caswall, Edward, 146
Cennick, John, 80
Chandler, J., 104
Chesterton, G. K., 95
Clark, Thomas, 41
Clarke, Jeremiah, 15, 119, 129
Claudius, Matthias, 143
Clayton, William, 26
Coffin, Charles, 104
Converse, Charles, 144
Cosin, John, 28
Cowper, William, 45, 93
Cox, Frances, 68

Croft, William, 102, 106, 127
Crosby, Frances, 19, 140
Crossman, Samuel, 88
Crüger, Johann, 24, 39, 51, 91, 125

Darwall, John, 111, 150
Davies, Walford, 22, 85, 132
Dearmer, Percy, 63
Dix, W. C., 9
Doane, William, 121, 140
Doddridge, Philip, 52
Draper, W. H., 3
Duckworth, F., 70
Dudley-Smith, Timothy, 122
Duffield, George, 117
Dykes, J. B., 34, 55, 64, 74, 89, 109, 112, 119, 123, 130

Edmeston, James, 75
Ellerton, John, 126
Elliott, Charlotte, 72
Elliott, J. W., 96
Ellor, James, 5
Elvey, George, 31, 32
Evans, David, 39, 65, 74
Ewing, Alexander, 62
Eyre, A. J., 94

Faber, F. W., 87
Farjeon, Eleanor, 86
Ferguson, W. H., 5, 14, 96
Filitz, Friedrich, 75
Francis of Assisi, St, 3, 84
Franck, J. W., 96
Fulbert of Chartres, St, 149

Gauntlett, H. J., 20, 68, 99, 149
Gellert, C. F., 68
Gerhardt, Paul, 100
Giardini, Felice, 136
Gibbons, Orlando, 40
Gillett, G. G. S., 50
Goss, John, 22, 107
Gould, Nathaniel, 33
Gounod, Charles, 134
Grant, James, 131
Grant, Robert, 102
Greatorex, Walter, 79, 122
Gurney, John, 150

Hall, W. J., 18
Handel, G. F., 22, 102, 111, 135
Hankey, Kate, 121
Harington, Henry, 94
Harris, W. H., 74
Harrison, Ralph, 70
Harwood, Basil, 77, 96, 139
Hassler, Hans, 100
Hatch, Edwin, 20
Hately, Thomas, 89
Hately, Walter, 16
Hatton, John, 36, 70
Havergal, F. R., 119
Havergal, W. H., 18, 111, 112, 119
Haweis, Thomas, 25, 94, 109
Haydn, F. J., 42, 105, 108
Heber, Reginald, 22, 41, 55
Herbert, George, 73, 77, 120
Hine, S. K., 97
Hodson, H. E., 23
Holland, Henry Scott, 71

Holst, Gustav, 60, 141
Hopkins, E. J., 22, 39, 66
Horsley, William, 134
How, W. Walsham, 38
Howe, Julia, 85
Hoyle, R. B., 135
Hughes, John, 48
Hull, Eleanor, 17
Hupton, Job, 30
Hutcheson, Charles, 93
Hutchings, Arthur, 101

Ingemann, B. S., 138
Ireland, John, 88
Irvine, Jessie, 131

Jackson, R., 20
James, F., 39
Jarman, Thomas, 94
John of Damascus, St, 125
Johnson, Samuel, 25
Jones, J. D., 73
Joubert, John, 39

Keble, John, 18, 90
Kelly, Thomas, 129
Kempthorne, J., 108
Ken, Thomas, 15
Kethe, William, 7
Kingham, Millicent, 44
Kirkpatrick, W. J., 148
Knapp, Phoebe, 19
Knecht, J. H., 119
Kocher, C., 39

Lahee, Henry, 29
Lee, H. G., 36, 37
Littledale, R. F., 27
Lloyd, J. A., 6
Lockhart, Charles, 20, 116
Lowry, Robert, 114
Luther, Martin, 1
Lyte, H. F., 2, 107

Madan, Martin, 64, 80
Mant, Richard, 21, 108
Marriott, John, 136
Martin, G. C., 14, 81

Mason, Lowell, 20, 89, 145
Matheson, George, 98
Milgrove, Benjamin, 78
Miller, Edward, 145
Milman, H. H., 112
Milton, John, 78
Monk, W. H., 2, 8, 14, 39, 49, 51, 77, 115, 119, 133
Monsell, J. S. B., 36, 103
Montgomery, James, 51, 116
Moultrie, Gerard, 76

Naylor, E. W., 115
Neale, J. M., 4, 23, 30, 62, 92, 125
Neander, Joachim, 6, 30, 110
Newman, J. H., 37, 74, 109
Newton, John, 10, 42, 57
Nicolai, P., 142
Noel, Caroline, 14

Oakley, C. E., 53
Oldham, Arthur, 14
Olivers, Thomas, 80, 128
Ouseley, Frederick, 8
Owens, Priscilla, 148

Parry, Hubert, 12, 33, 99
Parry, Joseph, 64
Patrick, St, 58
Pearce, Albert, 98
Perronet, Edward, 5
Phillips, Thomas, 94
Pierpoint, F. S., 39
Plumptre, E. H., 139
Pott, Francis, 133
Prichard, R. H., 9, 83
Purcell, Henry, 23, 47, 83
Purdy, C. H., 74

Rankin, J. E., 43
Redhead, Richard, 21, 113
Reinagle, Robert, 57
Richards, John, 21
Rinkart, Martin, 91

Roberts, John, 89
Routley, Erik, 77
Rowlands, W. P., 83

Schlegel, Katharina von, 16
Scholefield, Clement, 126
Schultz, J. A. P., 143
Scottish Psalter, 127, 131
Scriven, Joseph, 144
Shaw, Geoffrey, 39, 123
Shaw, Martin, 8, 44, 53, 77, 85, 138
Sibelius, Jean, 16
Siena, Bianco da, 27
Smart, George, 137
Smart, Henry, 39, 125
Smith, L. E., 56
Smith, W. C., 61
Somervell, Arthur, 109
Spedding, Frank, 122
Spring-Rice, Cecil, 60
Stainer, John, 20, 83
Stanford, C. V., 58, 83, 109, 126
Stanton, W. K., 22, 36

Stewart, C. H., 32
Stone, S. J., 124
Struther, Jan, 82
Sullivan, Arthur, 89, 105
Sweeting, E. T., 47

Tate, Nahum, 13, 137
Taylor, Cyril, 42, 82
Temple, Sebastian, 84
Tennyson, Alfred, 118
Teschner, Melchior, 4
Theodulph of Orleans, St, 4
Thomson, A. M., 127
Thorne, Edward, 66
Thrupp, J. F., 22
Tomer, W. G., 43
Toplady, A. M., 113
Turle, James, 87

Vaughan Williams, Ralph, 3, 14, 27, 35, 36, 37, 38, 43, 50, 95, 120, 147
Vulpius, Melchior, 133

Waghorne, W. R., 8

Warner, Anna, 69
Warner, Susan, 65
Watts, Isaac, 29, 70, 106, 145
Webb, G. J., 117
Webbe, Samuel, the younger, 25
Webbe, Samuel, the elder, 90
Wesley, Charles, 11, 24, 40, 49, 64, 80, 83, 94, 101, 111, 115
Wesley, Samuel, 116
Wesley, S. S., 9, 20, 62, 101, 124
Whiting, William, 34
Whittier, J. G., 33
Williams, Aaron, 20, 145
Williams, Peter, 48
Williams, Robert, 49
Williams, William, 48
Willis, Mrs L. M., 35
Wilson, Hugh, 13
Winkworth, Catherine, 91, 110